Handling of
Objects, Props

ADVANCED LABANOTATION SERIES

EDITOR
Ann Hutchinson Guest
Director, Language of Dance® Centre, London, UK

Vol. 1, 1:
Canon Forms
by Ann Hutchinson Guest
and Rob van Haarst

Vol. 1, 2:
Shape, Design, Trace Patterns
by Ann Hutchinson Guest
and Rob van Haarst

Vol. 1, 3:
Kneeling, Sitting, Lying
by Ann Hutchinson Guest
and Rob van Haarst

Issue 4:
Sequential Movements
by Ann Hutchinson Guest
and Joukje Kolff

Issue 5:
Hands, Fingers
by Ann Hutchinson Guest
and Joukje Kolff

Issue 6:
Floorwork, Basic Acrobatics
by Ann Hutchinson Guest
and Joukje Kolff

Issue 7:
Center of Weight
by Ann Hutchinson Guest
and Joukje Kolff

Issue 8:
Handling of Objects, Props
by Ann Hutchinson Guest
and Joukje Kolff

Issue 9:
Spatial Variations
by Ann Hutchinson Guest
and Joukje Kolff

Handling of Objects, Props

BY

ANN HUTCHINSON GUEST

AND

JOUKJE KOLFF

DANCE
BOOKS

©2002 Ann Hutchinson Guest. All rights reserved

Dance Books Ltd,
4 Lenten Street, Alton, Hampshire GU34 1HG

ISBN: 1 85273 090 0

This book was written and produced at the Language of Dance® Centre:
    The Language of Dance® Centre
    17 Holland Park
    London W11 3TD
    United Kingdom
    T: +44 (0)20 7229 3780
    F: +44 (0)20 7792 1794
    web: http://www.lodc.org
    e-mail: info@lodc.org

Ann Hutchinson Guest

Joukje Kolff

Contents

Introduction to the Series		xiii
Preface		xv
Acknowledgements		xvii
PART I BASIC INFORMATION ON PROPS		2
1	Definition of Props	2
	Hand Props	2
	Personal Props	2
	Stage Props	2
2	Indication of Prop	2
3	Forms of Relating to Props	4
4	Duration of Relationship, Validity	6
	Timing of Relationship	6
	Momentary Relationship	6
	Retained Relationship	6
	A Brief Passing (Moving) Relationship	6
	Continuous Moving Relationship	6
	Cancellation of Retained Relationship	6
5	Part of Prop Touched, Grasped, Carried	8
6	Placement of Prop on the Staff	10
7	Direction, Orientation of Object	12
PART II Hand Props		16
8	A Stick - Manner of Grasping, Holding	16
	Releasing a Hold	18
9	A Stick - Contact with the Floor	20

Handling of Objects, Props

	Leaning on a Stick	22
	Spot Hold for Object	22
	Spatial Retention for Object	22
10	A Stick - Simple Manipulations	24
	Hands Sliding on a Stick	24
	Dropping a Stick	24
	Throwing a Stick	24
11	Movements of a Stick	26
	Object Carried Along	26
	Specific Change of Direction for a Stick	26
12	Rotating, Turning a Stick	28
13	Circular Paths for a Stick	30
	Swinging Indian Clubs	30
	Independent Circles for a Stick	32
	Horizontal Circle Under the Legs	34
	Twirling a Stick	34
	Finger Twirl	36
14	Tracing a Design	38
15	A Stick - Figure Eight Patterns	40
	Sagittal Figure Eight	44
	Horizontal Pinwheel	44
16	Hitting Swords, Sticks	46
	Hitting Swords with a Partner	46
17	Relating to Sticks on the Floor	48
	Crossed Sticks on the Floor	48
18	Handling a Prop Gun	50
19	Handling an Umbrella	52
	Degrees of Opening (Spreading)	52
	Identifying Parts of the Object	54

20	Handling a Ball	56
	Juggling with Two Balls	58
	Rolling a Ball Along the Body	58
21	Relating to a Cup, Jar or Bottle	60
22	Handling a Book	62
	Identifying Parts of a Book	64
	Rotating a Book	66
23	Handling a Basket	68
	Penetrating	68
	'Inside', 'In the Center'	68
24	Skipping Rope	70
	Skipping Rope, Sagittal Circles	70
	Reading Example for Skipping Rope	70
	Skipping Rope with Three People	72
25	Handling a Hoop	74
26	Handling A Tambourine	78
27	Handling a Pillow	80
28	Handling a Cigarette, Apple	82
29	Circling Lighted Candles	84
30	Handling a Fan	86
	Representation of a Fan	86
	Dance with a Fan and Handkerchief	88
	The *Sensu*	90
	Parts of the *Sensu*	92
	Points of the *Sensu*	92
	Intermediate Points	94
	Areas of the *Sensu*	94
	Intermediate Areas	94
	Augmented Areas	94
	Area Surfaces of the *Sensu*	94

	The *Kaname* (Metal Pin)	94
	Identifying the Ribs (*Oyabones*)	96
	Rib Edges	98
	Rib Points	98
	Rib Surfaces	98
	Spaces Between Ribs	98
	Movements of the *Sensu*	100
	Direction of the *Sensu*	100
	Facing of the *Sensu*	100
	Open or Closed State of the *Sensu*	102
	Staff for the Fan	102
	Ways of Grasping the *Sensu*	104
	Grasping the Closed *Sensu*	104
	Ways of Grasping the Open *Sensu*	105
	Opening and Closing the *Sensu*	107
	Addressing	109
	Revolutions	110
	Cartwheel Revolution	111
	Manipulation of Open *Sensu*	112
	Lady Senda's Dance	116
	Closing the Fan - Lady Senda's Dance	120
31	Handling a Long Ribbon	128
32	Folding a Large Cloth	130
33	Handling a Blanket	136

PART III CLOTHING   138

34	Hat, Belt, Handkerchief, Sleeve, Pocket	138
	Hat	138
	Belt	138
	Handkerchief	138
	Reading Example - a Hat	140
	Reading Example - a Handkerchief	142
	Sleeve	144
	Pocket	144
35	Handling a Scarf	146

36	Handling a Veil	150
37	Handling a Skirt	154
38	Handling Long Sleeves	158
39	Using a False Leg, a Crutch	162
	Using a False Leg	162
	Using a Crutch	166
	Using Two Crutches	166

PART IV STAGE PROPERTIES — 168

40	Using a Chair	168
	Reading Study Using a Chair	168
	Reading Example - Chair, Pillow	170
41	A Table	172
	Contacting, Resting on a Table	172
	Supporting on a Table	172
	Reading Example - Manipulating a Table	174
42	A Rug	176
43	A Barre	178
44	A Wall	180
45	Stairs, a Ladder	182
	Moving Up or Down Stairs	182
	Climbing a Ladder	184
46	A Rope	186
47	A Pole	188
	Reading Material - Bamboo Grove	188
48	A Box	196
	Reading Material - New Dance	198

| 49 | An Imaginary Prop | 202 |

Appendix: Historical Background on Labanotation Textbooks — 206

Notes — 209

Bibliography — 219

Index — 221

Useful Contact Information — 236

Introduction to the Series

The <u>Advanced Labanotation</u> series provides a detailed exposition of the many topics introduced in the chapters of the 1970 textbook *Labanotation - The System of Analyzing and Recording Movement*. To make the material immediately accessible to the reader, each book in this series begins at a basic level, thus avoiding the need for immediate reference to other texts.

Within the series each topic is published independently as soon as it is completed in order to make the information immediately available. Topics for which there is at present a lack of information available, and those for which there is an immediate need, are being presented first.

Detailed theoretical exposition is supported by appropriate notated examples, and, where needed, figure illustrations of the movements and positions. A selection of reading materials from choreographic scores illustrates the different points, with the examples taken from various sources and styles of movement. Finally, a detailed index facilitates rapid access to required information and, for the researcher, meticulous endnotes and a bibliography indicate background and sources.

Preface

In many dances - indeed in many types of work and in daily life - objects are held and manipulated, for artistic or practical reasons. In many dance cultures around the world use of a particular object is essential to the dance and is an important source of movement. A general indication can be given of such use of an object, a 'property', but in many cases exact detail is required to ensure that the movements of object and dancer are correctly performed. The level of specificity depends on the usage and the context. When notating unfamiliar forms of dance the notator is wise to seek the advice of a specialist.

In his eight-volume *Dictionary of Kinetography Laban* (ca. 1948) Albrecht Knust devoted one whole volume, Section K, to this subject. While this book is in German and much of the notation needs updating, it has provided a valuable basis for this section of <u>Advanced Labanotation</u>. Only a selection of examples were included in his smaller English language 1979 *Dictionary of Kinetography Laban*. I had the advantage many years ago of working personally with Knust on this material and learned to appreciate the very logical general principles he had established.

Maria Szentpál, another brilliant mind, made a very significant theoretical and practical contribution to our system. In recording the many forms of Hungarian dance she found the need for specific indications of how the variety of objects involved were handled. Her detailed work provides another valuable resource for us. Several examples have been taken from her writings.

Theoretical discussions presented here with short, practical examples, some taken from dance scores, are followed by longer sections from scores in which use is made of particular objects and properties.

In facing the task of how best to present the many variations in types of objects, the manner of handling or relating to them, it was decided that, for ease in locating the information needed, the main body of this book should be organized according to type of property. In this way the reader can easily locate the kind of object for which information is needed. Reading Examples are given in or immediately following discussion on a particular property, rather than in a separate section at the end of the book.

Acknowledgements

As always, we have turned to information on advanced level Labanotation material contributed by Maria Szentpál and Albrecht Knust, who laid the groundwork on the notating of handling props.

Carl Wolz's expertise in Japanese dance, his organised notations on handling fans and his personal coaching in the art were an enormous help. We are also indebted to Lucy Venable and Odette Blum for their notation of *Ikkaku Sennin* from which we drew phrases of *Lady Senda's Dance*. Of particular help were Billie Mahoney, who contributed examples on baton twirling, and Sheila Marion, who provided the material on juggling.

For checking the drafts of this material and for actively taking part in discussions concerning issues and problems, we gratefully acknowledge the help given by our consultants, Jacqueline Challet-Haas, Ilene Fox, Janos Fügedi, David Henshaw, Sheila Marion and Lucy Venable whose detailed and judicious comments contributed much to the correction and clarification of working drafts.

Our thanks go to Helen Coxon and to Rosie Gerhard for contributing to the production of this book and to Roma Dispirito and Cheryl Hutton for producing the Labanotation examples on *Calaban*. It was Jane Dulieu who undertook the final reading and with her keen eye for accuracy found many instances where greater accuracy or clarity were still needed.

We are also grateful to the notators of the Reading Examples, who clarified details for us, and to the choreographers for giving permission to use excerpts from their scores.

The research for this issue of <u>Advanced Labanotation</u> and its production have been made possible through funding from the National Endowment for the Humanities, the Arts and Humanities Research Board and the John Simon Guggenheim Memorial Foundation. We are grateful for their generous support.

To conclude, we must also express appreciation to Andy Adamson who developed the *Calaban* software used to produce the Labanotation graphics.

Handling of Objects, Props

PART I BASIC INFORMATION ON PROPS

1 Definition of Props

1.1   An object handled on stage in a dance or drama production is known as a 'prop', an abbreviation of the word 'property'. This may be a 'hand prop', an object carried around by an individual. Typical of such props are a fan, flowers, a cane, or sword. Parts of a costume such as a hat, scarf, or skirt are sometimes called 'personal props'. Large objects such as furniture or draperies may be referred to as 'stage props'. Some objects fall between these three categories.

1.2.   **Hand Props.** These props come in many shapes and sizes. Some are hard, firm, and do not change shape, others (usually made of cloth) may change shape while they are being handled. A few props, such as a fan or an umbrella, may be open, closed or at some stage between the two. Amongst the most common props are: a stick, pole, walking stick, umbrella, fan, flower, basket, bowl, bottle, goblet, pillow.

1.3.   **Personal Props.** Clothing may be a hat, scarf, handkerchief, skirt, jacket, or a large shawl or cloak. Occasionally, pockets, belts, or other particular parts need to be specified.

1.4.   **Stage Props.** These may be a chair, stool, table, tree, door. Some of these may be manipulated, carried around (a chair for example), while others are usually touched or used as a support. Some are partly moveable, a door for instance, but many stage props, such as stairs or pillars are part of the stage set.

2 Indication of Prop

2.1.   Objects may be represented by a sketch drawn as pictorially as possible to represent the real thing, or by a simpler schematic pictogram which is easy to draw. In some cases a word or a letter abbreviation is used, such as B for book or S for stick. In the interest of international understanding a pictorial representation is preferable. Such sketches allow indication of which part of the object is handled. Explanation of the sketch of the object, prop or costume should be given in a glossary at the start of the score with an accurate, detailed drawing and other information, as required. The sketch may also be repeated within the score in a pre-staff indication. Repeated redrawing of the object may pose spacing problems on the page as well as difficulties in showing correct timing for the relationship bows; in such cases a detailed schematic representation on paper, in which the various parts of the prop are specified and given letters or symbols, is more practical. This should be given in the glossary.

2.2. Exs. **2a-2t** show typical drawings for commonly used objects. Such drawings may vary but are usually clear in themselves. However, they should still be given identification in the score. This is particularly true when an abbreviated or stylized representation is used or a letter identifies the object. Such a letter, e.g. a 't' for tambourine, may be written in a small circle, 2t.

Indication of Prop

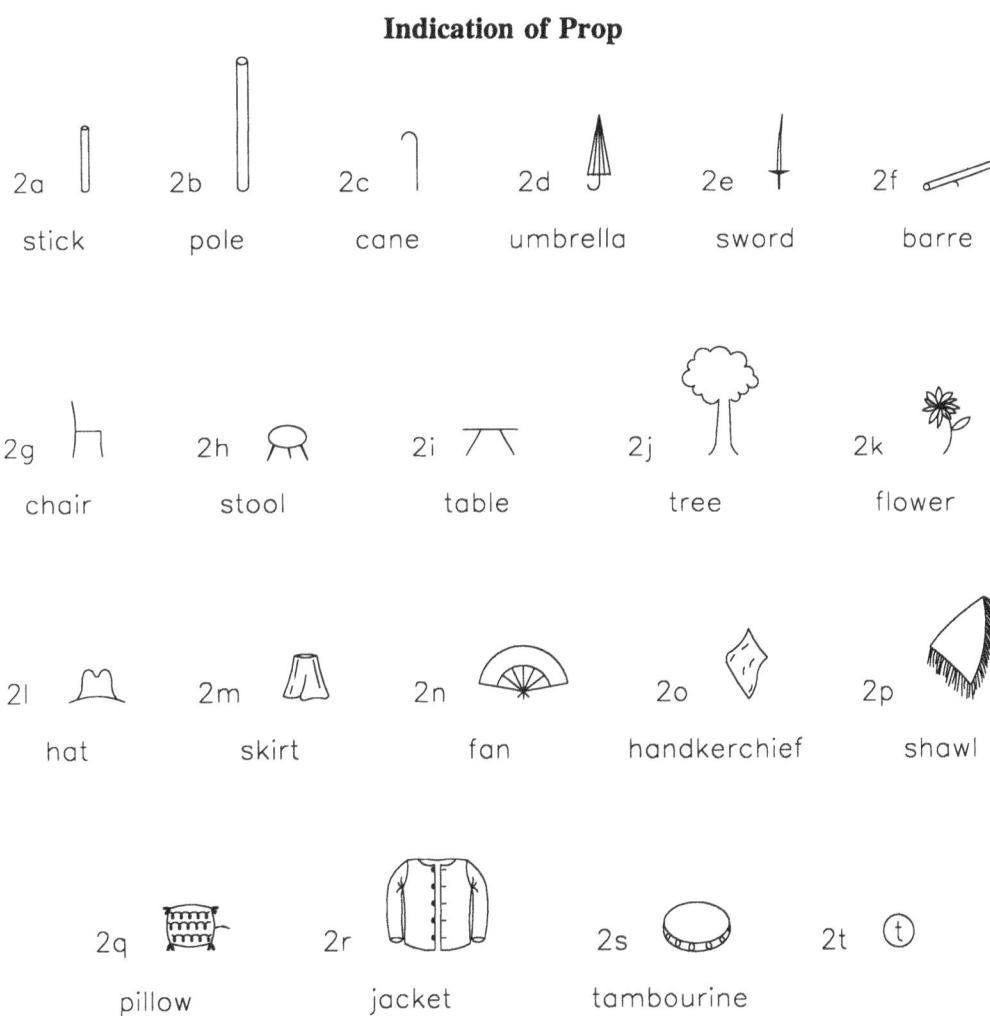

3 Forms of Relating to Props

3.1. A relationship to a prop may be one of:

3a: addressing
3b: nearness, proximity
3c: nearness and enclosing[1]
3d: penetrating nearness, e.g. inside without touching (a special meaning for the double X sign)
3e: actual contact, touching
3f: contact with enclosing (grasping)
3g: contact with penetrating, interlacing
3h: supporting, carrying
3i: holding support (carrying with grasping)
3j: holding (supporting) through extending (stretching)
3k: holding through body parts coming together

3.2. The above give the established terminology; the signs themselves readily convey what form is required.

3.3. In drawing the relationship signs certain modifications are also possible. For contact, and also for grasping, the center part of the bow may be drawn straight, as in **3l**; it is important that the ends be rounded. The curved ends may also bulge outward, as in **3m**, to allow room for a relationship pin or to avoid other symbols.

3.4. As long as the sign is angular the drawings of **3n** can be used instead of **3h**; swinging the sign to one side or the other helps to avoid other indications. Silmilarly, the drawings of **3o** are alternates for **3i**.

3.5. Either of the signs of **3h** and **3i** can be used when the context makes quite clear whether the object is being held (supported), or is itself the support for the performer or for another object, e.g. a book on a chair, or a chair on a mat. The drawing of the signs of **3p** clearly indicate that the person (or object) indicated at the lower end of the sign is the supporter and the indication placed at the upper end is the object (or person) being supported. This is true also for the grasping support signs of **3q**. To be explicit, the appropriate end of the bow can be thickened for the active part.

Advanced Labanotation

Forms of Relating to Props

3a	⌣ or ⌢		addressing
3b	` -_- ´ or ´ ¯¯ `		near
3c	` -x- ´ or ´ -x- `		near enclosing
3d	` -※- ´ or ´ -※- `		within, not touching
3e	⌣ or ⌢		contact, touch
3f	⌣x or ⌢x		touch with grasp
3g	⌣※ or ⌢※		contact with penetration
3h	⌣ or ⌢		support, carry
3i	⌣x or ⌢x		hold, carry with grasp
3j	⌣ʜ or ⌢ʜ		carry through extending
3k	⌣△ or ⌢△		carry through lateral closing
3l	⌣ or ⌢	3m ⊂⊃ or ⊂⊐	
3n	⌣ or ⌢	3o ⌣x or ⌢x	
3p	⌣ or ⌢	3q ⌣x or ⌢x	

4 Duration of Relationship, Validity

4.1. **Timing of Relationship.** The end of the relationship bow for the active part (person) indicates the moment the relationship takes place.

4.2. **Momentary Relationship.** Certain relationships may be only momentary, i.e. specifically of brief duration.[2] The following are typical of relating briefly: **4a** shows a brief nearness, the active part or person immediately moves away. Similarly, a touch may be momentary, as in touching a hot stove, **4b**, and a grasp may be brief, as in grasping something that hurt and immediately letting go, **4c**.

4.3. **Retained Relationship.** All forms of relating can be held, retained. Placement of the hold sign above the particular indication establishes such retention. In **4d** addressing is retained; in **4e** it is nearness; in **4f** a contact; in **4g** the grasp is to be held. Carrying (supporting) is held in **4h**, and in **4i** a grasping support is to be retained.

4.4. **A Brief Passing (Moving) Relationship.** A movement may cause a relationship to continue briefly; doubling the sign indicates a passing relationship. Ex. **4j** shows a passing addressing; in **4k** it is a passing nearness; in **4l** a passing touch results in sliding, as in brushing a fleck off a garment. A brief moving grasp is indicated in **4m**, while **4n** show a brief sliding support as when a book slides off your lap; a similar brief sliding occurs in **4o**, but here an object was being grasped, as might happen with a pencil slipping out of your hand.

4.5. **Continuous Moving Relationship.** Instead of being momentary, as explored above, the form of passing, moving relationship may continue. In the following examples a short action stroke is used to indicate that some form of movement is involved in connection with the stated relationship. Ex. **4p** shows an addressing which moves, as in looking at the contents of a shop window. Passing the hand near, but not touching, is expressed as **4q**. Continuous contact, stroking, smoothing something would be shown as **4r**. Ex. **4s** states a moving grasp as in squeezing out water along a rope. A sliding support, as in skating, is shown as **4t**, while **4u** could be a supporting grasp as you slide down a rope.

4.6. **Cancellation of Retained Relationship.** The cancellation for a hold sign is the release sign, **4v**. This sign is placed above the hold sign for general statement of relationship, as in **4w**, **4x**, **4y** and **4z**. The same appropriate placement is used for canceling a passing, moving relationship, as in **4aa**, **4ab**, **4ac** and **4ad**. The release sign is placed above the body part sign when such is used (see **8u**, **9e**, **9o**).

Duration of Relationship, Validity

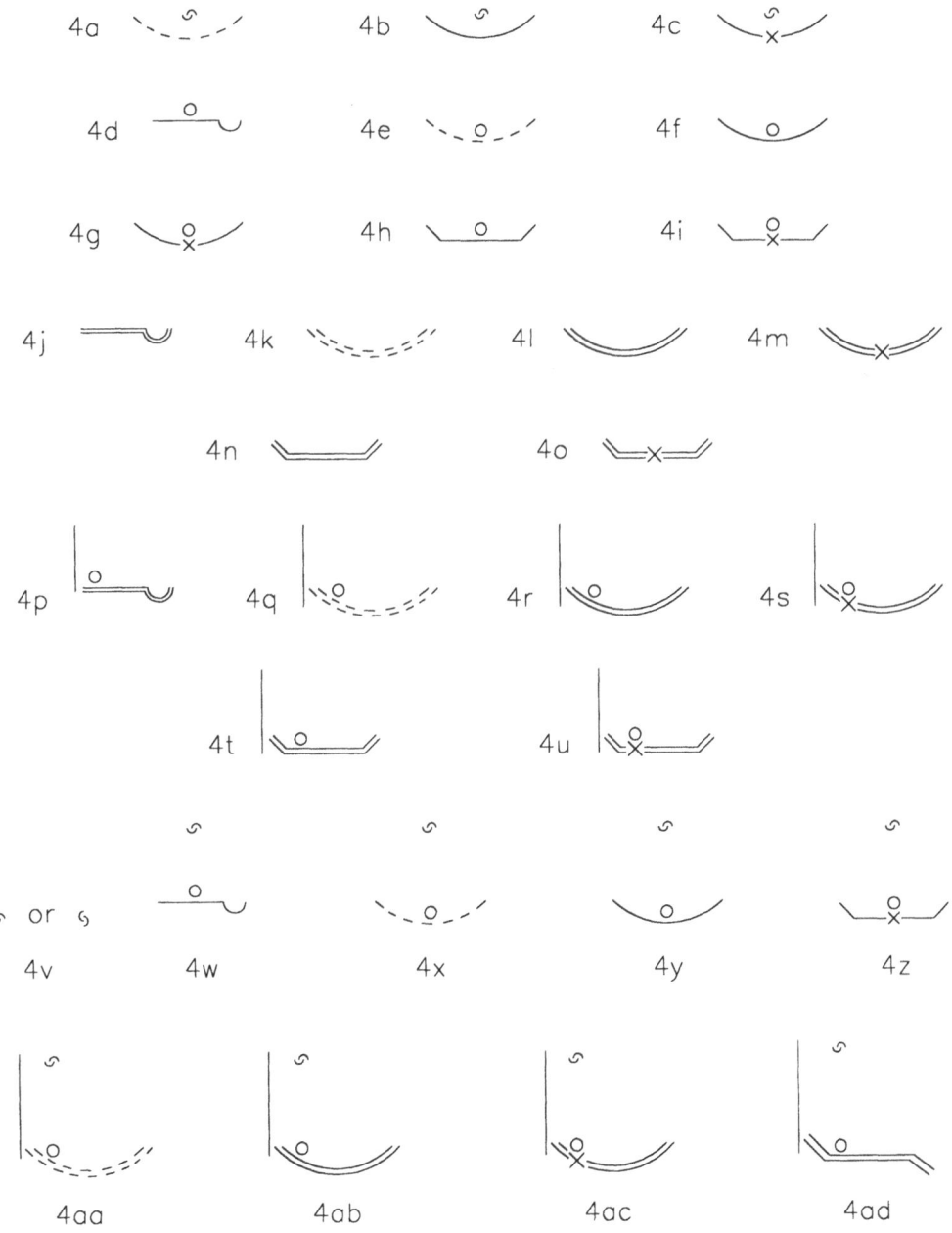

5 Part of Prop Touched, Grasped, Carried

5.1. Whenever possible, the drawing of the relationship sign (touch, grasp, etc.) should indicate visually to what part of the object the relationship refers. Parts of an object may be identified by using letters, numbers or special signs. For examples see an umbrella (19.4), a book (22.6-7) and a fan (30.2).

5.2. In **5a** the hand touches the back of a chair. In **5b** the index finger touches the center of the seat. The right foot contacts the front edge of the chair in **5c**.

5.3. A three-dimensional drawing of the chair allows greater specificity. Ex. **5d** shows grasping the center of the top strut of the chair. In **5e** the center strut is grasped, while in **5f** the right foot kicks (contact with a strong accent and an immediate release) the right back leg of the chair.

5.4. In **5g** the right hand grasps and carries a cane near the bottom. Grasping at the center of the cane is shown in **5h**, while **5i** shows grasping the handle. In **5j** the bottom of the vase is supported by the palm of the left hand, while both hands grasp the sides near the base to support the vase in **5k**. The right thumb and first finger grasp the edge of the tumbler to carry it in **5l**.

5.5. In **5m** a pencil is grasped by the thumb, index and middle fingers. When writing, people vary in the configuration of the fingers used to hold a pencil.

5.6. Most scores require specific statements of where an object is to be touched, grasped or carried, but sometimes freedom is needed. If it does not matter where an object is to be touched, grasped or carried, the ad lib. sign is written between the end of the bow and the drawing of the object.[3] In **5n** the right hand touches a table; where it touches does not matter.

5.7. Note the different ways in which the supporting bow can be swung to show pictorially the part of the stick being held. In **5o** the stick is grasped in the middle, in **5p** near the top and in **5q** near the bottom. To grasp the very bottom with the hand (rather than the fingers), **5r**, a cupped hand may be needed, as it is for **5s**, grasping the top end. How the hand is used depends on the shape of the object, the part that is being grasped and the direction from which the grasp takes place.

Part of Prop Touched, Grasped, Carried

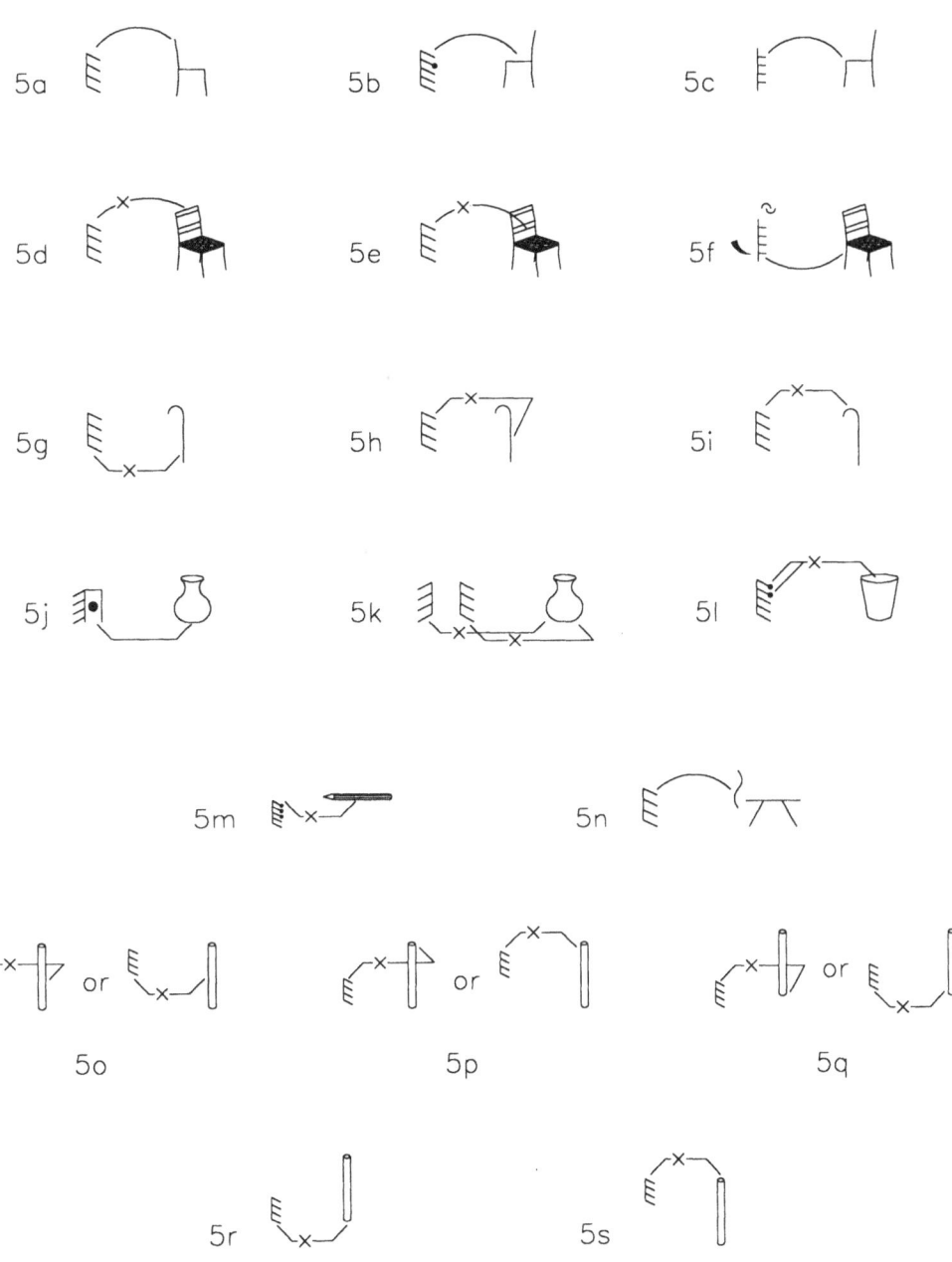

6 Placement of Prop on the Staff

6.1. Prop indications are usually placed to the right of the main staff, beyond any movement instructions relating to the person, i.e. beyond indications for the head and path signs. Hand props may also be placed on the left (see **13a-13e**). It can be more practical to redraw the indication for the prop on the appropriate side of the staff when right or left hand is involved to avoid contact bows crossing the staff. If need be, the prop can be drawn on both sides of the staff, as when quick alternation of hands grasping takes place (see **20b**). For a starting position the object can be written below the staff, as in **6a**, which shows each hand grasping the side of a skirt.

6.2. In **6b** indication of the prop, in this case a table, is placed at the right side of the staff. Because the subsequent contact bows end above this drawing, it is understood that the same object is being touched. It is as though the prop has its own column. An actual 'column' can be drawn for it, as in **6c**. A prop column may be on the right or left of the staff, but always outside all columns relating to the performer.[4] Here there is no question that the contact is with the table and not with the floor. When no prop is stated, the usual meaning for a contact or support bow which ends beyond the staff, is that reference is to the floor.

6.3. In **6d**, while sitting on the floor, the right palm hits the floor twice before weight is put on that hand. Here the floor is understood. The specific sign for the floor is a letter T in a box, **6e**, the T standing for *terra*, i.e. earth. Because the T may look like a middle level 'tack' and could be mistaken for a Front sign, it is often drawn with a slanted top line, as in **6f**. Ex. **6g** shows a specific statement of hitting the floor.

6.4. When a prop is used by the left hand, for example an exercise at the barre which starts with the right leg, it is obviously more appropriate to place the indication of the barre at the left side of the staff, as in **6h**. Here the performer is standing with the left side next to the barre. Note that in this example the level for the arm gesture is left blank as the height of the performer and also the height of the barre may vary. Placement of the hand above the barre is correct for most barre exercises. (See Part IV for details on use of static properties such as barres, steps, ladders.)

6.5. The prop may be redrawn each time it is needed; this is especially true if contact with another part of the prop occurs, or if the spatial placement of the prop changes (see 36b, 40a).

Placement of Prop on the Staff

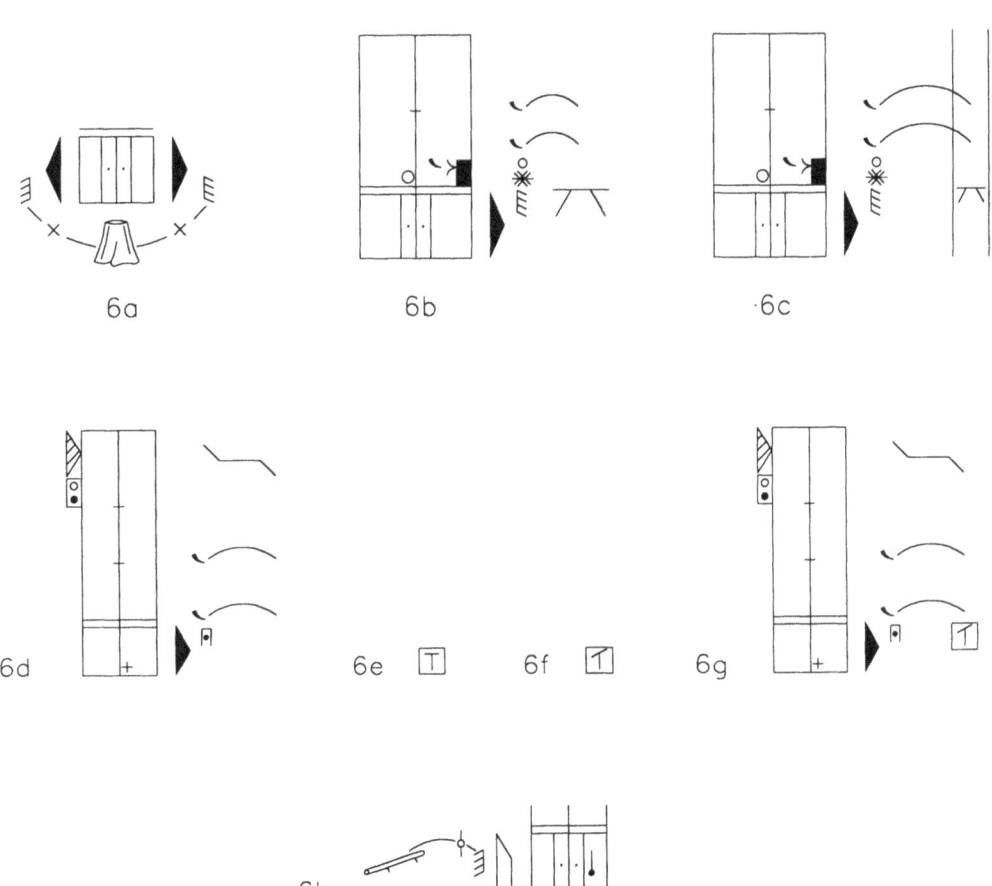

7 Direction, Orientation of Object

7.1.   To determine the orientation of a prop we rely on the identification of particular features of that prop. The simplest object which has no front or back, no up or down, is a ball, for which specific orientation does not matter. In **7a** a ball is being held on the performer's palm. Grasping the ball with the hand is shown in **7b**, while in **7c** it is being balanced on the index finger.

7.2.   The orientation of an object, such as a stick which has no defined end or front surface, must be stated with direction symbols. Let us take a stick lying on the floor or on a table. Ex. **7d**, which can also be written as **7e**, shows the stick lying horizontally sideward, these directions being in relation to the performer's Standard Cross of Axes. This placement could also be written as **7f**, where one direction symbol will suffice, because, for a rigid object of this kind, the other end will automatically be in the opposite direction.

7.3.   While it is visually helpful to illustrate a horizontally placed object with a horizontal drawing, as in **7d**, **7e** and **7f**, the necessary information can be written next to a vertical drawing as in **7g** or **7h**; the message is the same. Sagittal placement can be stated, as in **7i**. Compare this with **7j** in which the stick is vertically up and down. The oblique drawing for the diagonal placement in **7k** facilitates reading, although **7l** provides the required information. All these direction signs can be written quite small.

7.4.   Placement of objects on the stage must be described according to the Constant Cross of Axes for directions, as in **7m**. This gives orientation but not location; location is indicated by addition of a floor plan.

7.5.   When various manipulations of a stick take place, it can be hard to keep track of how the stick is changing directions and at which end it is being held. For such needs the ends are identified: in **7n** they are called A and B. The drawing may also be as in **7o**. Following the orientation of the A end will usually suffice, but when hand grasps change, which end is being grasped by which hand may need designating. Another device is to darken one end of such a prop, as in **7p**. (See *Bamboo Grove*, Section 47)

7.6.   A long rigid object with a distinctive end may be a cane, a sword, a broom, etc. The drawings of **7q** and **7r** give some idea of horizontal or vertical placement. Some objects have an inbuilt top and bottom, for example a vase or a hat. To some extent the drawing can indicate whether these are upside down or lying horizontally as in **7s**, **7t**. Other objects have an obvious front and back, for example a chair, **7u**, a jug, **7v**, or an embroidered pillow, **7w**. A change in the position of an object can be indicated by redrawing it in its new orientation, as illustrated here. However, this device is limited and not always practical; specific directions may need to be added.

Direction, Orientation of Object

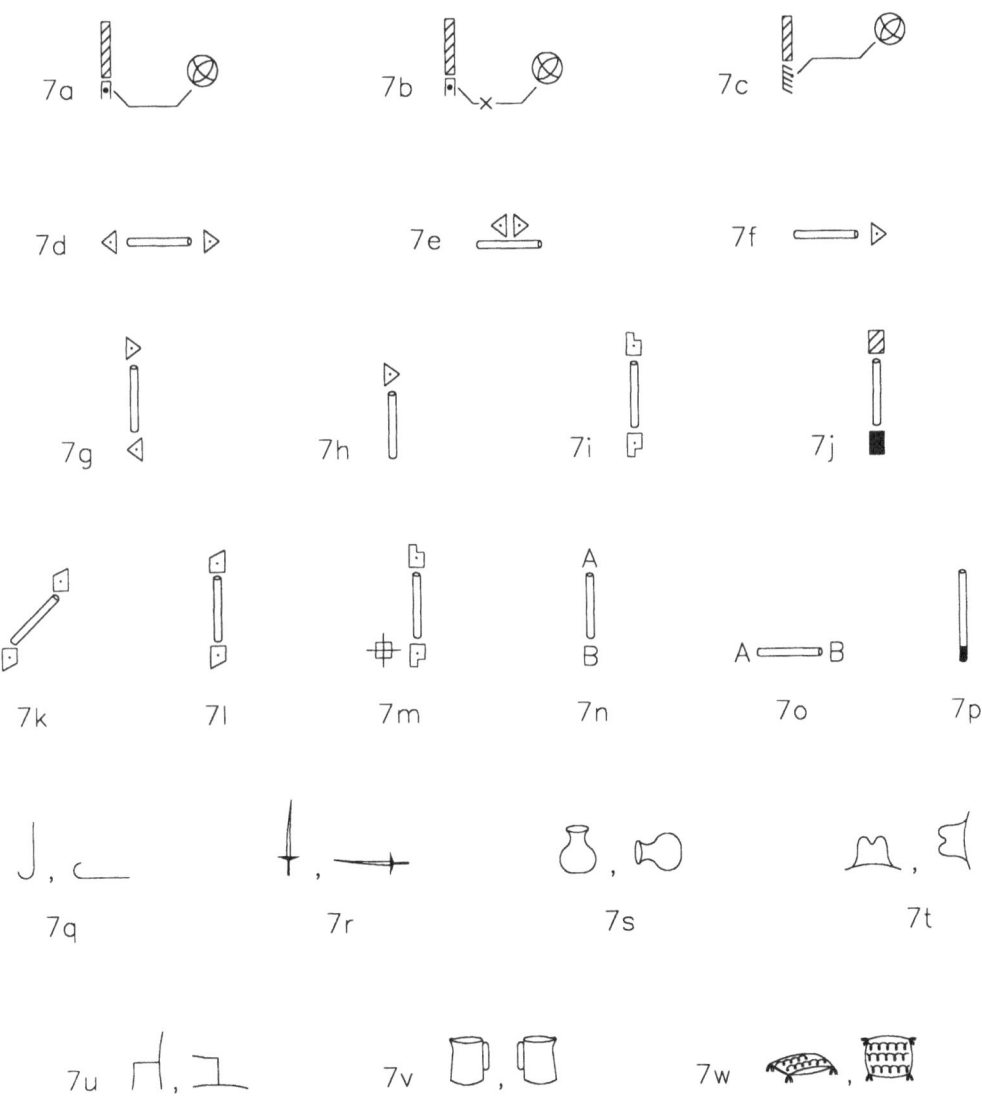

7.7. The direction indicated for an object is determined by where it is held, the 'point of attachment'. If an object is held at one end, as in **7x**, that end is usually drawn pointing toward the bottom of the page, the free end being drawn toward the top of the page. However, the reverse may be practical (see **9g** and **9h, 9k, 9l**).[5] For objects in which one end has a particular function, the hand usually holds the opposite end. In **7y** the right arm is forward holding a sword vertically. This direction sign is written just after the free end or, if space decrees, adjacent to it, **7z**. In **7aa** an umbrella, held by the handle, is pointing forward. Ex. **7ab** shows a shepherd's crook with the crook end backward high. Subsequent directions will relate to this free end. In **7ac** the brush end of a broom is shown to be forward low. Note that the right hand grasps nearer the end of the stick.

7.8. The following examples show simple changes in orientation for the props concerned. (See Section 10 for simple manipulations of sticks.) At the start of **7ad** the cane is hanging down, as the drawing suggests. However, to be quite clear, the free end direction is stated. On count 1 the cane points forward middle; on count 2 it points straight up.

7.9. The drawing of the walking stick in **7ae** suggests that the free end is up; this has also been specifically stated. On the lunge step the walking stick points forward low. In **7af** a hat, carried by the edge of the brim, hangs down. An unwritten wrist action causes it to move side horizontal and then down again.

7.10. For an object held in the middle, **7ag**, the direction sign is given for the end drawn toward the top of the page; only one direction sign is needed for a rigid object such as a stick. The stick starts pointing left diagonally forward. As the arm moves the same end of the stick comes to point side high.

7.11. Certain objects, such as an axe, have a functioning end and also a functioning edge or surface. In **7ah** the axe has its 'head' end pointing left side middle; nothing is designated for the blade. Where the blade edge faces, can be added; in **7ai** the blade points forward. This placement can be shown more visually by a horizontal sketch, as in **7aj**.

7.12. When an object such as a stick is held at both ends, as in **7ak**, the direction of the arms and placement of grasping indicate clearly that the stick is horizontal; this fact is even more quickly recognized because of the horizontal sketch. Similarly, in **7al** arm and hand placements make the vertical orientation of the stick obvious. If the object is smaller, arm placement may not convey sufficient information, therefore direction symbols are needed, as in **7am**. As shown in **7an**, one direction symbol can suffice.

Direction, Orientation of Object

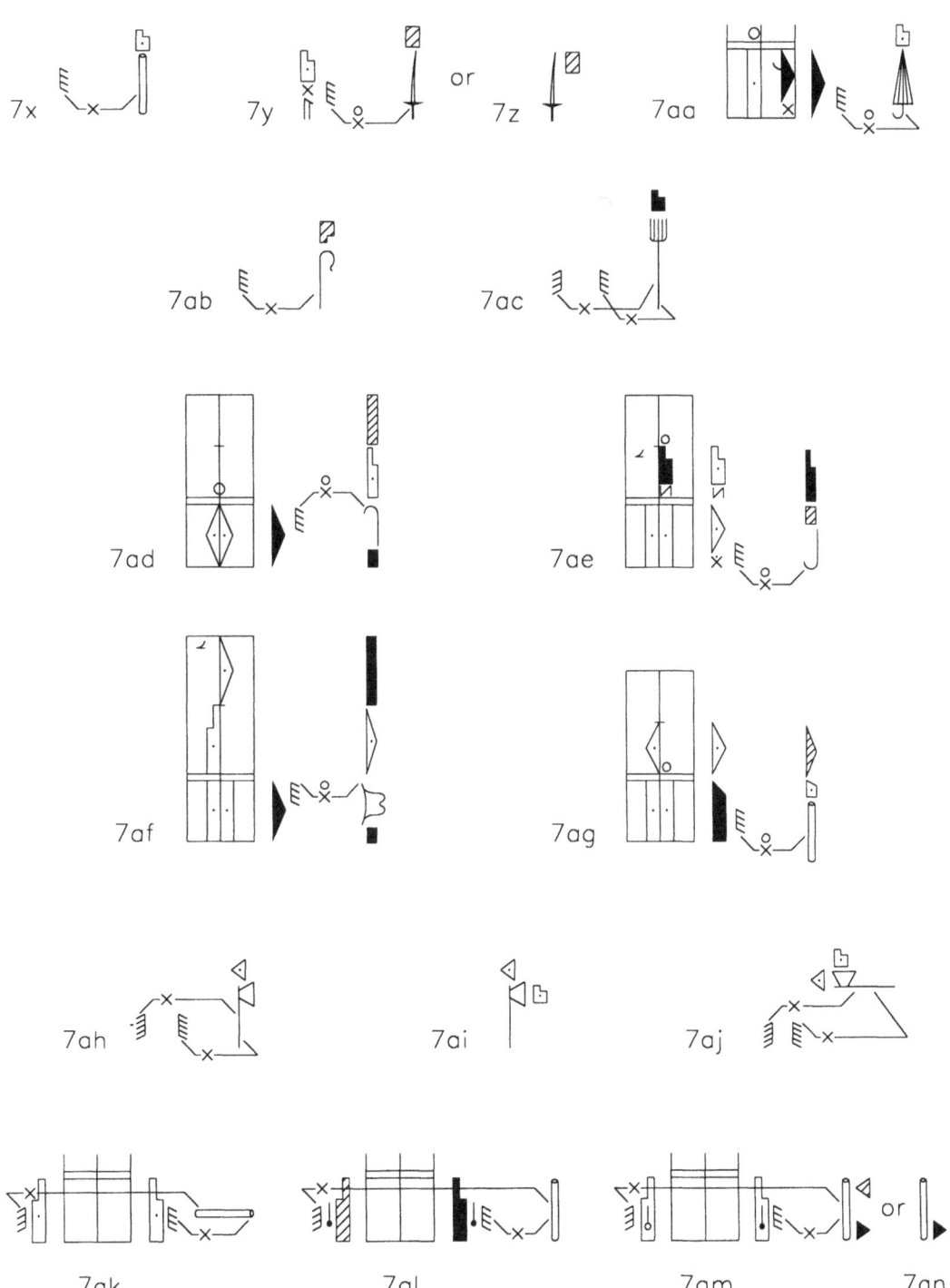

PART II Hand Props

8   A Stick - Manner of Grasping, Holding

8.1.   Because many props are in the general shape of a stick or pole this type of object is being investigated first. Aspects investigated in relation to a stick are often applicable to other shapes but particular needs can vary. For specific explanations on hand movements and positions and use of pins to specify the direction of relationship, see the <u>Advanced Labanotation</u> issue on hands and fingers.

8.2.   In examples such as **8a**, whatever the direction of the stick, the direction of the hand (i.e. the hand grasp) is usually at right angles to the shaft of the stick. In **8b** the right arm is forward, the stick is upright and held in the center, it is expected that the hand is grasping from the right.

8.3.   How the hand is used to hold a stick, i.e. the shape it takes, will vary according to the direction of the stick in relation to the direction of the arm. In general the hand adjusts as little as possible when directions for the stick change. Because the hand and the object are at right angles to each other in **8b**, the hand will be in the general shape of a fist, the palm facing to the left. This is illustrated in **8c**, seen from the left. Another simple holding of a stick may be as in **8d**; the arm is side low, the stick slanting upward side high and an ordinary fist grasp is being used.

8.4.   For a general statement no pin is required - a logical, comfortable grasp will take place. When used, the appropriate pin is placed between the hand symbol and the relationship bow. This is true whether the bow is swung upward or downward. It should be noted that a pin pointing to the right indicates the *direction from which the grasp takes place,* i.e. the direction from which the hand approaches the object. To achieve this grasp, the hand must be slightly to the right of the object to contact it from the right. When grasping an object from above, the hand must approach that object from above, and so on.

8.5.   In **8e** the broom is sideward horizontal and the hand hold is from below, i.e. palm faces up, resulting in hand and object being at right angles. This right angle relationship is also true for **8f** where the hand grasps from above. For the right hand to grip the upright stick from the left side, shown in **8g**, the arm has to be twisted inward.

Advanced Labanotation

8.6. With the arm forward middle, the stick of **8h** is now slanting forward high. Thus the hand hold has involved a wrist flexion toward the little finger edge, as noted in parentheses. When arm and stick direction are the same, as in **8i** (here forward horizontal), the fingers will be rotated outward, as noted in parentheses, illustrated in **8j**. Placement of the stick slanting backward (toward the thumb edge), **8k**, will mean that the hand hold will be in a different position, the little finger and fourth finger being less bent, the index finger being more bent. In these three last examples the direction of the grasp is from the right, the pin being placed between the hand and the supporting bow.[6]

8.7. A different hold for the stick and the hand is for them to be in the same direction but not with the palm facing the object. In **8l** the palm is facing to the left and the grasp is from below, this will result in the 'bunched finger' position for the hand, illustrated in **8m**.

A Stick - Manner of Grasping, Holding

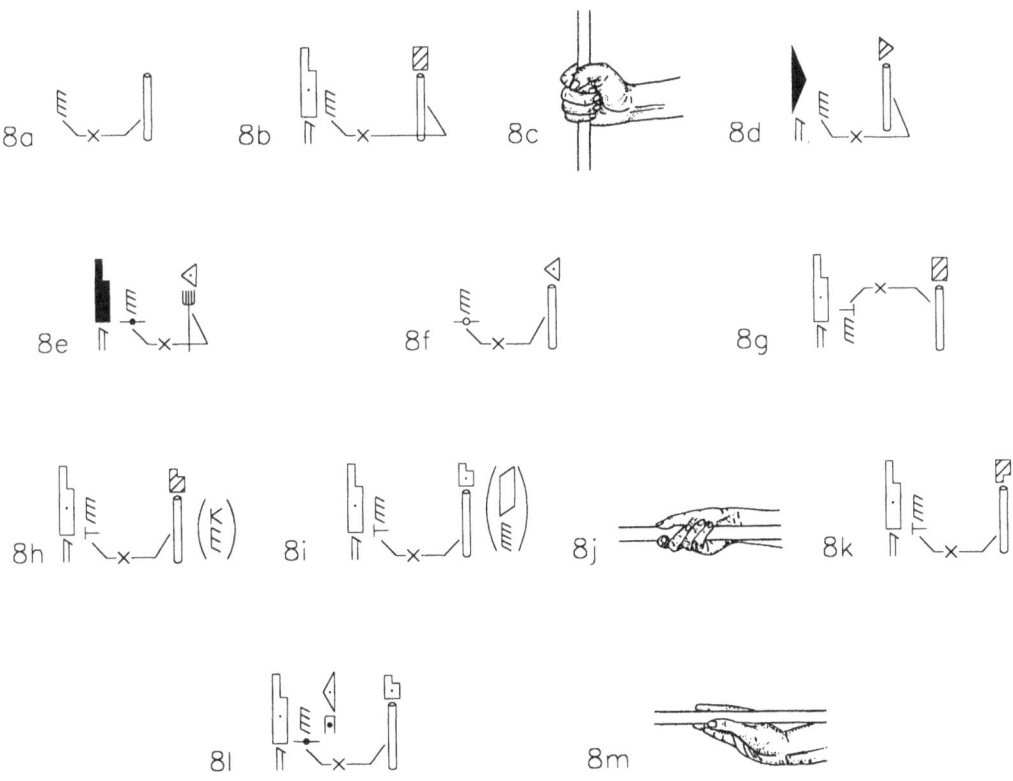

8.8. A stick held horizontally may be written as **8n** or as **8o**, the latter having the advantage of the visual image of the horizontal placement. As mentioned in Section 7, with a rigid prop, once one end is spatially oriented, the other end will automatically be in the opposite direction.

8.9. Contact of an object with part of the torso is shown in **8p**. The stick is held horizontally at both ends and the middle of the stick touches the back of the shoulder section; it is therefore behind the body.

8.10. In **8q** the right hand holds the stick with a forward low relationship, the grasp being near the middle, while at the same time the section near the end is held (grasped) by the armpit. As it is only the hand which is supporting (taking the weight of) the stick, there is only one angular bow.

8.11. An almost identical configuration is shown in **8r**. Here it is the armpit which supports the stick, while the hand merely touches the other end. If the stick were placed lower at the side of the chest it would not be the armpit but instead the upper arm and the side of the chest that would achieve the grasping, **8s**. A more specific description of this would be that of **8t**, in which the grasping action is shown to be one of adduction, the upper arm closing in to the side of the chest.

8.12. **Releasing a Hold.** In the sequence of **8u** the stick is held at first with both hands, then only with the left hand, the right hand releasing in order to make the sideward arm gesture. The right hand then grasps again as the feet close. A similar action then takes place with the left hand and arm. It is assumed that the hand will return to grasp at the same place unless otherwise specified. Each hold sign on an object must be canceled; there is no automatic cancellation rule. Note use of the space hold above the indication for the stick; this states clearly that the stick does not change its spatial placement.

A Stick - Manner of Grasping, Holding (continued)

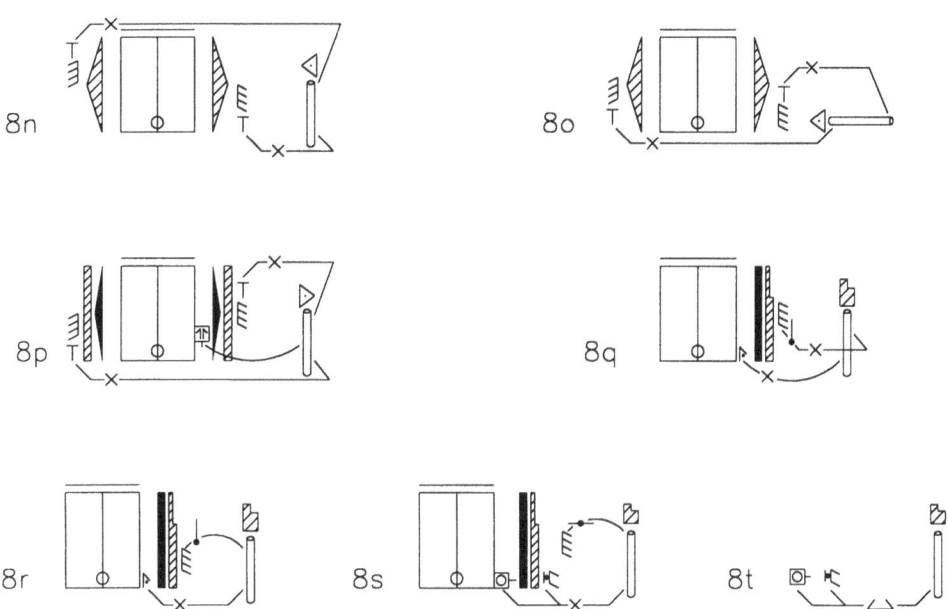

Releasing a Hold

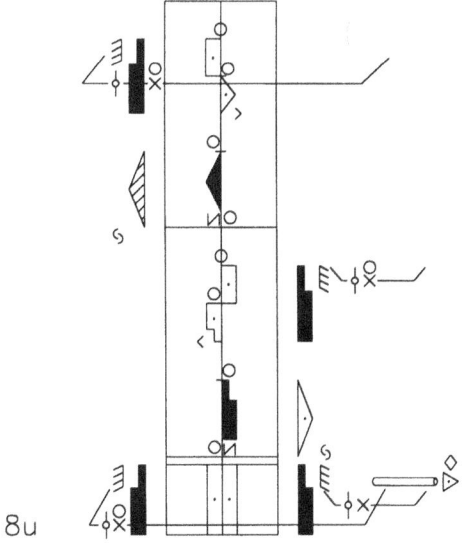

9 A Stick - Contact with the Floor

9.1.   A stick may be lying on the floor; until it is related to a performer there is no way of identifying its direction except with the Constant Key. In **9a** the stick lies parallel with the front of the room, i.e. the one end pointing to the right side of the room, the other to the left. The floor is represented by the letter T (for *terra*) in a box (see **6e-6g**).

9.2.   The bottom of the vertical stick in **9b** and **9c** is supported on the floor. Use of this form of the angular supporting bow gives the image of what is being supported by what. The direction of the stick is judged from where it is being supported. When use of the floor is obvious, it need not be stated; in **9c** supporting on the floor is understood.

9.3.   In **9d** the right palm rests on the end of the stick, probably helping it to balance. In ordinary parlance such assisted balance is sometimes called 'holding' or 'supporting', but this is not to be confused with a real action of supporting. The support bow for the base of the stick should be drawn out beyond the object to show supporting on the floor.[7]

9.4.   Placing the stick on the floor is shown in **9e**. The torso bends forward, the arm lowers, the hand releases and the object is shown to support on the floor. In **9f** the relationship of the stick on the floor to the performer is indicated by use of the meeting line. Here the stick is placed to the performer's right.

9.5.   Hitting the floor with the end of the stick is shown in **9g**. Note that the 'free end' of the stick is drawn downward; similarly, use of the contact bow in which the end is pointing downward gives a better visual impression of the end contacting the floor. If the support column is used to represent the floor, as in **9h**[8] (a familiar usage in the past), it might give the impression that the foot is being tapped. A stick tapping the end of the gesturing foot is shown in **9i**.[9] In **9e** and subsequent examples, note the use of a hold sign above the grasping indication in the support bow. This statement alerts the reader to the fact that the object continues to be held.

9.6.   Brushing the floor with the end of a stick is given in **9j**. The brief duration for the contact which results from the arm gesture is shown by the double bow (see 4.4). (For larger movements of sticks see Section 10-15.)

Advanced Labanotation

A Stick - Contact with the Floor

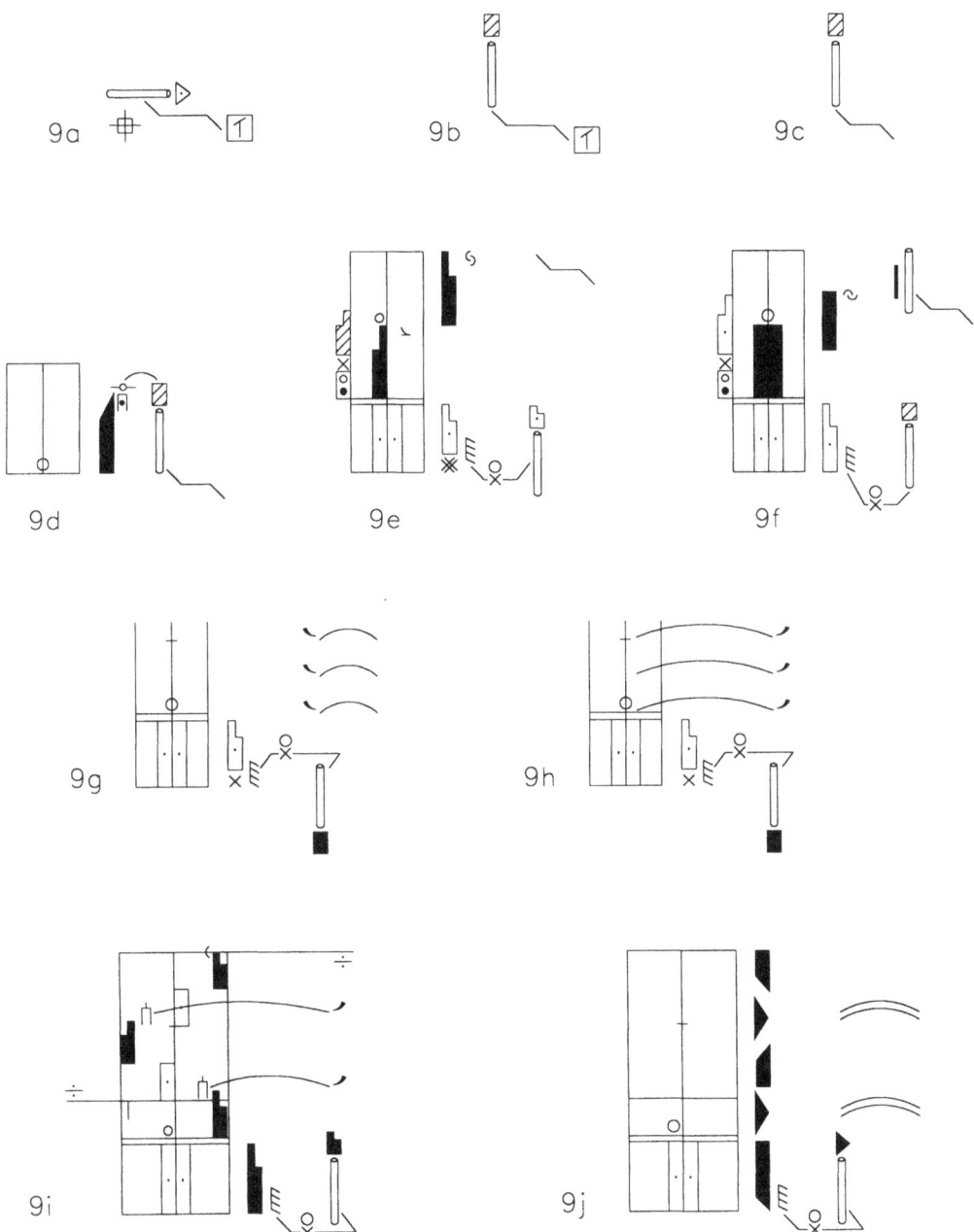

9.7. **Leaning on a Stick.** In contrast to being carried, an object may partially or sometimes totally support the person. In **9k**, as the body from ankle to chest leans to the right, some weight is taken onto the cane which is held in the right hand. In **9l** the lean is greater so that weight is now shared by the right foot and the right hand, which still holds the cane. Because it has become a major support, the hand sign is now placed in the support column. (For indication of weight distribution among supports see the Advanced Labanotation issue on floorwork.)

9.8. **Spot Hold for Object.** In **9m** a man leans on a stick (his left hand is on top of his right) in order to perform a high *cabriole*. Note the spot hold for the hands and for the stick, which remain where they are. During the hop, weight is taken on the hands; on landing weight is released.[10]

9.9. The broom head in **9n**[11] is resting on the floor and the handle is held in the right hand, grasped from the right side. The broom stick is slanting backward high. Note the spot hold indicated for the end supporting on the floor. In this case it is written before the action for which it is required takes place, but the retention applies throughout the sequence. While the dancer is moving side to side the broom handle is passed from the right hand to the left and then back again.

9.10. **Spatial Retention for Object.** In the next example, **9o**, the stick is shown to be a shepherd's crook. Starting with the arms held upward, the crook is at first held upright, being grasped near its base by the right hand. As the arms lower and come together the left hand grasps the crook near the bottom and immediately the right hand releases. The arms are again raised and, as they lower and come together, the right hand grasps the crook and the left hand releases. To indicate the exact moment of the new grasp, the sketch has been repeated so that the part to be grasped lines up with the moment the grasp is to take place. Note that the hand sign does not need to be repeated because the contact sign ends in that column. The crook is to remain upright all the time, as made clear by use of the space hold sign. Without the space hold the direction of the prop will be affected by arm and body movements, being carried along.

Leaning on a Stick

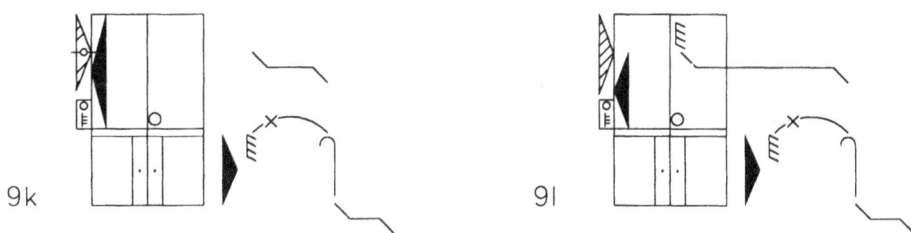

Spot Hold for Object

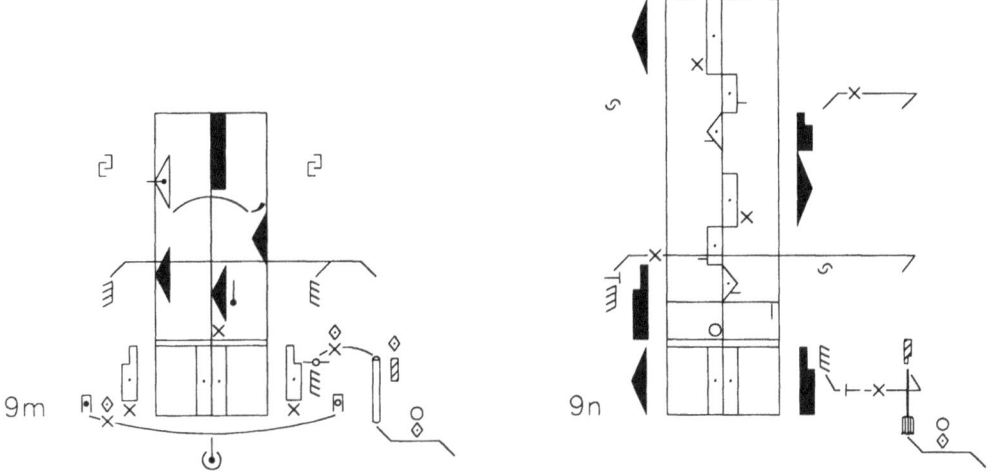

Spatial Retention for Object

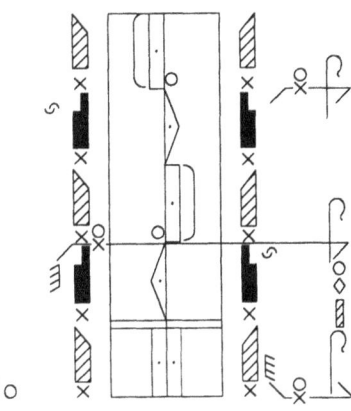

10 A Stick - Simple Manipulations

10.1. **Hands Sliding on a Stick.** While holding a stick in both hands, the hands may slide along the stick, as in **10a**. The stick is grasped in the middle from above (palms facing down), then, as the arms open sideways the hands slide while still supporting the stick. This is shown by the doubled supporting bow, the sliding being maintained. The resulting position with the hands at the ends of the stick is shown.

10.2. With a long enough stick it is possible to allow it to slip within the hand and to support it again before it falls completely. In **10b** a vertical stick is held near the bottom; the top end is marked A. The supporting bow changes to a sliding grasp (the weight of the object is no longer held). As a result the stick slips toward the floor (as shown by the path sign) until it is supported again at part A.[12]

10.3. **Dropping a Stick.** When the hand releases, as in **10c**, the stick will automatically fall to the floor. This downward path for the stick can be assumed and need not be written. If the arm moves while the release takes place the path of the object will be affected. In **10d** the stick will travel somewhat sideward as a result of the arm gesture. Here its path is not stated, only the subsequent support on the floor.

10.4. **Throwing a Stick.** When throwing an object, the performer can control the path and direction of the object. If this is important the path of the object should be designated. A stick is thrown upward in **10e**, it rises vertically before descending and being caught. Note the quick, accented, small upward motion of the hand as the stick is released. The upward and downward path for the stick is shown in the path sign. If nothing is stated concerning where the stick is to be caught, then this detail is not important.

10.5. Two boys face each other in **10f**, each having a stick in his right hand. They throw the stick to the partner who catches the stick with his left hand. The aim for the path of the stick is horizontal; because of gravity it will need to be given a slightly upward arc. The pattern is then repeated to the other side.

Hands Sliding on a Stick

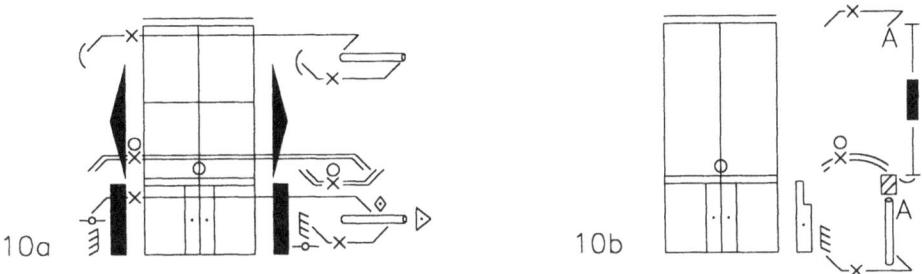

Dropping a Stick

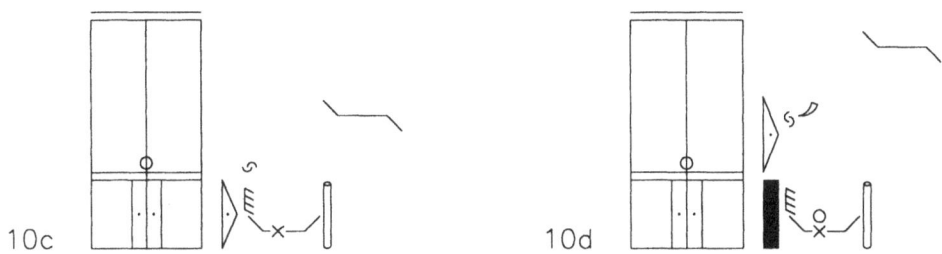

Throwing a Stick

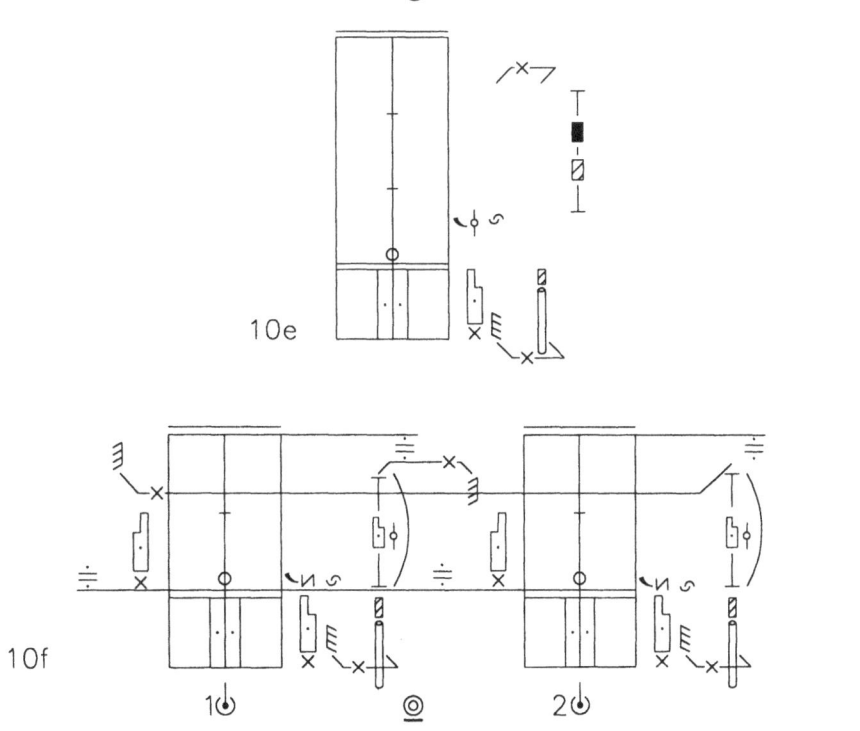

11 Movements of a Stick

11.1. In writing the movements of objects there is the choice of either describing the changes in the arm, wrist and hand, which make such movements possible, or directly describing the desired change for the object. In most cases the latter is more practical and focuses directly on what is important; the specific hand and wrist movements needed to achieve this result are understood and not written. When intricate manipulations occur, specific details such as the rotational state, hand grip, and use of the fingers will also need to be described.

11.2. **Object Carried Along.** When the arm moves in space the stick will automatically be carried along. In **11a** there is no change in the position of the arm or of the stick while the dancer turns. When the arm moves horizontally to the other side in **11b**, the stick remains upright, and no change takes place. The stick is pointing forward middle at the start of **11c**. As the arm moves across to the left, the stick is carried, and its direction will change to pointing to the left side and then pointing backward.[13] There is no change in the hand grasp.

11.3. The stick is also carried along when arm and object are in line, i.e. in the same direction, **11d**; as the arm moves, the stick maintains the same direction as the arm. In this example the stick will end pointing in line with the lower arm. The same is true for **11e** in which the stick is carried as the arm lowers, the stick ending pointing forward low.

11.4. In contrast to **11e**, **11f** states that, as the arm lowers, the stick is to remain vertical, indicated by the space hold. To achieve this retention of a direction for the stick, a marked change in the hand grasp must take place. Indication of a spot hold at the start for the grasp states that adjustment in the position of the hand at the point of contact is allowed.

11.5. **Specific Change of Direction for a Stick.** The change of direction for an object is written in the column above which the sketch of the object is drawn; this sketch usually appears in the starting position. The direction written refers to the free end, that is, the opposite end to which the object is grasped or held. If the stick is held in the middle, or at both ends, the end for which a direction has already been stated is the end to which subsequent directions relate. As mentioned before, for additional clarity the ends of the stick can be labeled as A and B.

11.6. In **11g**[14] a shepherd's crook is held in both hands; the direction is given for the crook end. The object changes direction simultaneously with the change of direction for the arms. In contrast, in **11h** the fairy's wand, held upright at the start, is waved to left and right as the dancer does a little curtsey.

Object Carried Along

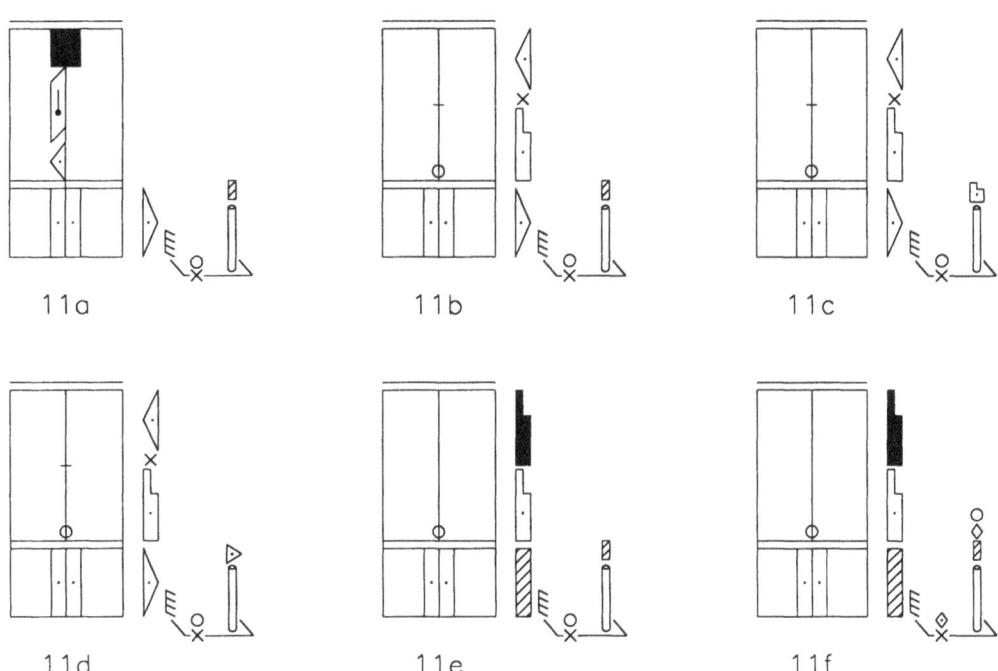

Specific Change of Direction for a Stick

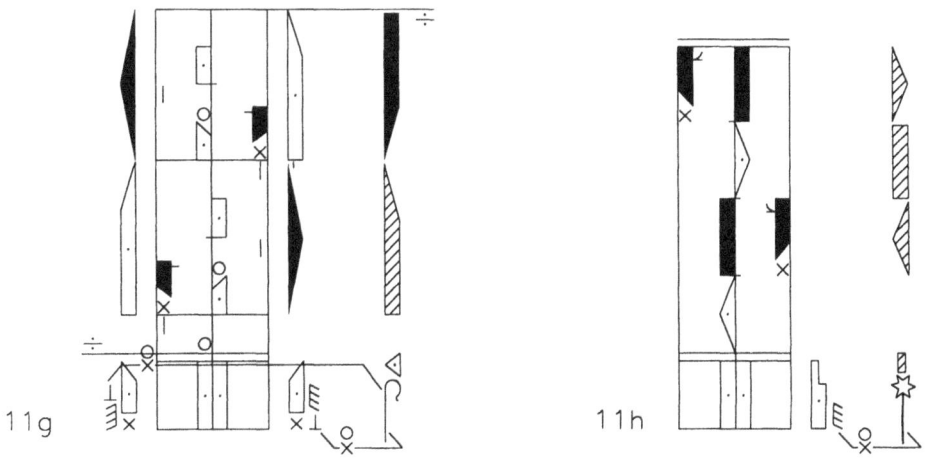

12 Rotating, Turning a Stick

12.1. Movements of the arm carrying a stick may make it rotate. The arm is down in **12a** and the stick being held is also down. As the lower arm rotates outward and inward the stick rotates in the same way, being carried along. If focus on the prop is important, this same action can be written as **12b**. In **12c** stick and lower arm are both vertically up. As the lower arm twists outward and then inward the stick automatically turns at the same time. Note that it may appear to the observer (and also to the performer) that lower arm and stick are *turning inward (to the left) instead of outward (to the right)*; the movement is, in fact, exactly the same as in **12a** but is seen here from *a different perspective*. This question of the direction of a rotation is also met when the arms are overhead.[15] Ex. **12d** describes the same movement as **12c** for the stick, the lower arm producing this result.

12.2. Spatial relationship of the prop to the performer may change the form of description. In **12e** the stick is horizontally side-to-side, the right hand grasping it in the middle from above; the stick is then shown to make a cartwheel rotation to the right and left. This is, in fact, made possible by the outward and inward twist of the lower arm, but this need not be mentioned.[16] Somersault rotations are shown for the stick in **12f**, made possible through flexions of the wrists.[17] These directions are judged from the performer's Standard Cross.

12.3. The arm rotation in **12g**, in which the arm is out to the side and the stick is at right angles to it (pointing forward horizontal), will produce a somersaulting action for the prop, written as such in **12h**. It is assumed in these examples that there is no adjustment in the hand grasp.

12.4. While the rotations in **12h** are judged from the performer's Standard system of reference, if the same action is to occur while the arm is moving in space, relationship to that system changes. In such cases a Body Key can be used for the prop and the direction or rotation relate to the point of attachment. In **12i** the stick rotates right and then left while the arm is moving up, across to the left and then returns to the side. The turning direction is judged in the same way as we describe a rotation of the arm - a body reference. In the case of a stick a longitudinal rotation can be identified and hence described.

12.5. In **12j** the stick is held by the fingers. In making it roll (forward and backward somersault rolls), the fingers can manipulate the stick without any spatial displacement of the hand. Note the use here of the spot hold to allow adjustments in the grasping.

Rotating, Turning a Stick

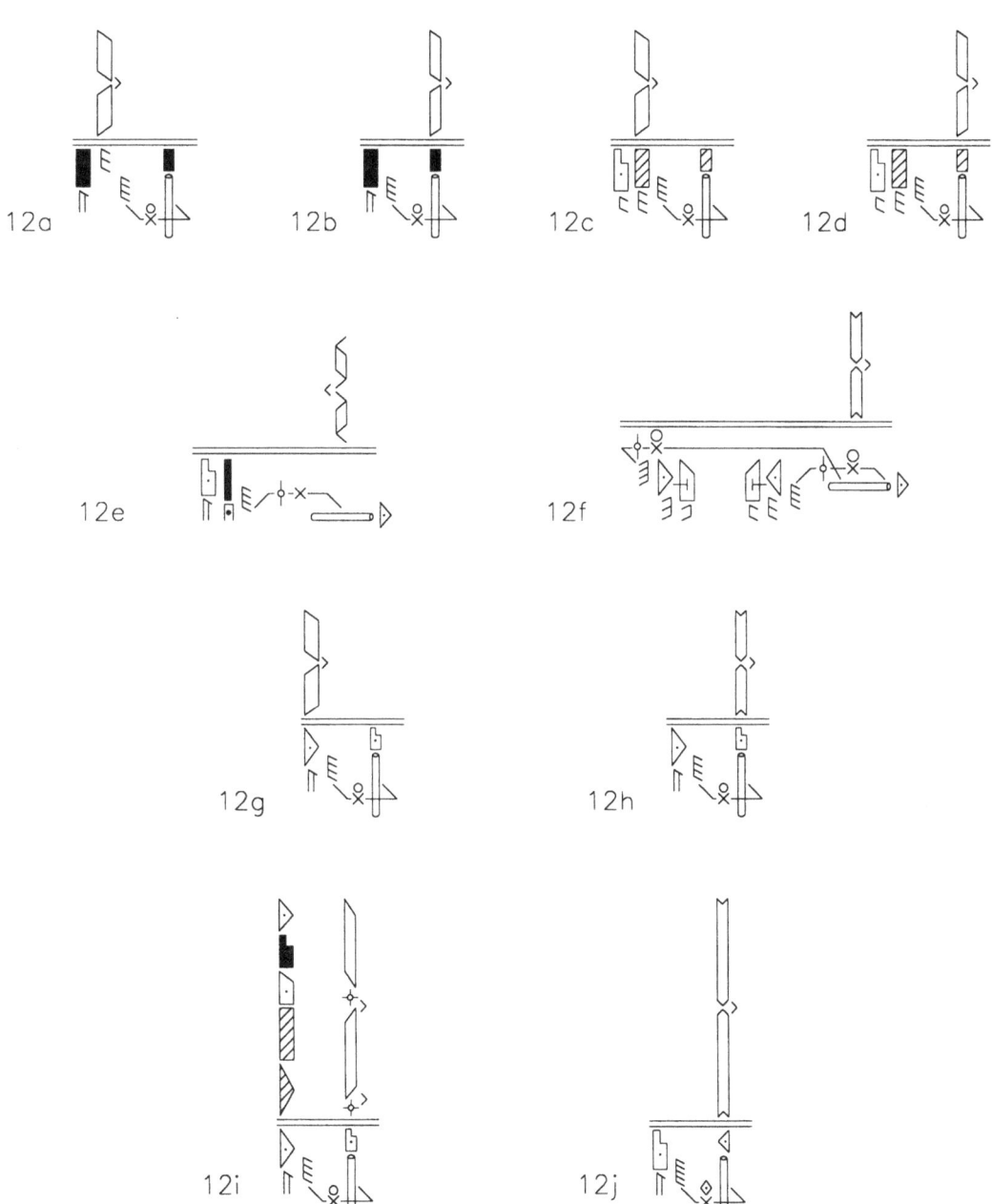

13 Circular Paths for a Stick

13.1. As with circular paths for arm gestures, circular paths for sticks can be written either with a series of direction symbols or through using the appropriate path sign. The latter often gives the message more quickly as well as showing fluent continuity. Such circles are produced through the appropriate whole arm, lower arm and wrist folding actions, this last often aided by passive inclusion of the lower arm. The following examples show frequently met circles.

13.2. **Swinging Indian Clubs.**[18] When swinging Indian Clubs, the club is often in line with the whole arm or the lower arm as these circle. In this case no individual movement needs to be recorded for the club, just the indication that spatially the prop equals (is an extension of) the lower arm. The smaller circles for the clubs require wrist manipulation, the neck of the club being held so that it can slide within the hand's grasp. Use of the spot hold over the carrying grasp indicates that such adjustments are allowed.

13.3. Ex. **13a** shows the technique for performing small 'wrist' circles for the club. The club starts by being held forward, in line with the arm. As it circles downward and backward the arm flexes slightly to accomodate this and the lower arm twists outward. During the second half of the circle the arm and wrist return to normal. Note use of the slightly diagonal backward direction, this makes clear that the club passes on the outside of the arm. While a forward somersault path sign could be used, as in **13b**, the timing is indicated more precisely with the direction symbols. The reverse circle is given in **13c**.

13.4. Here note the starting position, where the clubs are 'at the ready' in the following examples. Whole arm and lower arm open lateral circles are combined in **13d**, the lower arm circle on the right side passing in front of the left, and both passing in front of the body. The clubs should maintain the line of the lower arm, hence the indication of the space hold sign combined with the equal sign linked to the lower arm signs. In **13e** 'closed' circles (moving across the body first) are given.

Advanced Labanotation

Swinging Indian Clubs

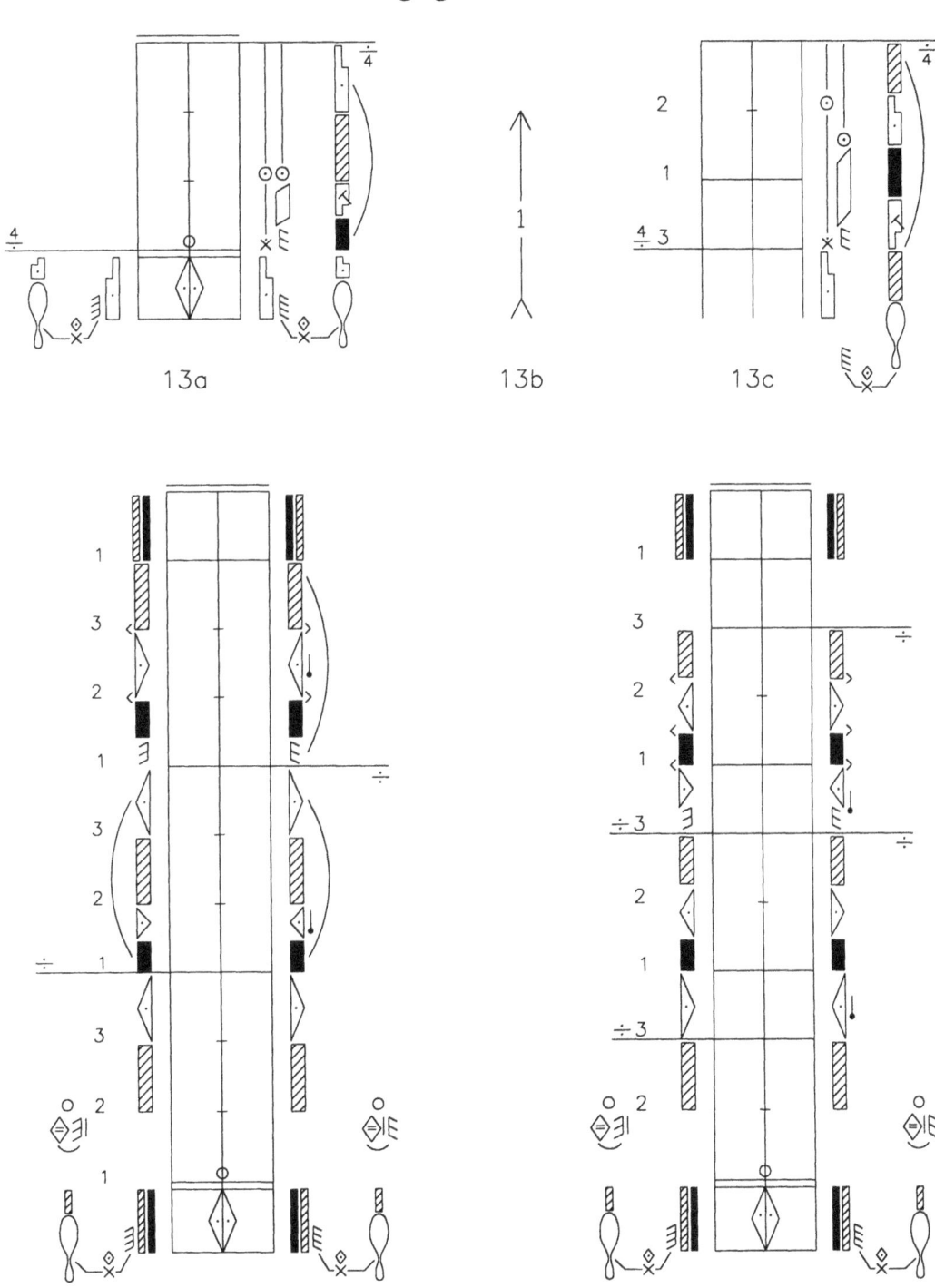

13.5. **Independent Circles for a Stick.** As in **13a** and **13b**, sticks are often manipulated independently, i.e. without a specific movement of the arm occurring at the same time. With the arm in front and the stick held upright, **13f** shows a lateral circular path for the end of the stick. In **13g** the same is written with a cartwheel path sign. The cartwheel path sign used in **13g** is the abbreviated form, the full sign is given in **13h**. An advantage of using the path sign is that multiple circles, which occur quickly, can be easily read; **13i** shows two and a half such circles. By using a spot hold for the grasp, change in manner of holding and finger manipulation are allowed to occur, as needed.

13.6. In a similar way the backward sagittal path of **13j** can be written as **13k**. The horizontal circle of **13l** can be indicated as **13m**. In these basic circles the axis of the circle is automatically understood: a sagittal axis for a cartwheel, a lateral axis for a somersault, and a vertical axis for a horizontal path.

13.7. Diagonal circles are not so familiar and need specific indications.[19] The specific axis, **13n**, abbreviated to **13o**, is stated and then applied to the more appropriate of the standard circular path signs. The standard axis for the somersault path of **13p** is side-to-side. By indicating a different axis, as in **13q**, we show that the path is to be deviated to the right to circle around this axis. In **13r** the stick is to follow this diagonal path, spelled out here with direction symbols. This same diagonal path is shown in **13s** with the somersault path of **13q**. This same path could equally well be expressed as **13t**, in which the standard forward-backward cartwheel axis has been deviated to the left; both the axis and the direction of the circling are clear.

13.8. If the path lies at a three-dimensional slant, the appropriate pins can be shown, **13u**. This path is spelled out in **13v** in which the stick begins in the right backward high direction. Should the stick start vertically and circle around the same axis, the path would be parallel to that of **13v** but lying slightly more toward the left front diagonal.

13.9. In many instances, the surface on which such paths are to be drawn provides a ready reference, a device established for Design Drawing (see the <u>Advanced Labanotation</u> issue on spatial variations and *Shape, Design, Trace Patterns*). The surface stated in **13w** is an imagined vertical wall at the performer's left front diagonal. It is on this surface that the circles of **13r** and **13s** are performed, notated in **13x**. By tilting this surface upward, as in **13y**, the appropriate circle can be drawn. This surface indication provides an alternative method of writing the circle in **13u**.

Advanced Labanotation

Independent Circles for a Stick

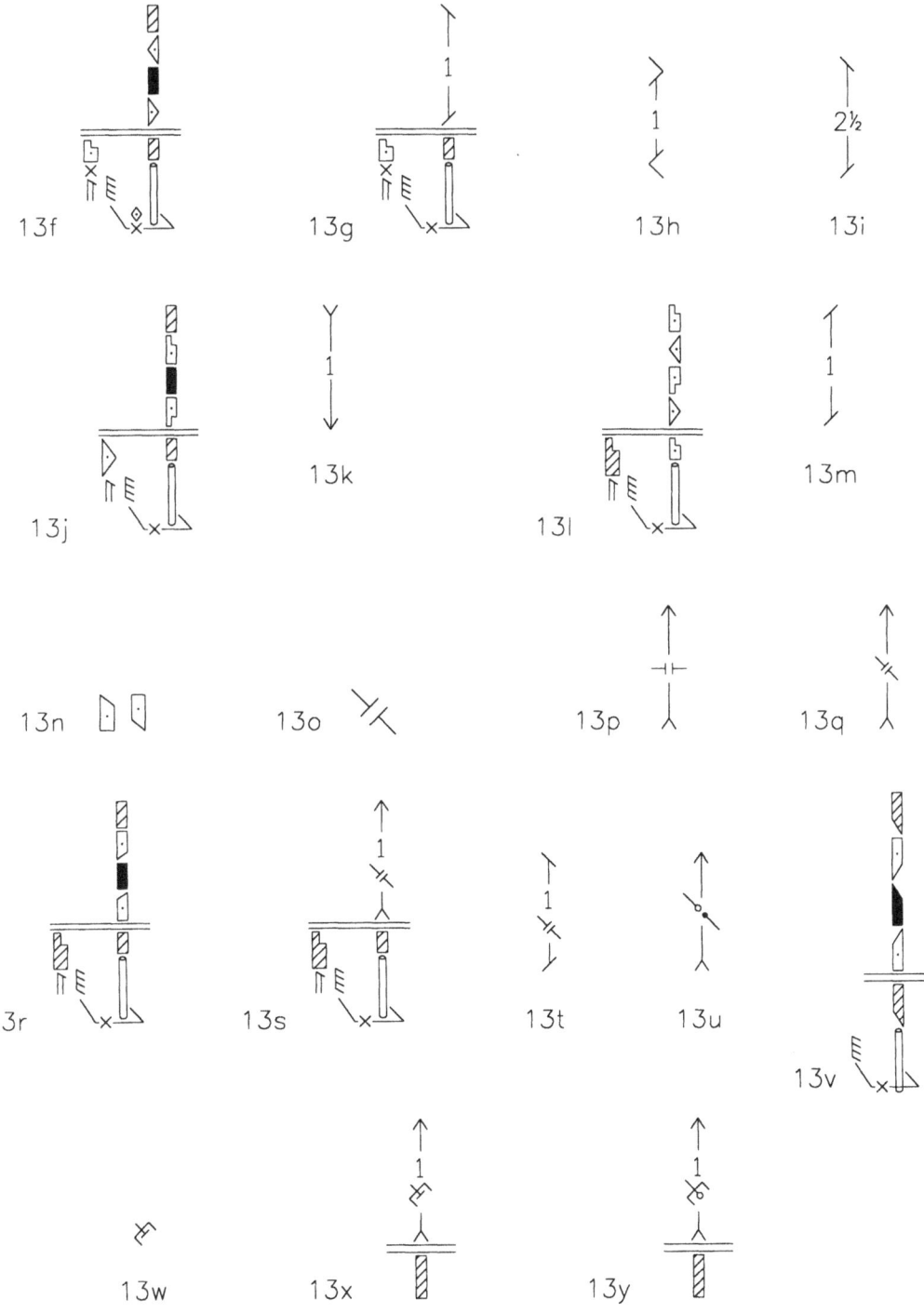

13.10. **Horizontal Circle Under the Legs.** Manipulating objects often involves relating to parts of the body, the path of the object passing over or under a limb, for example. In **13z**[20] an axe (basically a stick-like object) is held horizontally forward with the arm down. As the man springs up the axe circles counterclockwise, passing under his raised right leg and then under his left leg. The movement for the arm is shown but not the wrist flexion and rotation needed to produce the horizontal path for the axe. A dotted nearness bow could also have been used instead of the addressing sign in this example; either conveys the needed message.

13.11. **Twirling a Stick.** Another typical manipulation is twirling a stick in a cartwheel pattern with both hands, one hand taking over and replacing the other; this is shown in **13aa**.[21] Start by holding the stick in the middle with the right hand, grasping from above. One end of the stick is pointing side left. Directions from here on refer to this end.

13.12. Outward rotation of the right arm causes the stick to cartwheel to the right. As the marked end of the stick approaches being down, the right hand releases, with the result that only the thumb and index finger are holding the stick and helping it on its way. In preparation for taking over, the left arm rotates outward so that the inside of the wrist contacts the outside of the right wrist from below. The left thumb and index finger take over, the hold transferring to the whole hand as the left arm begins to rotate inward, keeping the stick moving continuously. As the stick nears its second complete circle, the right arm rotates inward to the point where the inside of the right wrist is touching the inside of the left wrist from above. At this moment the left hand releases its hold, the right hand grasps the stick from above, as at the start, and the whole sequence can be repeated. This double cartwheel for the stick is done at a very quick tempo; the two hands must be kept close to each other all the time to facilitate grasping the stick. These movements should be performed swiftly. Because it is not possible to provide all these details without the symbols consuming space on the page, the Time Sign for much speed has been added.[22]

Horizontal Circle Under the Legs

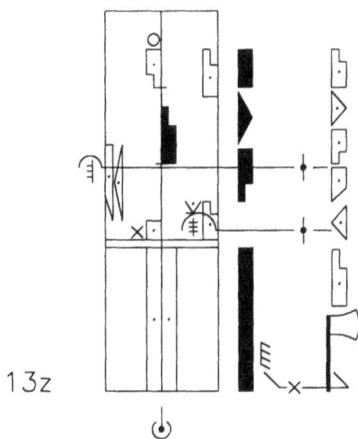

13z

Twirling a Stick

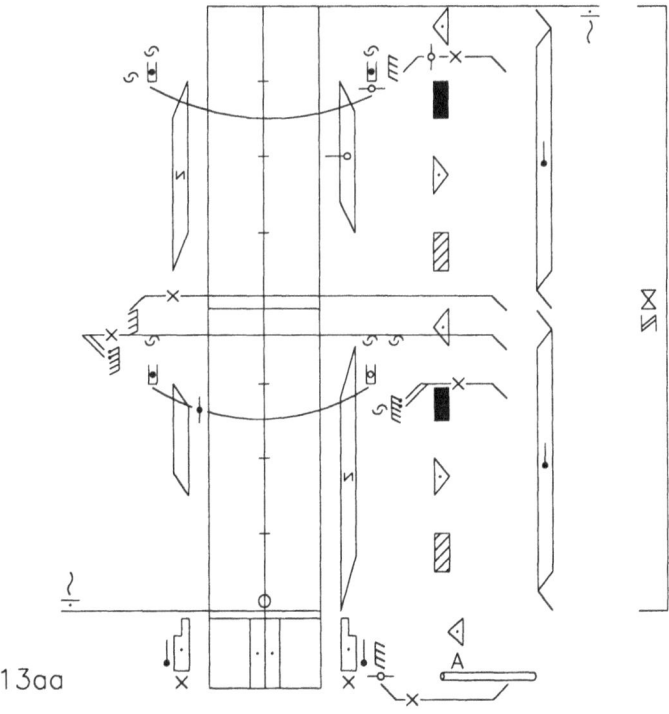

13aa

13.13. **Finger Twirl.** When twirling a baton, cane, or stick of some kind in one hand, the stick may pass through the different fingers. In **13ab**[23] the cane is held in the right hand between thumb and first finger, the other fingers are folded and behind the cane, i.e. nearer the performer. The palm starts facing up and remains so until near the end. As the cane makes cartwheel rotations to the left, it travels between each finger in turn until it reaches the little finger as the palm faces side left; it then rolls over the back of the fourth, middle, and first fingers as the palm faces down. Continuing the revolution the cane then rolls into the palm of the hand, now facing side left as the thumb grasps from the left and the fingers grasp from the right for the final $\frac{1}{4}$ turn (2 $\frac{1}{2}$ full revolutions).

Advanced Labanotation

Finger Twirl

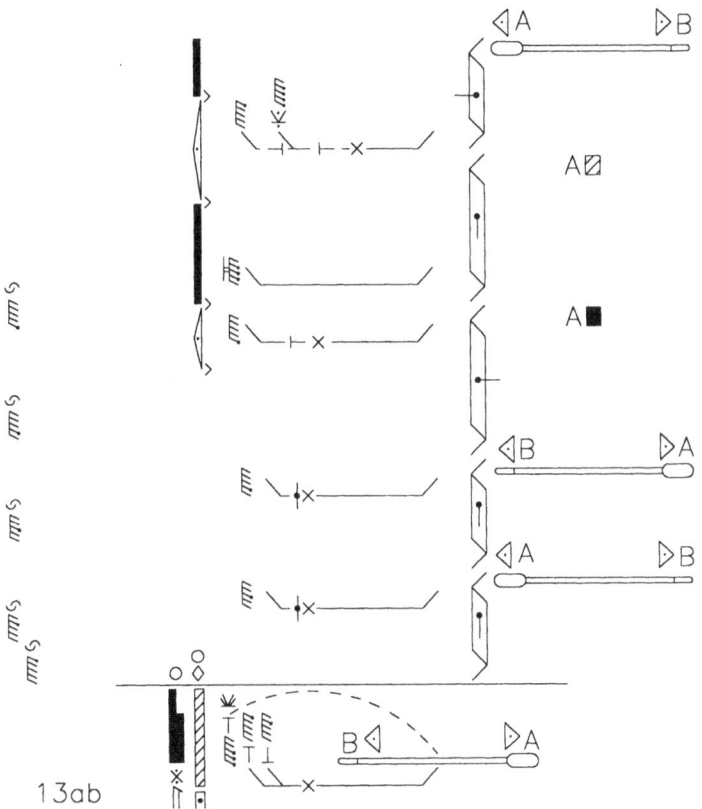

13ab

14 Tracing a Design

14.1. The aim may be for the end of a stick-like object to trace a design in the air. In **14a** it is a sword. Taking a lunge position, the performer traces a Z in the air on an imaginary surface, such as a wall, in front of him. The arm starts slightly across the body to start the design. This can give some idea of the size of the design; to be more precise the ending location for the arm can be given. (See also **15a-15c**. For details on Design Drawing see the <u>Advanced Labanotation</u> issue *Shape, Design Trace Patterns*.)

14.2. A design may also be traced on the floor with the end of a stick or other similar object. In **14b**, while turning, the performer repeats the loop-like design four times in front of her. This is followed by traveling sideward and at the same time making a wave-like pattern. This sideward traveling is then repeated to the left side.

14.3. In manipulating various objects it is helpful to include information on the design being made. This is further explored in the next section.

Tracing a Design

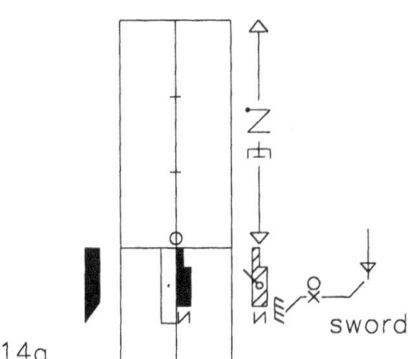

14a

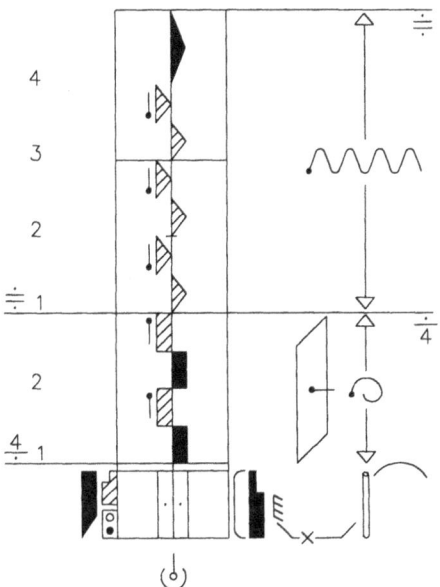

14b

15 A Stick - Figure Eight Patterns

15.1. The most direct way of writing figure eight patterns for a stick or other object is to use Design Drawing.[24] Ex. **15a** shows a figure eight, starting clockwise. This design is being drawn with the free end of the stick on the imaginary vertical surface in front of you. The stick is held near one end. The hold sign for the arm emphasizes that it does not move. The size of the design will depend on length of the stick and degree of flexion in the wrist and lower arm twist. This also applies to the following examples.

15.2. With the arm held out to the side, the figure eight of **15b** is shown to be 'drawn' on the imaginary wall to your right. This produces a sagittal design which starts forward and then continues backward.

15.3. In **15c** the arm holding the stick is higher and the surface in front of you on which the design is being drawn is at a tilt; thus the slant of the figure eight will be toward backward high and then toward forward low on each section of the 'eight'.

15.4. A sagittal figure eight can occur when the arm is held forward, in front of the body. In **15d** the stick is held in the middle, the designated end starting up. The movement is described as somersault paths, the first part of the eight is a forward circle in which the stick passes on the 'inside' of the arm; note the meeting line for the stick showing the arm to be at the right. The second half of this folded figure eight is a similar circle which passes on the outside of the arm. To perform this last part the arm has to adjust, flexing a bit more with the elbow moving toward the center line of the body.

15.5. This pattern could also be written with design drawing as in **15e**, where the surface changes for each part of the design. Note that, although the circle moves in the same direction - forward and downward, the change of surface requires that the design be drawn the other way. (For sagittal figure eight patterns see also **15k**)

15.6. This same figure eight pattern for a stick, found in male Hungarian dances for which 'lopsided' figure eight designs are typical, is written out in the standard way in **15f**, as is the reverse version in **15i**[25] The 'active' end of the stick is shown to start up; this end is usually heavier. The wrist flexions needed to produce this sagittal figure eight are not written, the wrist automatically adjusts to produce the design. The direction symbols show the need to deviate diagonally from the sagittal line. To help 'push the stick through' at the 'dead point' in the circle, the hand makes a downward pressing movement. The extra bending of the arm and its gradual return to being only slightly bent is shown for the second half of the pattern. Note that in these forward circles the hand movement is led by the thumb edge throughout.

A Stick - Figure Eight Patterns

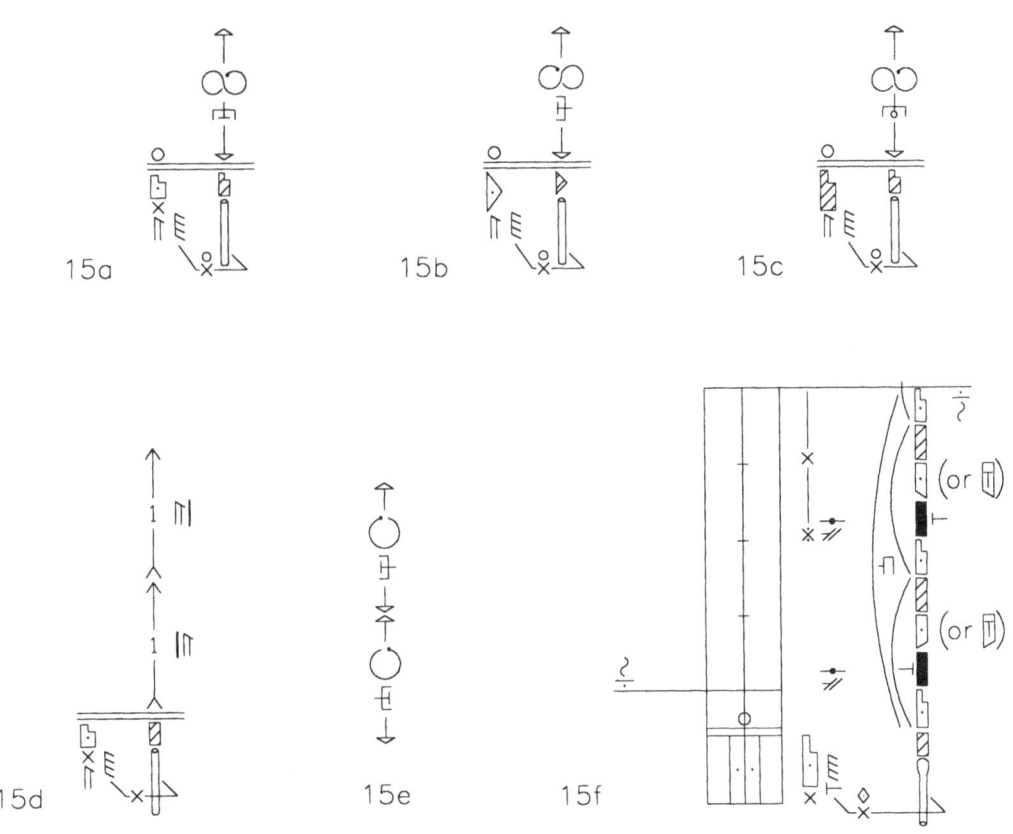

15.7. The reverse circle is shown in simplified form in **15g**. Again the stick passes on the inside of the arm in the first half and on the outside on the second half. Ex. **15h** gives the design drawing description of this reverse circle, which is fully spelled out in **15i**. The end of the stick must start pointing up. To start the circle the hand must turn outward. It is now the little finger edge which leads the whole pattern.

15.8. Ex. **15j** comes from *The Green Table* score.[26] The performer is holding a flag in his right hand, waving it in a figure eight pattern while performing specific steps and gestures. In general the flag follows the movement of the arm, producing a curved, flowing movement. Note use of the statement that the spatial aspects of the flag more or less equals that of the right arm (see 13.4). In this case, the ad lib. sign is added to state 'more or less'. It is clear in the design where the dancer dips and where there is an angular change into a straight-line gesture. It is important to note that the directions for the arm and the design are both related to the Constant Cross of Directions, they are not affected by the turns on the supporting foot.

A Stick - Figure Eight Patterns (continued)

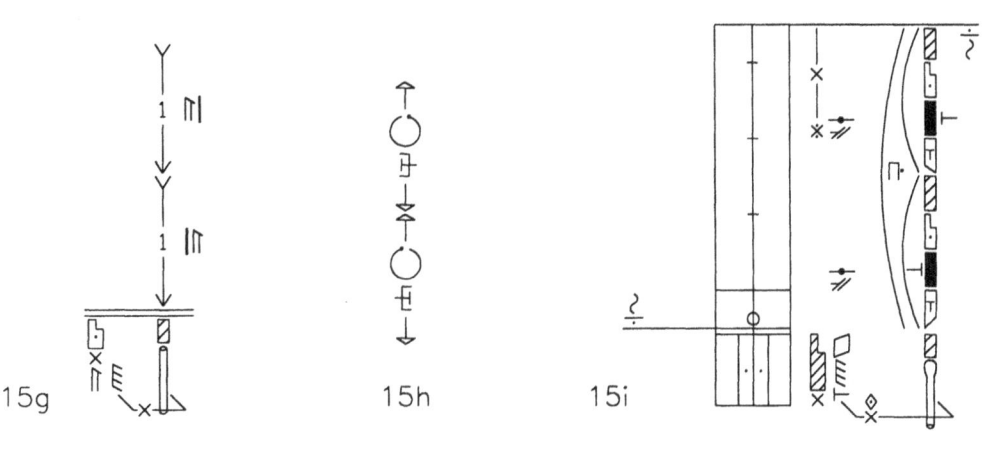

15g   15h   15i

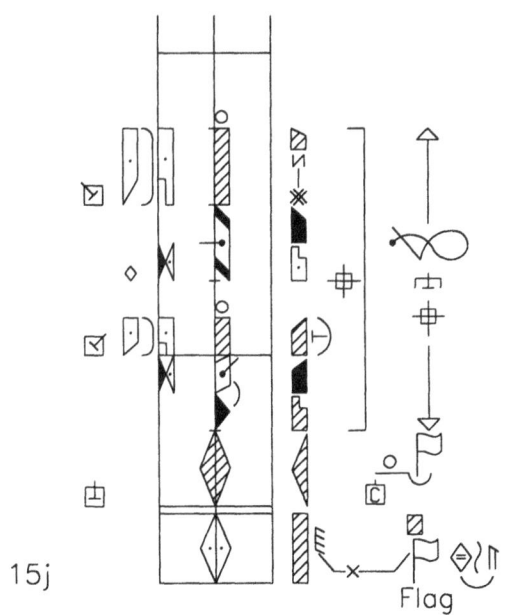

15j

Flag

15.9. **Sagittal Figure Eight.** Ex. **15k**[27] shows a sagittal Pinwheel pattern made while handling a baton or stick, a flat 'figure eight' being the result. Held at the balance point in the right hand in the 'valley' between the base of the thumb and base of the index finger, the baton starts with the ball pointing forward low. Wrist flexion and lower arm rotation cause the baton to describe a forward sagittal circle, the ball passing first on the inside (to the left) of the arm; then, on the second circle, the ball passes on the outside (to the right) of the arm. It is the flexion and rotation in the wrist and lower arm which propels and guides the direction of the baton.

15.10. **Horizontal Pinwheel.** Flexion and rotation of the wrist and lower arm are also involved in the horizontal wheel of **15l**. The ball of the baton, marked A here, always passes above the arm, the 'tail' always below.

Sagittal Figure Eight

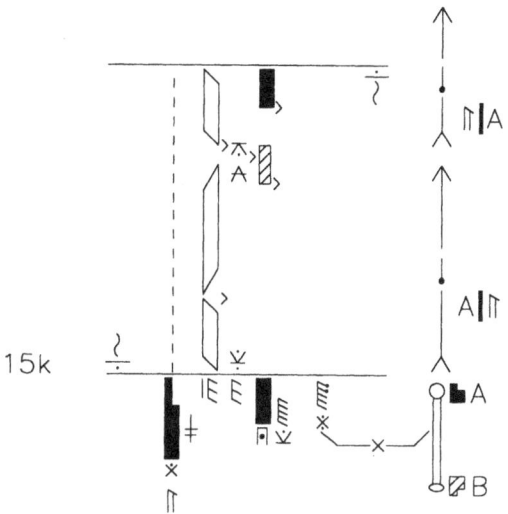

15k

Horizontal Pinwheel

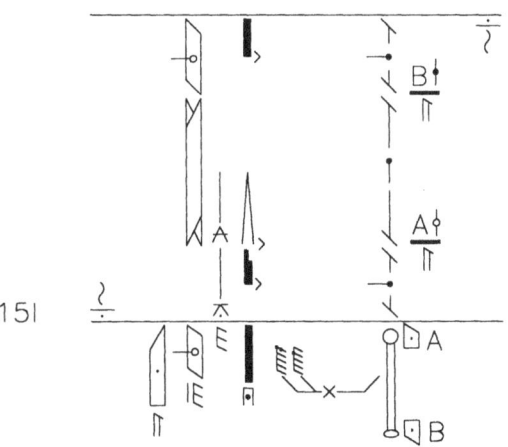

15l

16 Hitting Swords, Sticks

16.1. In many dances, the clashing or beating of sticks or swords adds visual as well as aural interest. In **16a**[28] the performer holds a sword up in each hand. He then rhythmically beats the swords one against the other, alternating which sword beats in front of the other.

16.2. **Hitting Swords with a Partner.** In fencing there are many different ways for one sword to contact the other; a simple choreographed example is given here. The protagonists in **16b** both perform the same movements. They start facing in opposite directions, each right side to right side (stated between the staves), each having a sword in each hand. With a backward flourish, the right hand swords hit while held sideward high. The right arm then moves down so that the same sword can hit the sword in their left hand. Note the small backward deviation for the right-hand sword to move away from the partner's sword.

16.3. In partner dances with sticks there are many ways in which the sticks may be hit. The men identified as 1 and 2 in **16c**[29] are facing each other. Note the center of the stick is identified as C. First one 'attacks' the other, then the other 'attacks'. No. 1 begins in a defensive position, holding his stick in both hands, his right arm across so as to protect his face. The stick (judged from the right hand) is pointing diagonally back low. As he advances he releases his left hand, extends his right arm in an arc diagonally up and hits No. 2's stick in the center, while No. 2 simultaneously retreats and takes up the defensive position which No. 1 had at the start. They then reverse rôles.

Note use of the sign for shoulder and hip inclusion in a step, **16d**. As this sign is not commonly known it should be glossarized in a score. This indication brings the right shoulder and hip (i.e. the right side of the body) slightly forward as the step is taken. In this sequence the inclusion is to be retained during the next two steps, hence the hold sign; it is automatically canceled by the left hip-shoulder inclusion which occurs with the backward step. Normally such hip-shoulder inclusion is not retained but is automatically canceled with the next step. The double accent sign is used to indicate that the striking of the other stick should be very loud.

Advanced Labanotation

Hitting Swords, Sticks

16a

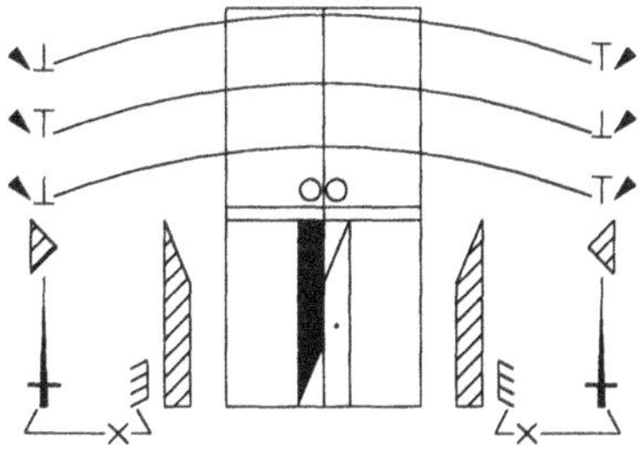

Hitting Swords with a Partner

16b

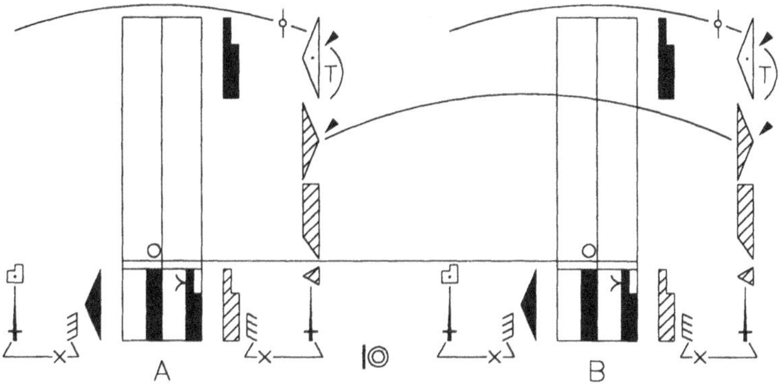

16c

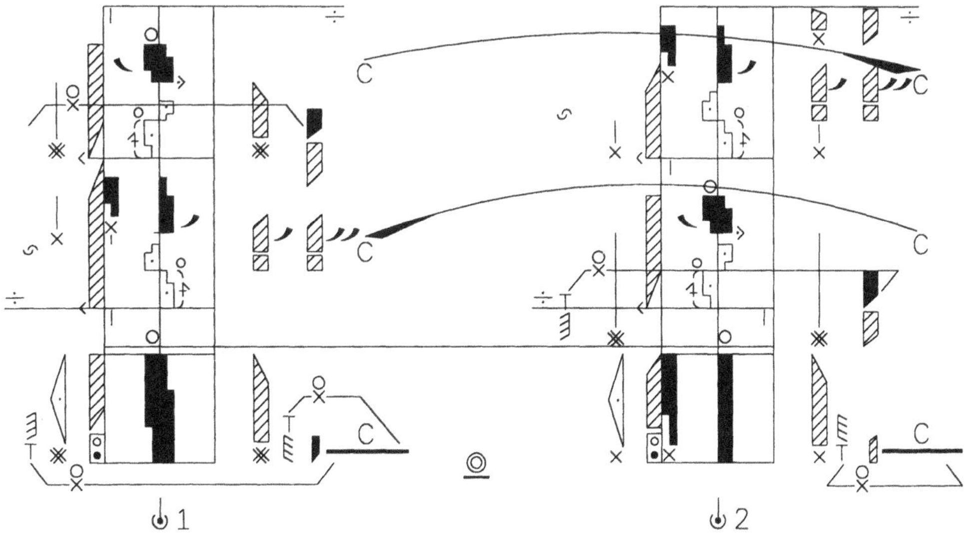

        1   2

C = center of stick

16d

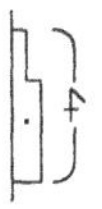

17 Relating to Sticks on the Floor

17.1. **Crossed Sticks on the Floor.** In **17a** the pre-staff diagram indicates that the big X represents two crossed sticks on the floor; these have been designated as B.[30] The dancer starts facing front with the sticks in front of him. With sideward steps to the left he makes a complete circle around B clockwise, always facing the sticks. Note the indication of B as being the focal point of the circle.

17.2. In contrast, in **17b**[31] the dancer circles the sticks but without change of front, thus he is always facing the audience. This circling without turning is shown by the space hold sign within the path sign and also the fact that the amount of circling is given as $1/1$ instead of a black pin, which for the body-as-a-whole indicates a change of Front. A single number 1 can be used to show a full circle but it can too often be mistaken for a pin.

17.3. Placing one's feet between the sticks to make particular patterns is familiar in Hungarian dance as well as in Scottish dance in which two crossed swords are placed on the ground. For this the spaces between the sticks need to be identified. The pre-staff drawing of **17c**[32] designates the identification of the spaces by using the letters **a**, **b**, **c** and **d**. The dancer starts facing front with space **a** in front of him. Leaping forward he lands on his right foot in space **c**; this is shown by the support bow linking his support to space **c**. During the two steps in place it is understood that the dancer stays in space **c**. He then springs into a 2nd position traveling backward and arriving with his right foot in space **d** and his left in space **b**. This is followed by a $1/4$ turn in the air, which lands in 2nd position with his right foot in space **c** and his left in space **a**.

Advanced Labanotation

Crossed Sticks on the Floor

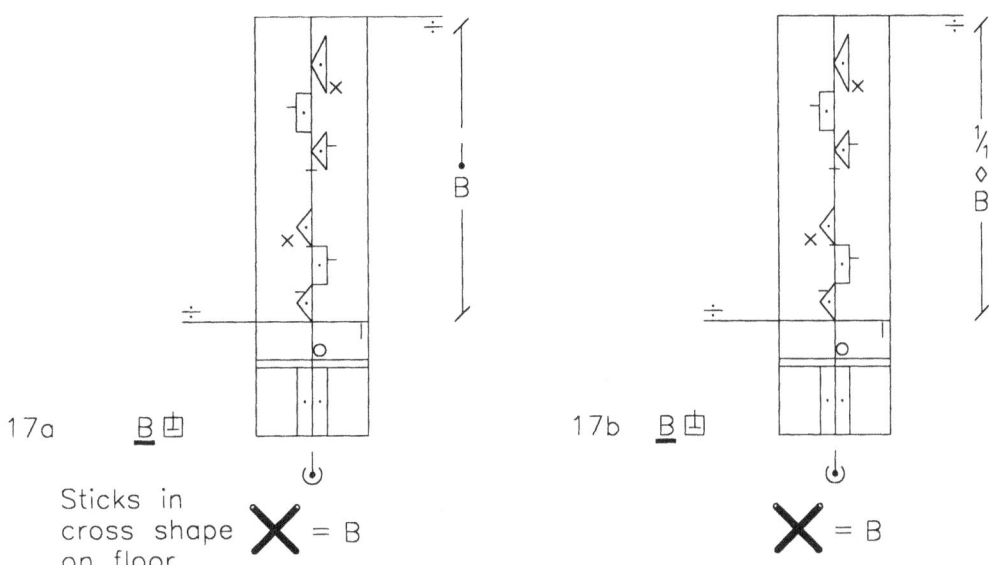

17a Sticks in cross shape on floor. X = B

17b X = B

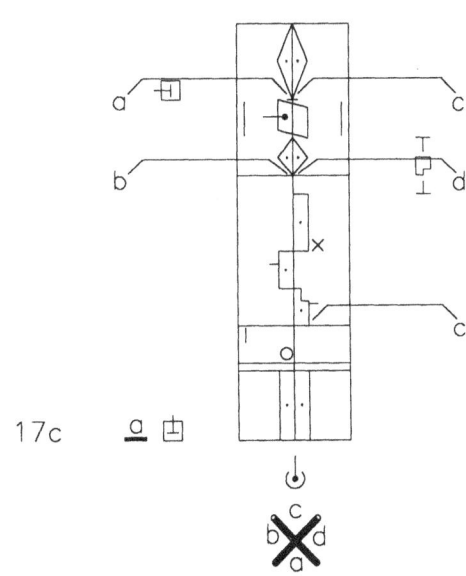

17c

18 Handling a Prop Gun

18.1. A dance for a boy with a toy rifle,[33] pretending to be a soldier, brings up the need to show different placements and moves with this prop. In the glossary to this dance, the gun is shown by a drawing of the gun, as in **18a**. In the following presentation, example numbers are given for reference. Moves with the gun use a visual representation of the prop. As these are excerpts, no footwork is given until the very last action.

18.2. In the opening, 'marching' position, **18b**, the gun is 'shouldered'. The butt of the gun is in the left hand, the barrel rests on the boy's left shoulder, and the direction for the gun is backward high. The gun is then placed in the aiming position, as shown in **18c**. The right hand grasps near the butt, palm grasping from in front, fingers from the left, bringing the gun horizontal; the left hand then grasps the barrel near its base.

18.3. The end of moving into aiming the gun is shown in **18d**. The direction of the aim is left front diagonal. The chest twists to the right, which then allows the butt to be supported at the front of the right shoulder. The left hand slides along the barrel, the right hand grasps at the trigger, the head inclines and the eyes look in the direction of the gun.

18.4. Once this passage is over, the boy returns the gun to its original 'marching' position, **18e**. To do so, while still supporting the gun, he lowers his right arm, the gun being moved to point backward high again. The left hand then releases to grasp the butt, the barrel again resting on the left shoulder, the right hand releases and the arm returns to his side. Another aim is taken in **18f**, this time to forward horizontal. A similar change of grasps takes place.

18.5. In **18g** the gun changes to being carried horizontally, side to side in front of the body. Both hands change their grasp to holding the gun from above. Note the right hand sliding into position over the butt of the gun.

18.6. In **18h** there is a return to the opening shouldered gun position, while **18i** shows the change at the end of the dance to hold the gun vertically, grasped by the barrel, the left hand higher than the right. A sharp upward displacement prepares for the sharp downward motion, which, with the quick movements of his right leg and the counter head movement, gives a clear, strong ending to the dance.

Advanced Labanotation

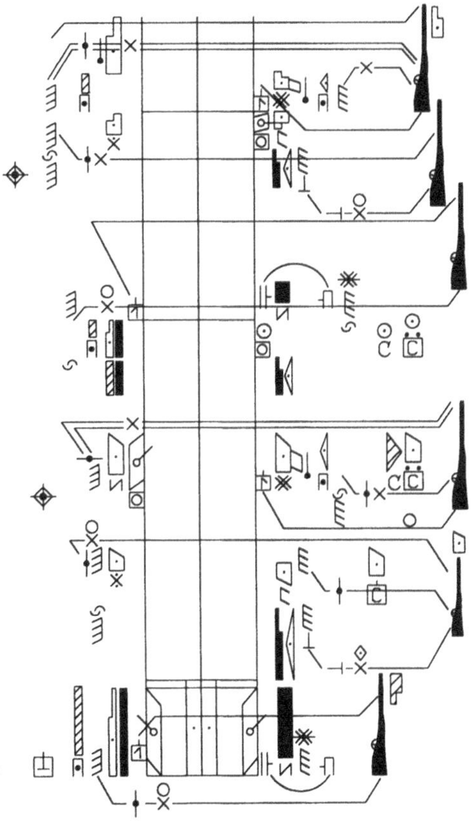

Handling a Prop Gun

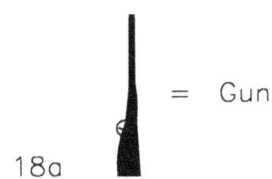

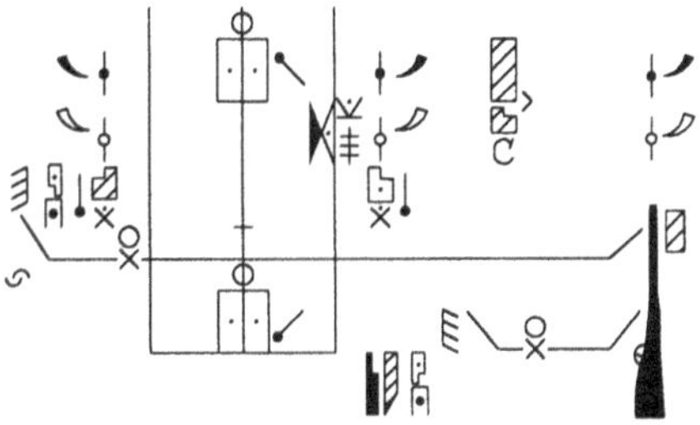

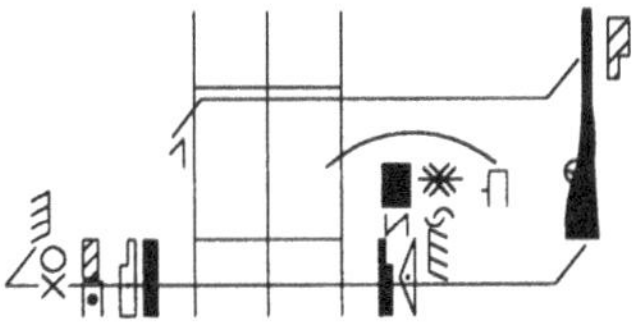

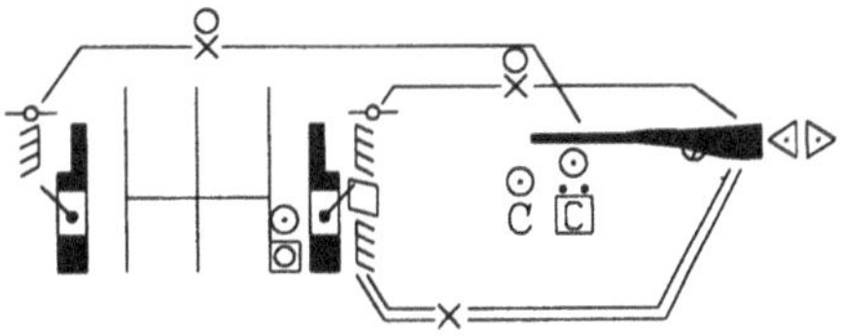

19 Handling an Umbrella

19.1. Similar to a sword, an umbrella has a 'working' end. In addition it may be carried open or closed (furled). This is also true of a parasol. The drawing of the umbrella can convey at once its closed or open state: in **19a** it is closed; in **19b** it is open.

19.2. As with other props, the drawing of this object on the page can suggest its vertical or horizontal placement. In **19a** and **19b** the impression is of its being upright, while in **19c** it appears to be downward. However, this does not always follow. Ex. **19d** adds the information that the tip is pointing backward; the tip is clearly pointing to the left in **19e**, as it is also in **19f** where space has not been taken for a lateral drawing. While it is usual for an umbrella or parasol to be held by the handle, it may be held by the tip, **19g**, or in the middle, **19h**.

19.3. **Degrees of Opening (Spreading).** For the following pictograms the degree of openness is given next to each drawing. For its closed state, the neutral, the umbrella is shown to be elongated, **19i**. Opening is shown by degrees of three-dimenional extension - **19j** being slightly open, **19k** halfway and **19l** fully open.[34]

19.4. A pictogram of the umbrella or parasol is given whenever possible, but if room for a full drawing does not exist in the score, the letter U can be designated to represent the umbrella, **19m**, and the appropriate degree of opening can be indicated. In **19n** the umbrella has been given a vertical staff in which is placed information concerning its state. Here it starts closed and then is halfway open. Ex. **19o** shows labeling the staff as U; the prop starts fully opened and then approaches the closed state.

19.5. An umbrella or parasol has no front or back. Therefore, where a particular part of the 'cover', the shade part, is facing is usually not designated. It may, however, be grasped by the edge of the cover, as in **19p**. In a fancy routine with a parasol, parts of the cover may be touched. In **19q** the parasol is held upright while the left palm touches (from the direction high left) the center area of one section of the cover.

Advanced Labanotation

Handling an Umbrella

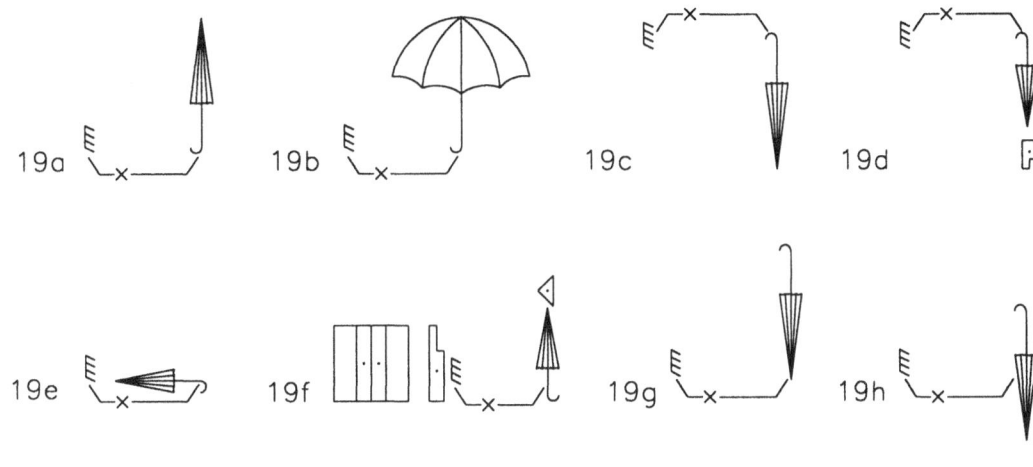

Degrees of Opening (Spreading)

19i 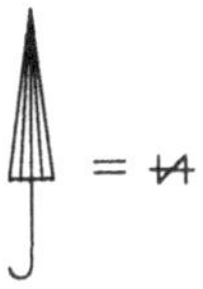 19j 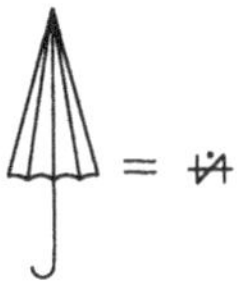 19k  19l

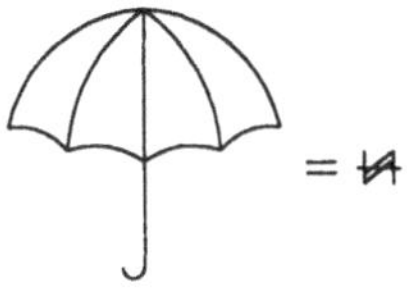

19m U = Umbrella

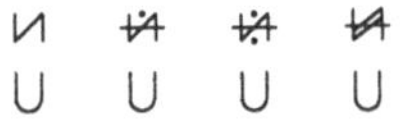

19n

19o

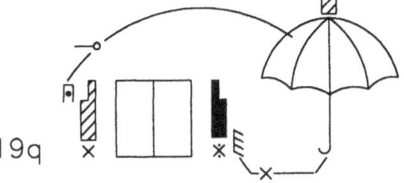

19.6. **Identifying Parts of the Object.** When space is not available to allow representational drawings of an object, it may be necessary to make a schematic drawing at the start of the score designating specific parts through numbers or letters. This information is usually given in a glossary at the start of the score. In **19r** we see a diagram of a parasol indicating H for the handle, T for the tip end, C for the cover and E for the edge of the cover. Lower case letters are used for specific parts of the cover: a = area near edge, b = center area, c = area near tip. If the examples provided in this book do not suffice, the choice of these identifications is up to the notator. Specifying parts of the handle may also be needed, as shown in **19s**.

19.7. With such abbreviations it is practical to use a staff for the prop with specific columns for the parts. Here the direction of the parasol is given in the right column, while letters identifying parts of the object are written in the left column in order to show touches, grasps, etc. A small parasol, identified as P, is being used in **19t**. Held upright in the right hand, it is moved across toward the left side and then 'batted' back to the right side by the left hand, which then moves across to grasp it by the edge and carry it out to the left, the right hand letting go. Note the space hold for the vertical direction of P, showing that the object is carried in space but does not change its vertical orientation. The traveling for the parasol is not written as such, as it results from the movements of the carrying arm.

Identifying Parts of the Object

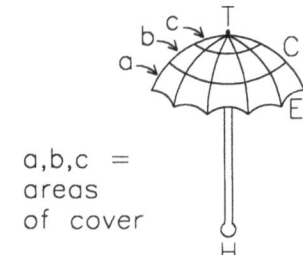

19r   a,b,c = areas of cover

E=Edge
T=Tip
C=Cover
H=Handle

19s

Parts of Handle

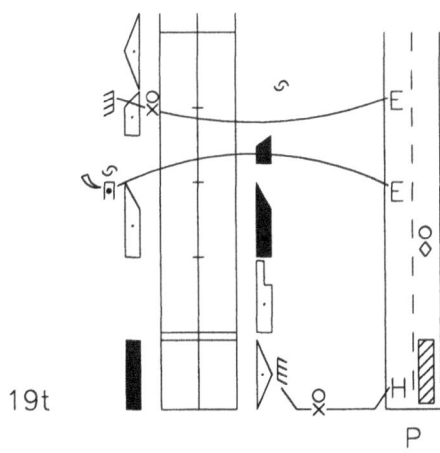

19t

P=Parasol

20 Handling a Ball

20.1. Using or playing with a ball may involve tossing it up, catching it, throwing it, rolling it along the floor, and so on. In the following examples no specific timing is indicated. Were the actions to be co-ordinated with music or some basic beat, then timing would need to be specific. The finger and wrist motions required to produce a particular spin on a ball as it is thrown are not being investigated here.

20.2. The pre-staff indication in **20a** identifies the drawing of a ball. The person grasps the ball from below in the right hand. With a small upward motion the ball rises in the air, falls down and is caught in the left hand. Here, although the throwing action has been written, the path of the object would in itself presuppose the required action to produce this result.

20.3. In contrast, **20b** shows the ball to be released downward, hitting the floor and then bouncing up to be caught in the left hand. Starting by grasping the ball from below, the hand is turned and a sharp downward action occurs just as the ball is being released. Note the path for the ball, the contact with the floor (T in a box for *terra* could be used here, if needed) and the resultant rising. In this example, because it is being caught by the left hand, the ball has been drawn again on the left of the staff for convenience.

20.4. In **20c** the ball is on the floor. It is hit from behind and rolls forward, traveling a long distance. The number of revolutions is not important. The form of rolling is judged from the person's point of view, the ball not having a defined front-back, right-left, or up-down. As there is no indication of leaving the floor, it is assumed that the ball rolls along the floor; rolling indications, as in **20d**, could be added if it is not clear in the context.

20.5. The player in **20e** is watching the ball before jumping to try to catch it. The addressing sign is used to indicate watching as well as relating the hand to the ball.

Advanced Labanotation

Handling a Ball

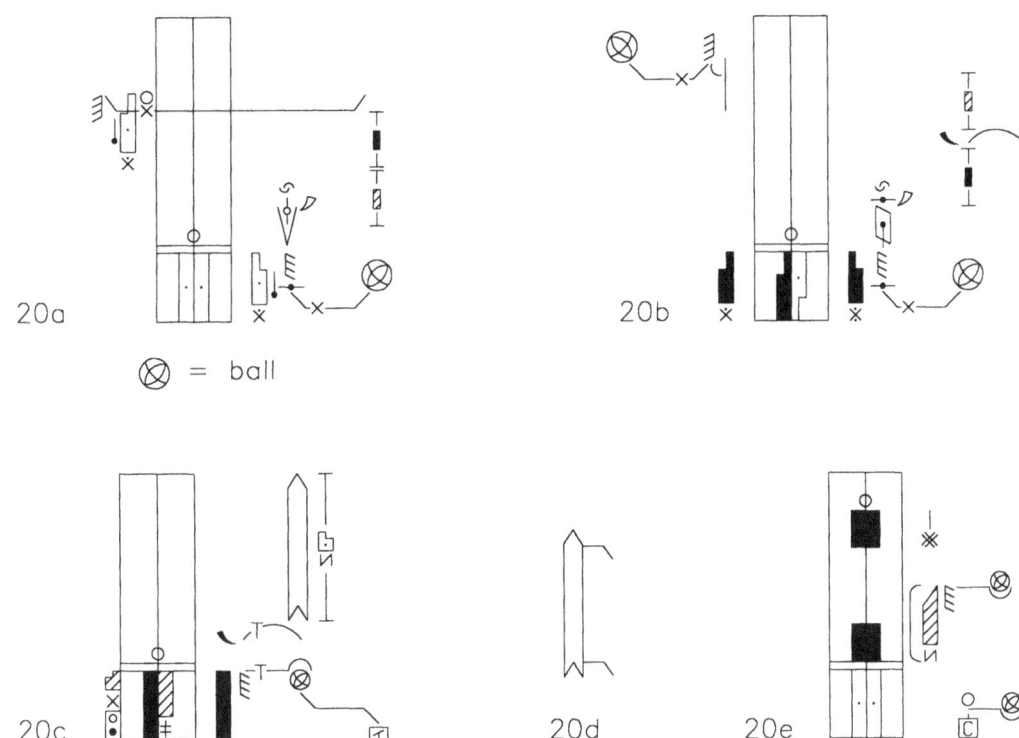

⊗ = ball

20.6. **Juggling with Two Balls.** Juggling with two balls may be done using only one hand, or with two hands, as shown in **20f**.[35] This exercise is, in fact, a preparation for juggling with three balls. The motions of the lower arm which prepare to send the balls up into the air and then to catch them mainly follow an eliptical track, an overcurve and then an undercurve. At the start of **20f** the palms face up, each holding a ball. While the upper arm is basically down, it is shown to have a passive reaction to assist the movement of the lower arm. The lateral displacement for the lower arms should be slight. A slight overcurve for the right lower arm as it opens slightly, is followed by an undercurve in preparation for throwing ball number 1. Ball number 2 is thrown in a similar manner while the first ball is in the air. The left hand then catches ball 1, and soon after, the right hand catches ball 2. The ball should stay in the lateral plane as it rises and falls. Note the path of the ball in the air, indicated through Design Drawing. As it is descending, ball number 1 passes at the left side high of ball number 2.

20.7. **Rolling a Ball Along the Body.** Many tricks in using a ball involve rolling it across part of the body such as a limb or the torso. The example given in **20g** shows a ball rolling along one arm, across the top of the chest and onto the other arm. The arms begin outstretched sideward with palms facing up. From being grasped in the right hand, a slight upward movement of the hand sends it rolling on its way. The upper spine, the shoulder section, is arched slightly backward thus providing the surface for the ball to roll over. The left hand catches the ball when it arrives at the end of the left arm. The notation indicates rolling over the unit of right arm, front of shoulder area, left arm with a supporting bow at the start and at the finish. The rolling progresses sideward with continuous contact.

Advanced Labanotation

Juggling with Two Balls

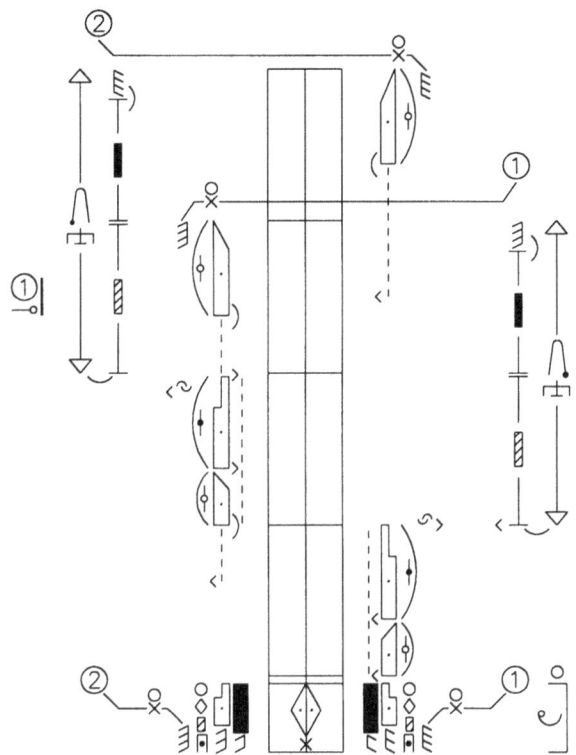

20f

Rolling a Ball Along the Body

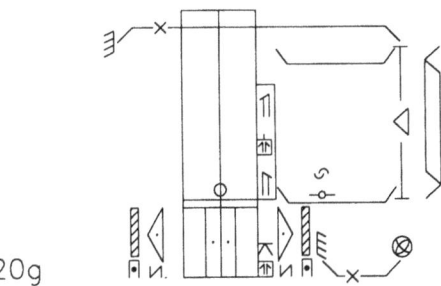

20g

21 Relating to a Cup, Jar or Bottle

21.1. A cup or mug is usually grasped and lifted by its handle, **21a**. A beaker however, having no handle, may be grasped in more ways. Using the right hand, these may be: from the right side, **21b**; from in front, **21c**; from above, **21d**; or from below, **21e**. By rotating the hand inward, the cup can be grasped from the left, **21f**; it can also be grasped from behind in which case the palm will automatically face forward according to the Standard Key, **21g**. Note that, in addition to the pin, the contact/supporting bow is drawn as clearly as possible to the appropriate part of the object.

21.2. Instead of the usual grasping an object by closing the hand, there is the possibility of lifting an object, such as a vase, by spreading the hand inside the opening, **21h**. The sign for inside (in the middle) is placed after the hand sign and three-dimensional extension is indicated in the supporting bow.[36]

21.3. A vase with two handles may be carried as in **21i**. Without handles, it may be picked up through a grasping action of the palms, **21j**.[37]

21.4. Hungarian dances often feature relating to a bottle,[38] identified in **21k** as B. At the start of **21l**, B is shown to be on the ground and the male dancer's relationship to it is stated, i.e. B is diagonally-right in front. During the first three steps the dancer passes behind B, and ends with B diagonally-left in front of him. On the next three steps he passes B on his left and ends with B diagonally-left behind. Compare this form of traveling around the bottle, always facing the same way, to **21m**, in which, as the dancer circles clockwise, the bottle is always on her right. The bottle is stated as being the focal point at the start of the circling. This focal point for circling can also be stated by placing the object (or its identification) within the circling sign, **21n** (see also **17a**).

21.5. In the next example the areas on either side of the bottle need to be identified. The small floor plan of **21o** shows the bottle and also area **a** and area **b**. The girl starts facing the audience with the bottle diagonally-left in front of her. She makes a small *rond de jambe* with her right leg above the bottle and leaps onto the **b** side of the bottle. After a rocking step the whole is then repeated symmetrically, the left leg circling over the bottle and the leap landing on the **a** side of the bottle. Note use of the support bow linking the landing step to the appropriate area. The $^1/_8$ turn during the 2nd and 3rd steps is written outside the staff; there should be no swiveling for the steps.

Relating to a Cup, Jar or Bottle

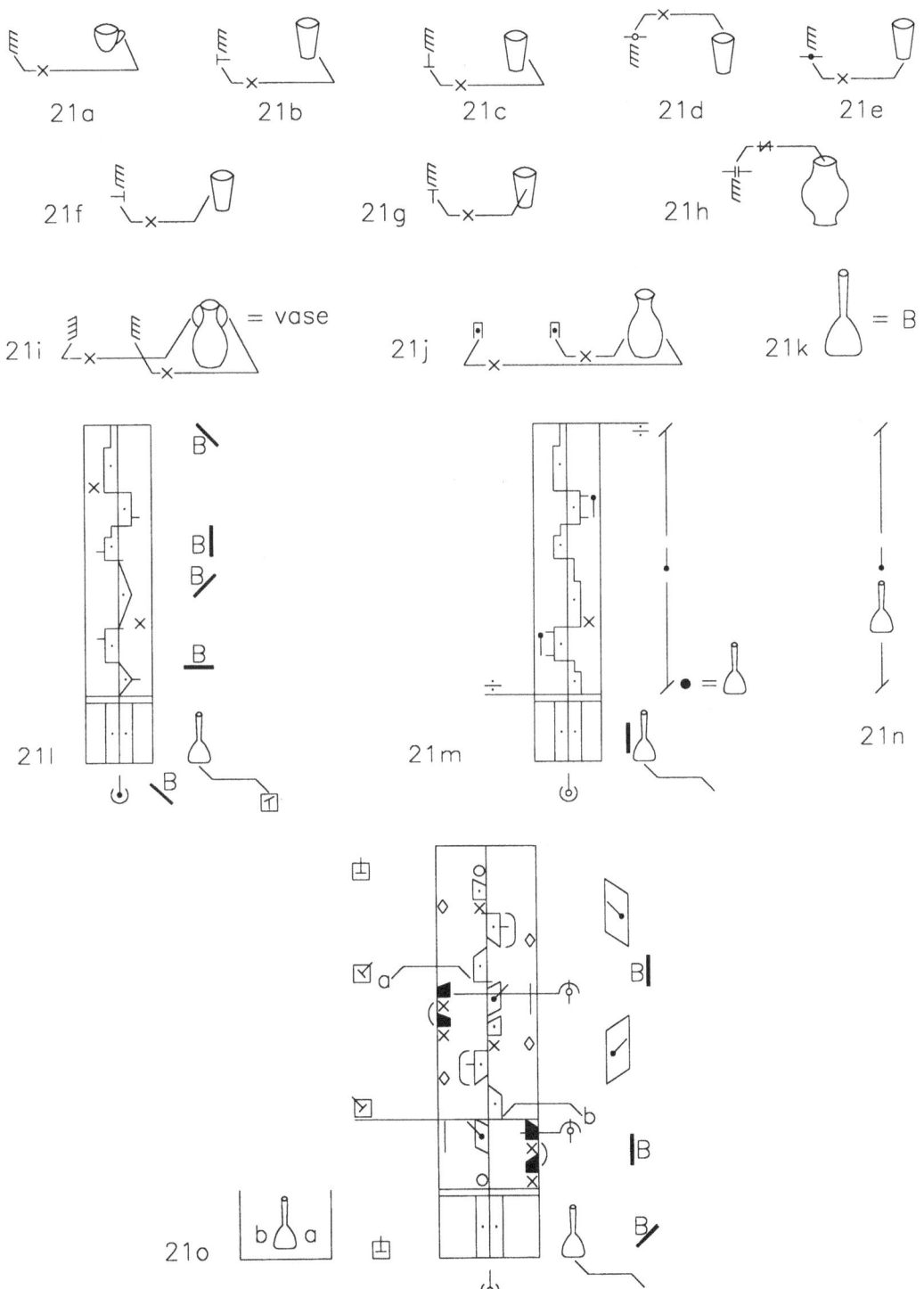

22 Handling a Book

22.1. A book being handled may be closed or open; **22a** shows a closed book. In **22b** the book is shown to be lying on a table. It is then picked up and placed on the head, balancing there as the person walks forward. In **22c** a book held in the left hand is tossed to the side in such a way that it turns as it travels.

22.2. The identification of an open book is given at the start of **22d**. One needs to know how it is held and how it is oriented. Here the open book is carried on the right palm without grasping. No 'above' or 'below' signs have been given, as the relationship is self-evident, the palm automatically facing up. In **22e**, with the arm forward, the right hand grasps the center fold of the half-opened book. Here the drawing of the book already indicates its state, although, to be specific, directions for the two edges of the book have been given. Holding an open book with the right arm is shown in **22f**. The book is at a slant, the top end pointing forward high; the hand grasps from in front (approaching from forward high) while the lower part of the book rests on the elbow.

22.3. Holding a book on both palms, **22g**, again needs no above/below indications but the book orientation is shown to be forward/backward. The open book is vertical in **22h**, with the printed side facing the performer, made clear from the drawing; both hands grasp the lower edge from in front, i.e. the palms are basically facing backward, toward the person.

22.4. The vertical book in **22i** is shown to be hanging down, grasped from behind (palm facing forward) by the right hand; the printed surface is again toward the performer. The hand will therefore be covering part of the text. The half-open book in **22j** is grasped on the horizontal part (the right part edge) by the right hand, the palm facing down (grasp is from above), while the left hand touches the edge of the part that is vertically up, presumably to balance it.

22.5. When orientation or movements of a book cannot be shown pictorially it can be given a column of its own, labeled B to designate 'book', **22k**. An open books is shown as laterally fully opened, **22l**. When both sides close in, the movement is one of contracting at the center, **22m**. When one side, here the left, closes, **22n**, the appropriate side of the adduction sign is thickened. For the appropriate state of being closed, the signs of **22m** represent the standard angles. If the book were folded backward the signs of **22o** would be used. A one-sided backward folding is indicated in **22p**.

Advanced Labanotation

Handling a Book

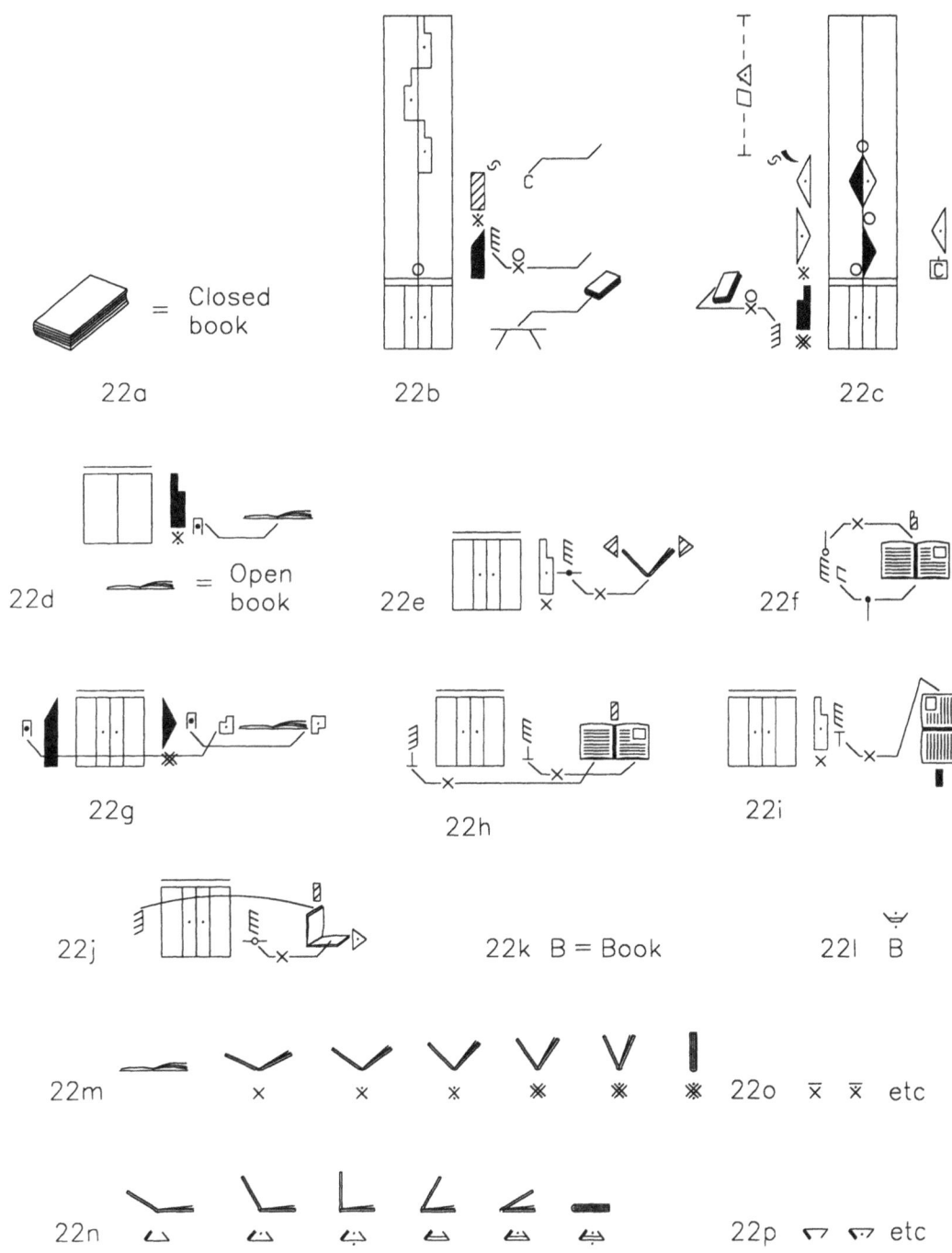

22.6. **Identifying Parts of a Book.** For more specific details in using a book as a prop, the various parts and surfaces can be identified. A book is partly a rigid object, partly moveable. The general orientation of the book in space can be determined by stating the directions for two parts which are at right angles to each other, for example, the top edge and the spine. In some cases, description of where the two surfaces (the pages) face may be preferable.

22.7. In **22q** the sign of i) represents the top edge of the book, ii) the bottom edge, while iii) is the right edge/'wing', and iv) the left.[39] The spine is indicated with a white circle (for outer surface) at the center of the indication for a book, v). The gutter, the inner center (spine), is shown with a black circle, vi). The recto page (right reading surface) is vii) and the verso page (left reading surface) is viii). The outside covers of the book can also be shown with a white circle, as in ix) and x). Ex. **22r** illustrates the outer spine and the sign used for it when the book is closed and when it is open; **22s** shows the outer edge when closed. The signs used should be stated in the glossary.

22.8. The notation of **22t** only states that the hands hold the book by the lateral edges (the 'wings'). With this simple manner of holding, many variations in its orientation and state of being, i.e. open or shut, are possible. In **22u** a staff for the book is given and the directions stated here provide a comfortable reading position for the person holding it. To get a better light for reading the recto page, the holder might change to the position of count 1 in **22v**. On count 2 of this sequence, the book is turned 'face down'; it is then closed and placed on a table. Note that when the recto and verso surfaces face in opposite directions the book is closed. Usually this is the natural, expected closing, but a paperback could be folded completely backward, inside out, this would involve the outside surfaces facing in opposite directions or shown to be contacting.

22.9. The movements of counts 2 in **22v** could be described as the inner spine opening laterally and then, for count 3, completely contracting to close up, as in **22w**. However, in this example the orientation of the book is missing.

22.10. For clear orientation of an open book, statement of directions for three parts which are at right angles to one another makes reading easier. The top edge or the outer spine can be combined with the two side edges, or with facing indications for the recto and verso surfaces. In **22x** the book is upside down and the two sides are at right angles to each other.

22.11. Indications for orientation can also be combined with degrees of contracting. In **22y** the book is half open, the top facing forward while the outside spine faces right side low.

Advanced Labanotation

Identifying Parts of a Book

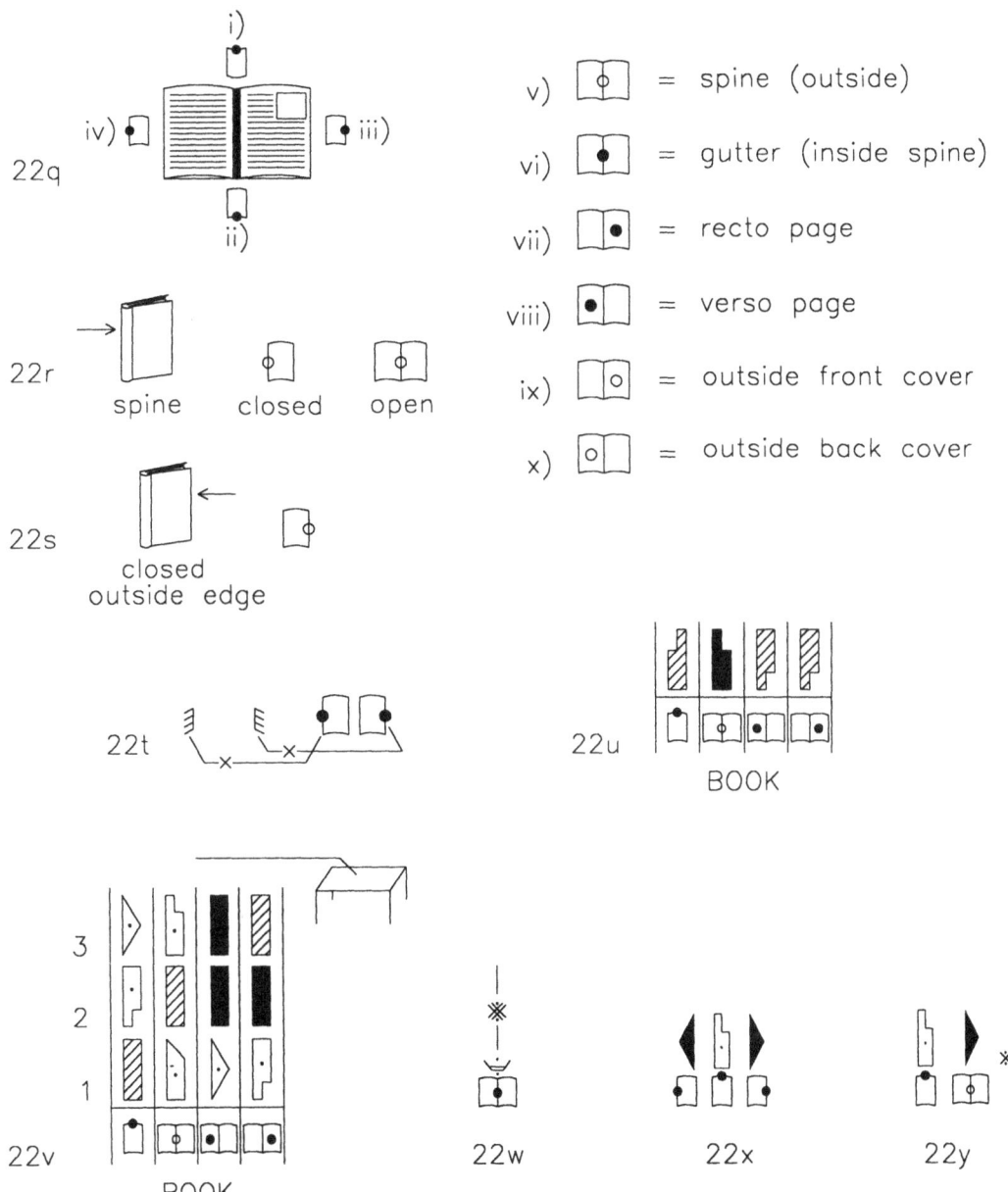

22.12. **Rotating a Book.** As we have seen, for objects such as a ball or stick which have insufficient identifying features, any turning indications have to be judged from the performer's system of reference. This is true also for a book. However, because a book has its own cross of axes - up-down, right-left, front-back, the different forms of revolving - the choice exists to write these from its own system of reference with the usual signs. This choice can be specifically stated with the Body Cross of Axes Key. In the following three examples in which the book is held in front of the performer, the forms of rotation for the book coincide with the performer's Standard system of reference.

22.13. With the book in its upright position, **22z**, the fingers manipulate the top and bottom to make the book revolve counterclockwise. The manner of achieving this is not spelled out, as the important thing is to produce the movement for the book, so only ad lib. lines are given for the fingers.

22.14. In **22aa** the upright book is held at the sides and made to somersault forward and backward. Similarly, by holding the corners as in **22ab**, it can be made to cartwheel to right and left.

22.15. Although not necessary, the performer's Standard Key is given in **22ac**. With the book held horizontally and grasped at its top and bottom ends, it is being made to perform somersault actions from the performer's point of view, these being rotations around the book's longitudinal axis. In the next example, **22ad**, the changing directions for the arms mean that the rotations for the book need to be judged around its own axis. Should there be any doubt as to which reference is being used, the Body Key can be placed next to the object column, as in this example, to show that reference is to the book's cross of axis.

22.16. When two forms of rotation occur at the same time, as in **22ae**, it is necessary that one of them be judged from the Standard or from the Constant Key, since only one can be related to the 'body' of the book. Starting with the top of the book up and the spine facing left, a half rotation clockwise combined with a half somersault forward causes the book to end with the top end downward and the spine pointing to the right. Note that these starting and ending directions are judged from the performer's Standard Key. Ex. **22af** gives a pictorial drawing of the beginning position and the end result of these combined rotations.

Advanced Labanotation

Rotating a Book

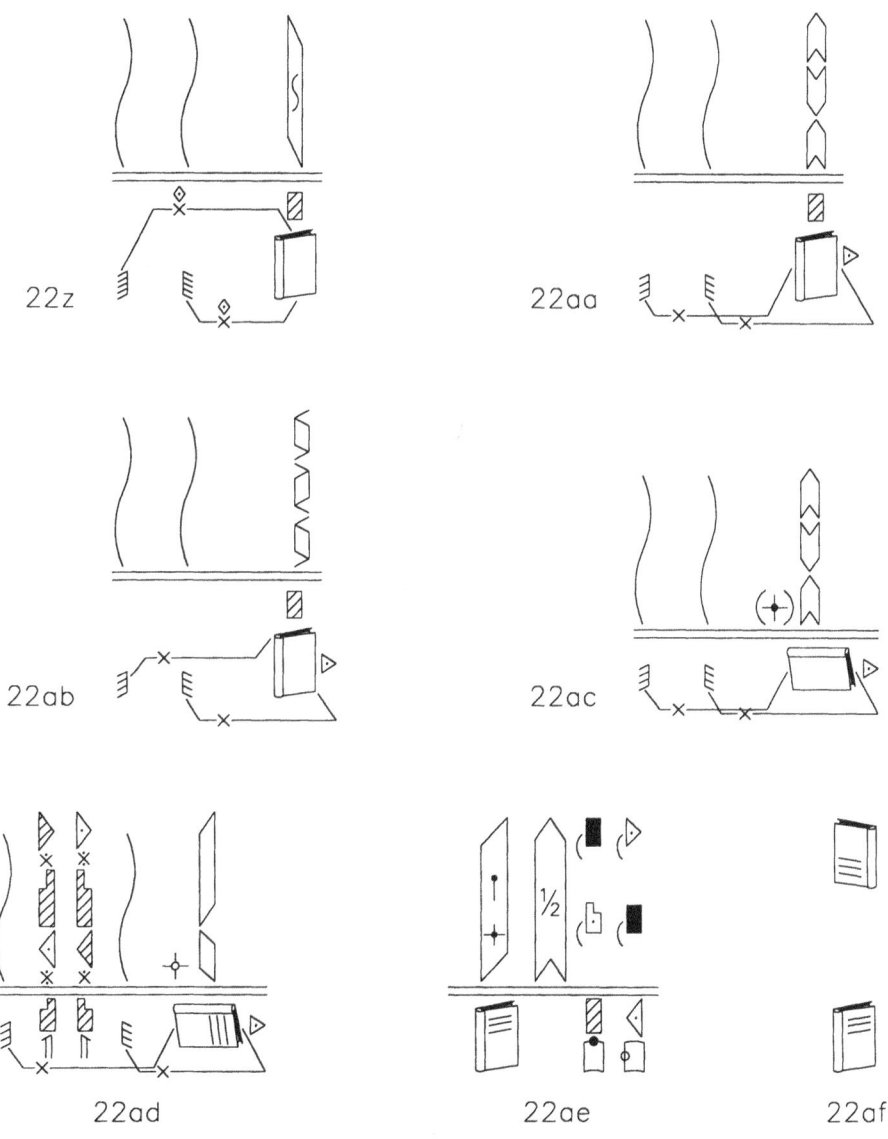

23 Handling a Basket

23.1. **Penetrating.** Objects such as baskets made of open wickerwork may be handled with the fingers penetrating the spaces. Use of the double X sign with grasping or supporting bows indicates such penetration.[40] In **23a** the right hand grasps the basket with penetration. Both hands carry the wastepaper basket in the same manner in **23b**. In **23c** the thumb of the left hand grasps the edge of the basket from above, the rest of the fingers carrying it with penetration.

23.2. Ex. **23d** illustrates grasping a lattice gate, no doubt to open it. Some gates of this kind require lifting in which case supporting bows and probably both hands would be used.

23.3. **'Inside', 'In the Center'.** Placing the hand (or an object) within a basket is shown by use of the sign of **23e** which means 'at center', 'in the middle', 'inside' or 'within' (whichever word is appropriate for the event).[41] The right hand is inside the basket at the level of the rim without touching in **23f**. In **23g** the hand is further inside without touching, the drawing being modified to indicate this. Because the sign for 'inside' is used, the object can also be drawn as though transparent, thus allowing the bow to indicate more exactly where inside it ends. In **23h** the hand touches the bottom of the object on the inside. Touching the center of one side is shown in **23i**. These examples are also applicable to china bowls or other objects of similar shape made of solid materials. For long objects the distance inside can be shown by the space measurement signs: **23j** shows far inside while **23k** states very far.

23.4. A bouquet of flowers is held in the right hand in **23l** while a bowl is held on the left palm. The flowers are dropped into the bowl: as the right arm with the flowers is held high above the bowl, and the right hand releases, a downward path results for the bouquet which ends inside the bowl.

23.5. At times there may be a question as to when to use the penetrating indication and when to state that something is 'inside' the object. For example, in placing the hand inside a pocket, or the arm inside a sleeve, the double pin for 'within' is appropriate. In **23m** the left hand is inside the pocket. In contrast, in **23n** the fingers of the right hand penetrate the hair at the temple and brush through it as the arm rises. In this example the white pin within the C sign for the head shows the upper right part of the head. The wide sign within the C indicates the hair.[42]

Handling a Basket

Penetrating

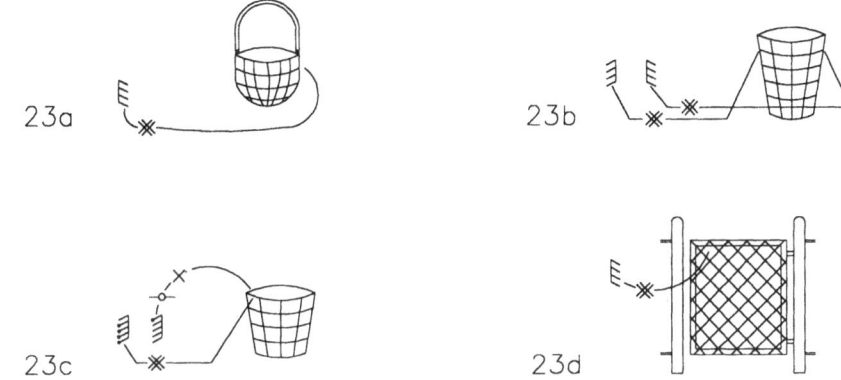

'Inside', 'In the Center'

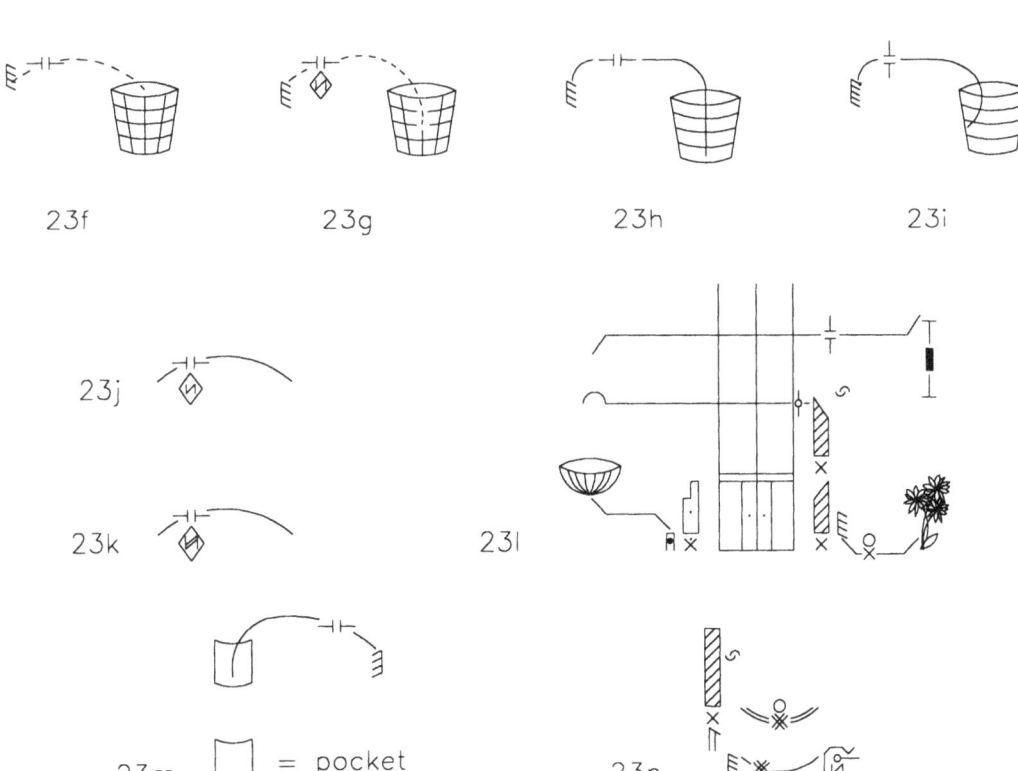

24 Skipping Rope

24.1. **Skipping Rope, Sagittal Circles.** An example of an object relating to the body is the act of skipping with a rope. For this sagittal circling of the object, either foward or backward circles occur. An ornamentation can be swinging the rope in a lateral circle between a standard skip; for this the hands are joined and the rope circled laterally at the side of the body. This ornamentation is not being shown here. In **24a** the jumping pattern includes the familiar rebound. The rope is shown to start behind the supports, at the end of the sagittal circle it passes under the legs and hits the ground at the same moment. After the second jump the performer stops, the rope does an additional $1/4$ circle and then drops. A double swing of the rope is shown in **24b** which, of course, requires a higher jump. Note the half circle before the increase in speed for the double, the rope hitting the floor twice while the performer is in the air. The rope concludes with the extra half circle. No actions for the arms are shown in these examples. For a skipping rope with ball bearings, very little arm and hand displacement is needed; for an ordinary rope, parallel but smaller circular hand movements must be made to produce the action for the rope.

24.2. **Reading Example for Skipping Rope.** The excerpt of **24c** is from the ballet *Le Beau Danube*.[43] In the opening scene in a park, various people are busy with their own activities. Two girls, designated as G1 and G2, enter side by side from upstage right, busily jumping rope. After a short time G1 falls, at which G2 stops. In the ballet she goes to help G1, but this last section is not included in the notation here.

Skipping Rope, Sagittal Circles

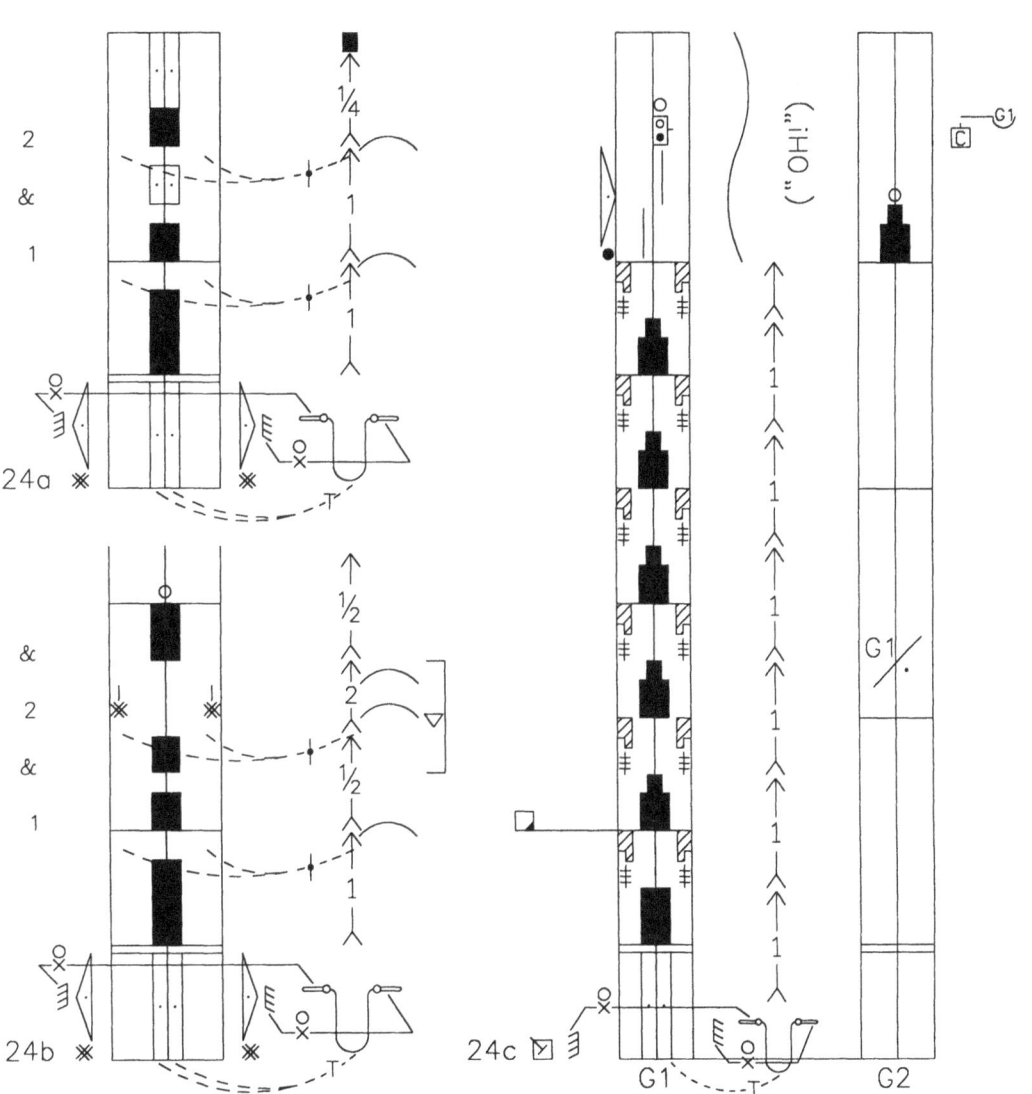

24.3. **Skipping Rope with Three People.** Ex. **24d** shows three people involved with a long skipping rope. Two of them, A and B, manipulate the rope, while the third person, C, runs into the center to jump. The turning of the rope is produced by movements of the lower arm. Note that, as A and B are facing each other, the circling direction into which each turns the rope is the opposite, this direction being judged from each one's individual point of view. From what is written for A and B, the direction for the rope itself can be determined; however it is easier to provide a staff for the rope and to state the direction into which it circles. Note that this direction is written from the Constant Cross of Axes, i.e. a forward somersault path toward the front of the room. To co-ordinate the path of the rope with C's springs, the moments when the rope's center is up or down are given. In this example the forward somersault paths for the rope are joined, in contrast to the examples on the previous page, where each circling is a separate sign immediately following the previous one without a break; either of these notations is correct.

Advanced Labanotation

Skipping Rope with Three People

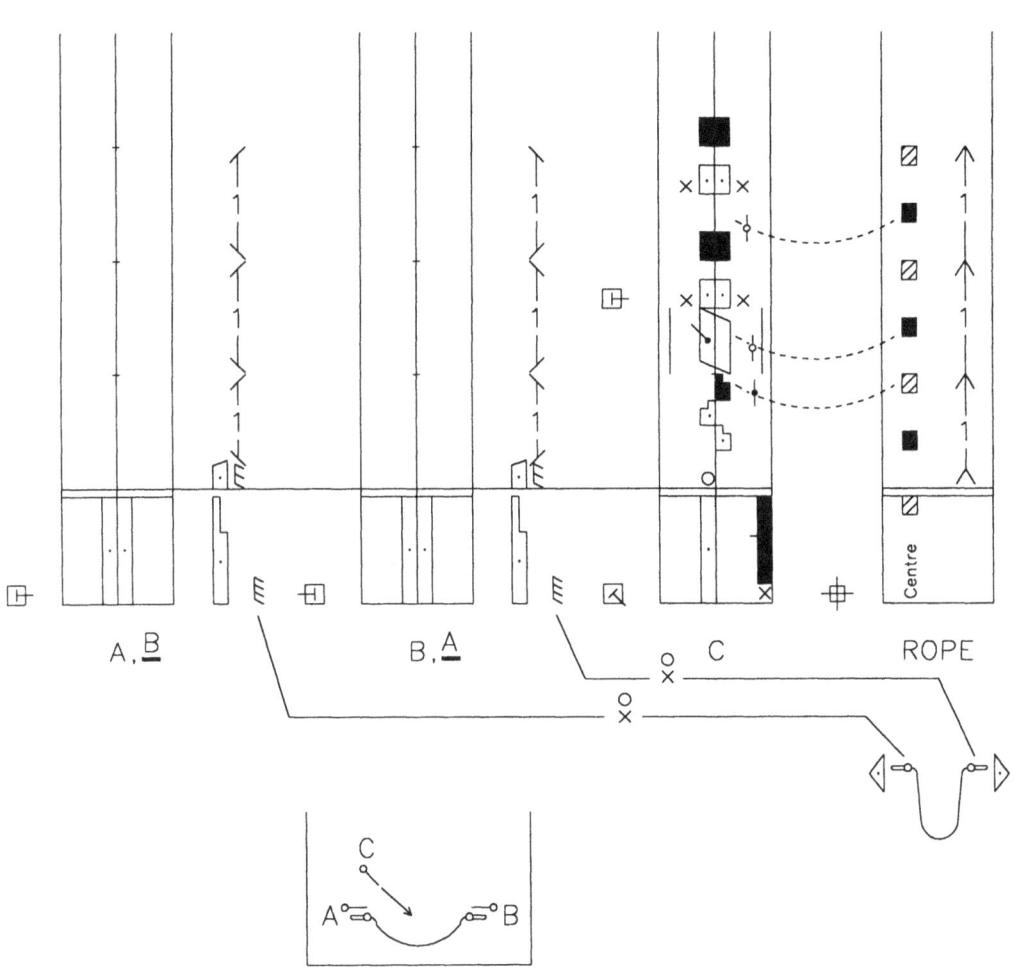

24d

25 Handling a Hoop

25.1. Circular props may be open objects such as a ring or a hoop, or they may have a functional central surface, as in a circular tray or a tambourine. With a hoop there is no front, back or identifiable side parts. Where it is held provides a point from which directions can be judged, thus establishing how it is being moved. A hoop may be used choreographically for display or used as a toy.

25.2. A hoop is being held up in **25a**, the hands grasping it on either side. Its orientation is indicated as vertical and sideward; directions for these two points is enough. Movement is then shown for the hoop, these movements being judged from the performer's system of reference. First a partial forward and then backward somersault rotation take place. This being the focus of the movement, the actions of the hands/wrists to produce this change are not given.
The change in arm placement is given for the turn of the hoop around its vertical axis and for the subsequent forward half somersault.

25.3. Throwing and then catching a hoop is shown in **25b**. The hoop is held upright in the sagittal plane (this direction being judged in relation to the performer), the hand grasping at the center back of the hoop. A sudden small upward movement of the hand and wrist flexion causes the hoop to rise in the air and at the same time to produce backward somersault revolutions.

25.4. A limb or the whole body may go through a hoop. To indicate the idea of 'through' in contrast to 'at center', the sign for 'within' is modified by the addition of an arrow, **25c**[44] A large hoop is designated in **25d**. Holding it either side of the bottom, the performer rotates it a half turn sagittally forward, placing the free end on the floor. The step forward is indicated to be through the hoop; the whole body passing through is shown by the addressing sign drawn across the whole staff, i.e. the body-as-a-whole.[45] As the hoop continues with this same rotation, it releases from the floor and passes behind the performer returning to the free end being up in front of the performer. Note use of spot holds for the hands to allow adjustments while holding the hoop at the same spot during the manipulations of the hoop. The torso bends forward as the hoop passes behind. The vertical lines following the wrist signs indicate 'an appropriate action', i.e. an action which relates to what else is happening; at the same time the arms react passively, so there is no an isolated movement of the lower arm. These movements are not spelled out as focus is on the manipulation of the hoop, and the person performs the actions that are necessary.

Advanced Labanotation

Handling a Hoop

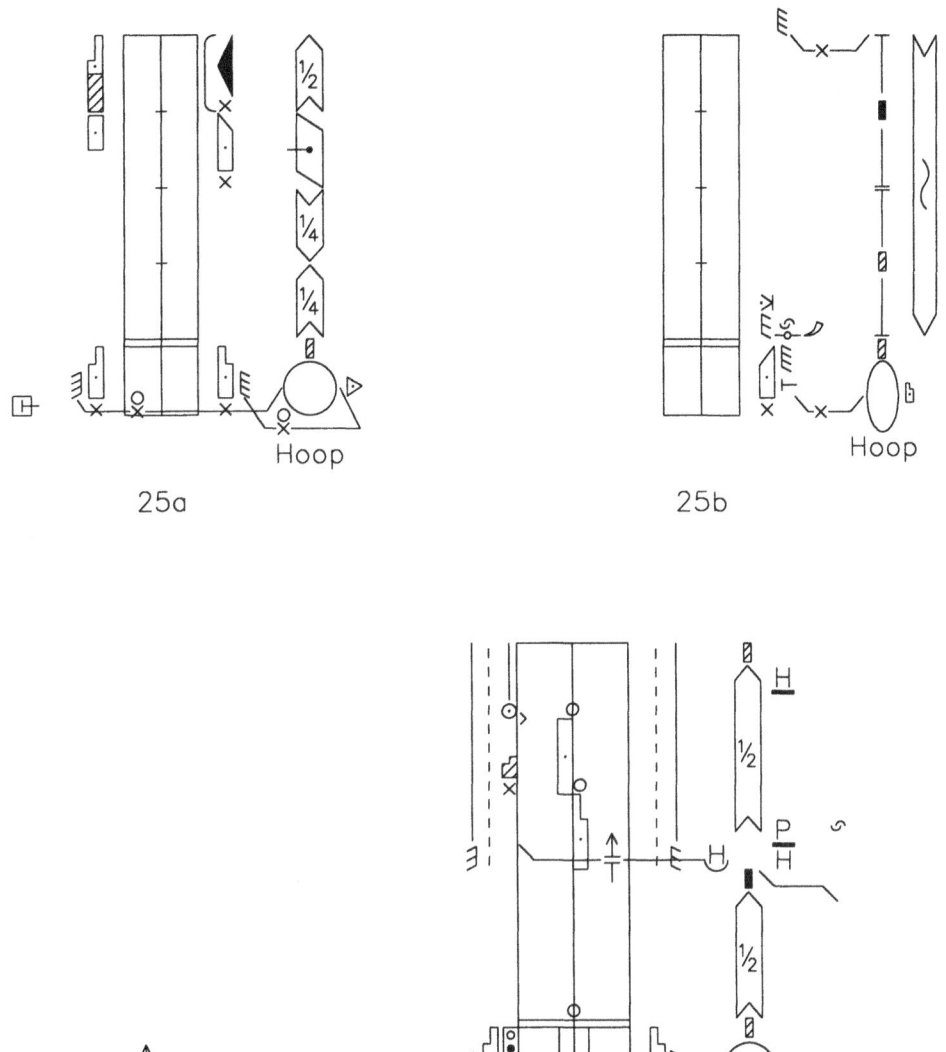

25a 25b

25c 25d

H = Large Hoop

25.5. Ex. **25e** shows a hoop being made to roll forward along the ground by being hit now and then by a stick. Each hit is a slight forward and upward movement. In contrast, in **25f** a large hoop is given a push and, as it rolls, the person running alongside ducks through it to the other side, and then through it again. Note use of the 'through' pin. Relationship to the hoop is shown with the meeting line at the left of the staff. No indication is given of the number of revolutions for the hoop.

25.6. Ex. **25g** shows a person to be facing stage left and holding a hoop at the top. Turning it $1/4$ to the right, the person then releases the hoop with a slight upward arm movement thus sending it rolling along the floor toward the audience. In this example the movements of the hoop are described in terms of the Constant Key. At the end the rotary movement dies out and the hoop comes to rest horizontally on the floor. The loss of momentum and verticality is not spelled out, just the end result.

Advanced Labanotation

Handling a Hoop (continued)

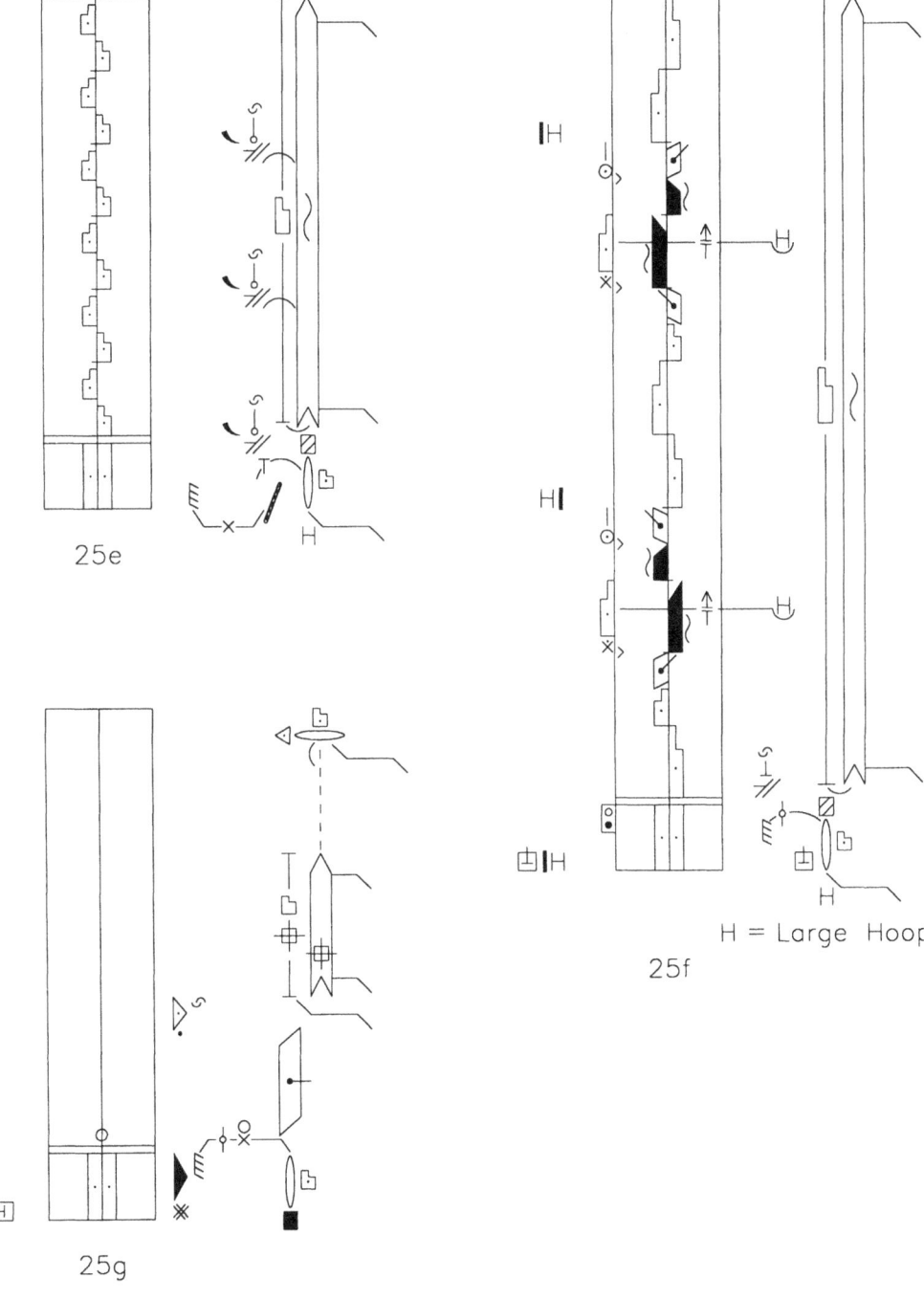

25e

25f H = Large Hoop

25g

26 Handling A Tambourine

26.1. In European and other folk dances a tambourine is a familiar object which embellishes the dance as well as providing additional accompaniment to the music. Some tambourines provide a slight hollowed-out edge for the hand to grip, while others may be grasped at any point on the rim. The 'front' is the parchment side, the drum which is beaten. Orientation for the object is determined from where the object is held, i.e. grasped, and by where the drum side faces. In **26a** the D in a circle identifies the drum (parchment) side of the tambourine. The tambourine is shown to be forward with the drum side up. In **26b** the tambourine is also forward but with the drum side to the left.

26.2. With the drum side of the tambourine facing down, a familiar grip in holding a tambourine is to grasp from above, thus causing the thumb to close in below at the edge, as in **26c**. This position allows much freedom in placing the prop at different angles and in different positions. There is usually no adjustment required in this form of grasp.

26.3. Hitting the tambourine may be with the mid-finger segments (the limbs above the third finger joints) as shown in the first part of **26d**, or with the palm of the hand as in the second part of this sequence. The palm side of the base of the hand (the heel of the hand) may also be used. Each part of the hand produces a different sound. (See the Advanced Labanotation issue on hands and fingers for parts of the fingers.)

26.4. A familiar feature in dancing with a tambourine is to shake it and thereby produce the loud attention-grabbing rattling sound. An up-down shaking is shown in **26e** during the running and then a rotary shaking during the 'spring points'.

Advanced Labanotation

Handling A Tambourine

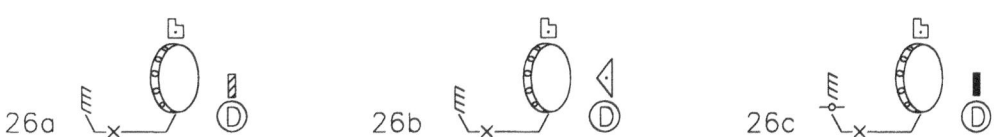

Ⓓ = drumside of tambourine

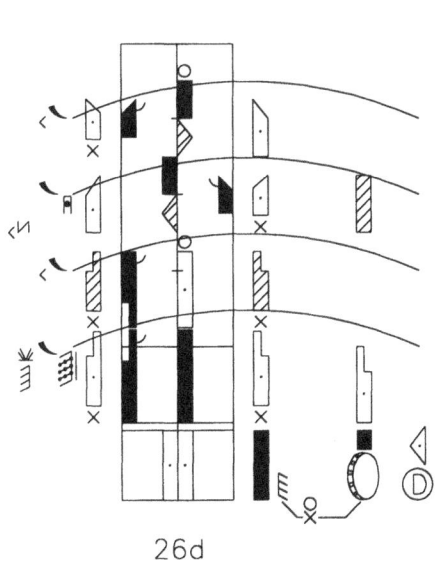

26d

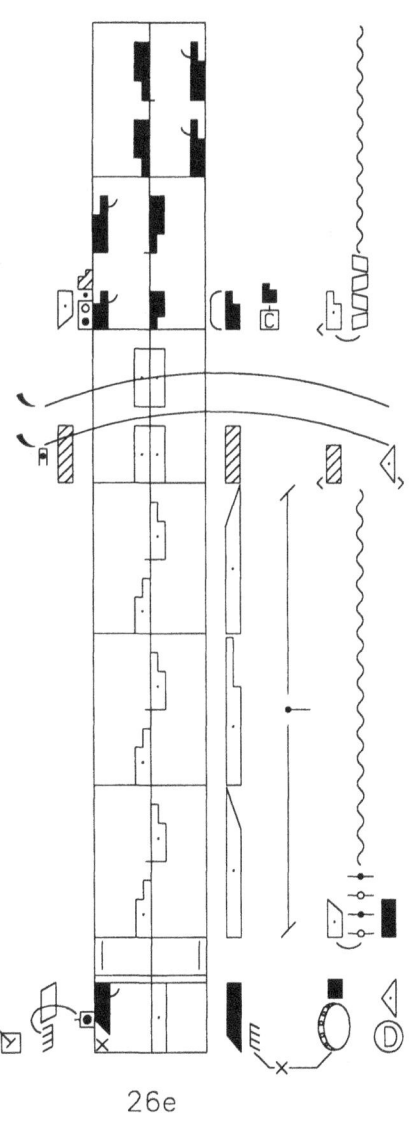

26e

27 Handling a Pillow

27.1. An embroidered pillow or cushion has traditionally been an object for a dance in countries such as Hungary. The embroidered front surface is often carried face up, but may be exhibited by holding it toward the audience or another person. The pillow may be placed on a chair horizontally or upright. Parts identified may be the front, the edges and, if need be, the corners. Statement of the orientation of any two sides which are at right angles to each other, provides precise orientation.

27.2. Ex. **27a** is a drawing of a pillow, the decorated surface representing the front, the embroidered surface. The front edge is shown here to be facing forward, the right edge facing to the right, as a result of which the embroidered side is facing up. Similarly, in **27b** the front edge is facing up with the right side still sideward, so that the decorated surface will be toward the performer. A horizontal placement of **27a**, can be shown in a perspective drawing as in **27c**. The pillow in **27d** is being held on the right palm.

27.3. The drawing of **27e** shows holding the pillow at the sides, the right side being sideward and the front edge facing forward high. That of **27f**, is held in a similar way but with the front edge pointing down. These are sufficiently clear. However, an abstract representation may be easier to draw. In **27g** the embroidered surface is indicated as an above sign within a circle (this surface frequently faces up),[46] and the four edges and corners are shown by ticks. If needed, a circled below pin can designate the under side of the pillow, **27h**.

27.4. In **27i** the front edge is to the right side, the left edge forward. In **27j** the front edge is to the left diagonal and the right edge down. With a square pillow, which may be tossed so that identification of the originally designated front edge is lost, there may be a need for clear identification on the pillow itself of the front edge. If it does not matter the new 'owner' can establish which edge is to be called front, judged from where it is being held.

27.5. In **27k** the pillow is held vertically by opposite corners; the left hand releases and, as a result, the pillow does a $^3/_8$ cartwheel to the left. The sequence of **27l** shows the pillow being displayed and then hugged with both arms. In contrast, in **27m** the pillow is being placed upright on a chair, the front surface facing to the left (direction taken from the performer). Note use of the Stance Key for the sideward arm directions.

Handling a Pillow

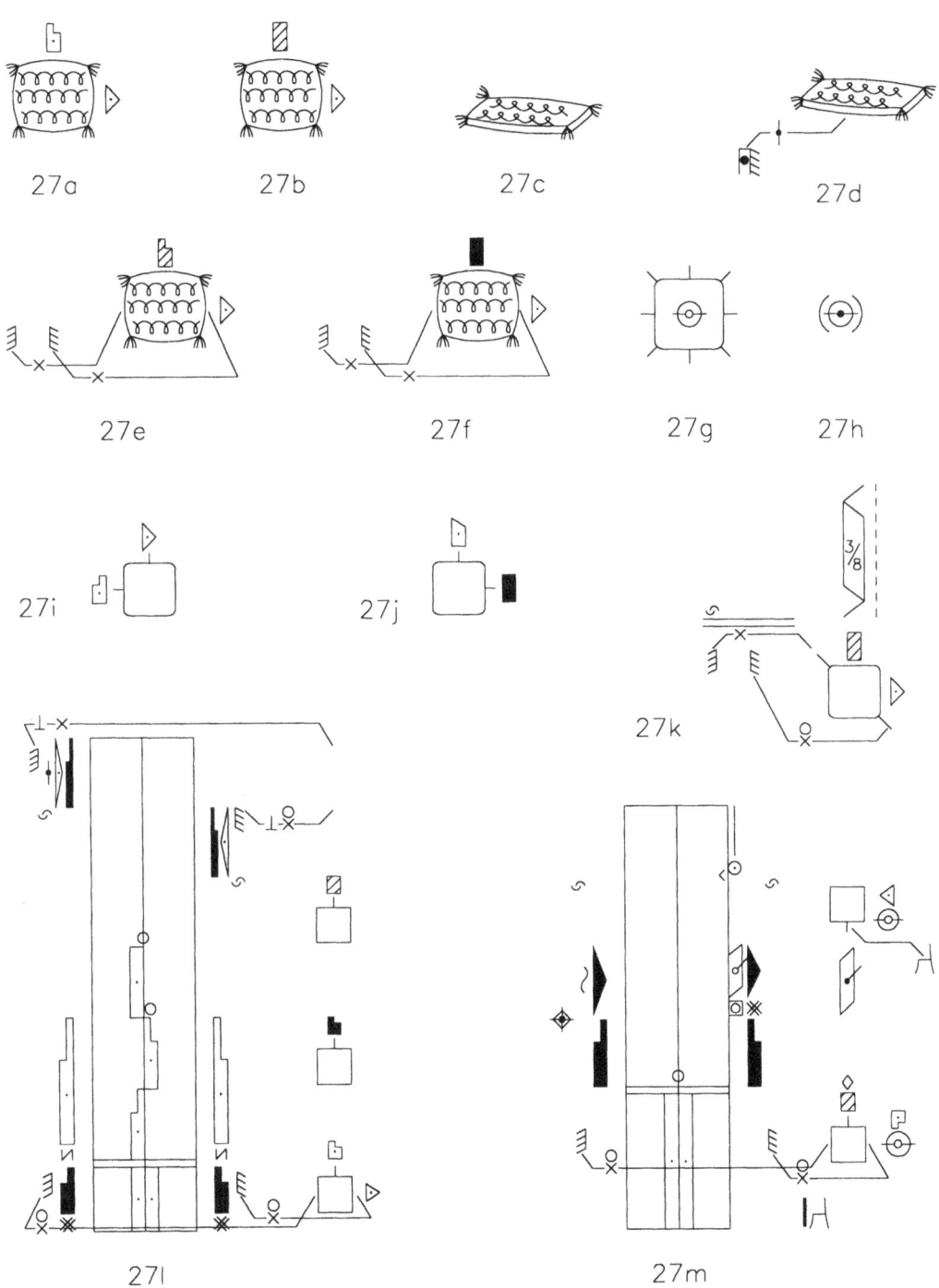

28 Handling a Cigarette, Apple

28.1. Two objects are being presented here which relate to the mouth. First is a cigarette. The parts of the cigarette are identified in **28a**: A for the lit end, B for the base end, and M for the middle. The sequence of events shown in **28b** involves changes in how the fingers hold the object. The numbers given during the sequence are for identification of the actions rather than counts showing specific timing. In the starting position the cigarette is held between the index and middle fingers, the 'grasping' support achieved by the two fingers pressing against each other, i.e. through adduction. Because the fingers are shown to be stretched, the usual grasping through flexion (use of the 'x' sign) cannot take place.[47] (See the <u>Advanced Labanotation</u> issue on hands and fingers for specific details in use of the hands.)

28.2 The arm moves on 1 to bring the B end of the cigarette near the mouth. The sign for the mouth used here is the simpler one. Note the stretching of the other fingers to get them out of the way. The mouth 'grasps' the cigarette on 2 and the lungs breathe in.

28.3. On 3 the arm moves the cigarette away, to above the ashtray. This is followed by breathing out on 4. On 5, with palm facing down, the manner of holding changes to the thumb closing from the left to hold the cigarette with the middle finger, allowing the index finger to be free. The index finger then taps the middle of the cigarette, tapping off the ashes in 6. On 7 index and middle finger resume their initial holding while the thumb releases and stretches.

28.4. Instead of another puff, the cigarette is to be stubbed out. On 8 thumb and first two fingers grasp the B end of the cigarette. The A end then points down and contacts the ashtray on 9. On 10 the hand presses downward and moves slightly from side to side before letting go the cigarette which, in 11 is then supported on the ashtray.

28.5. The sequence of **28c** shows biting into an apple. With the arm near the body, the hand, holding the apple, rises slightly so that it is near the mouth which has opened. The sign used here for the mouth is derived from Knust's more detailed set which provides indication of lips, teeth, tongue, etc. Parts within the mouth are shown by adding an 'x' within the sign, thus it is the teeth which penetrate the apple.[48]

Handling a Cigarette, Apple

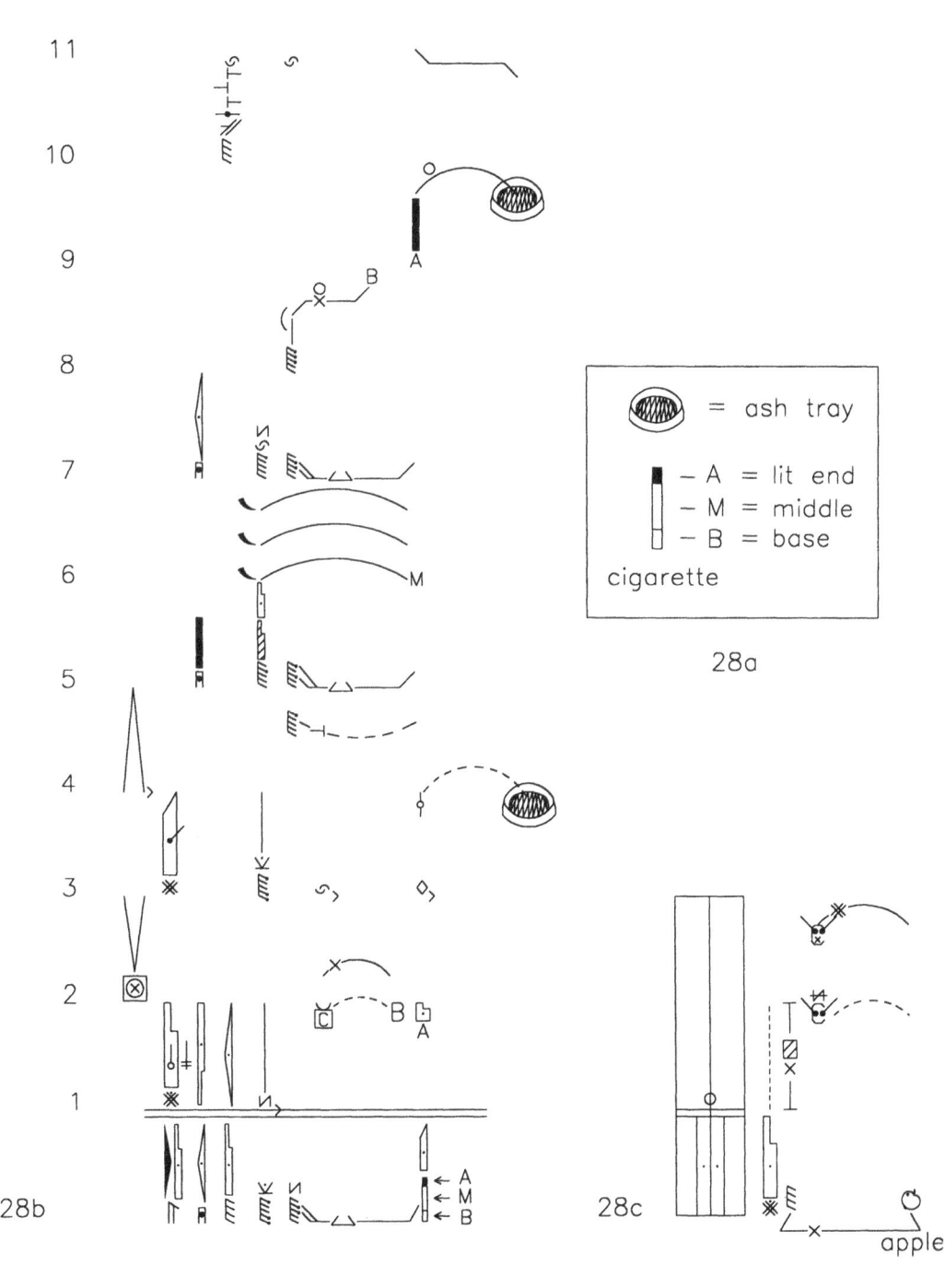

29 Circling Lighted Candles

29.1. Making figure eight patterns with lighted candles or saucers of water held on the palm is an ornamental movement used in certain Asian dances; it requires much arm flexibility. The objective is to keep the supporting palm facing up at all times during the arm gyrations. This display can be done with both arms moving in opposition or in co-ordination. Here the activity of only one arm is shown.

29.2. Starting with the bent arm held sideward at shoulder height, palm up and saucer with candle resting on it, **29a** shows the pattern of two clockwise circles led by the finger tips. During these circles the palm constantly faces up, while the hand, taking the arm with it, is raised and lowered. This rising and lowering is shown here as vertical displacements for the hand because the exact location of the arm may vary and is not important. During this action the arm twists inward to such a degree that it includes the upper body. After the first circle the arm passes through an inverted version of its starting position, i.e. the elbow is side high, the lower arm side low. With the second circle the arm rotates outward, lowering somewhat before rising to its starting position. To assist in the performance the chest is shown to react passively - it may need to lean slightly away from the arm at the end of the first circle and then return to normal.

29.3. From the same starting position, **29b** shows the reverse circling. Here again the first full circle ends with the arm twisted inward with upper body inclusion. The pattern involves lowering at the start followed by rising. When performed with both arms moving symmetrically the body may need to participate slightly to accomodate the movement.

Advanced Labanotation

Circling Lighted Candles

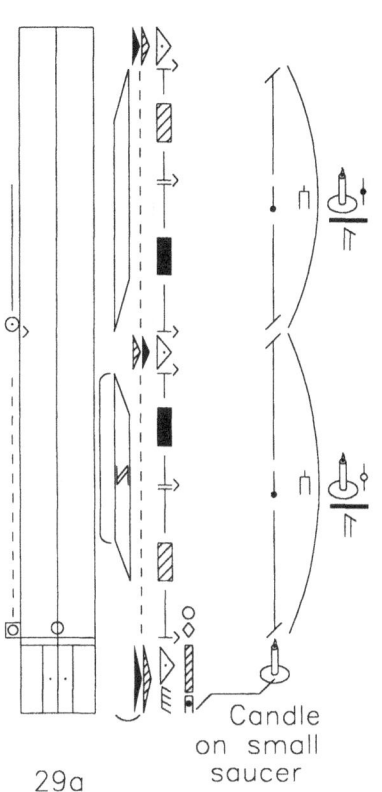

29a

Candle on small saucer

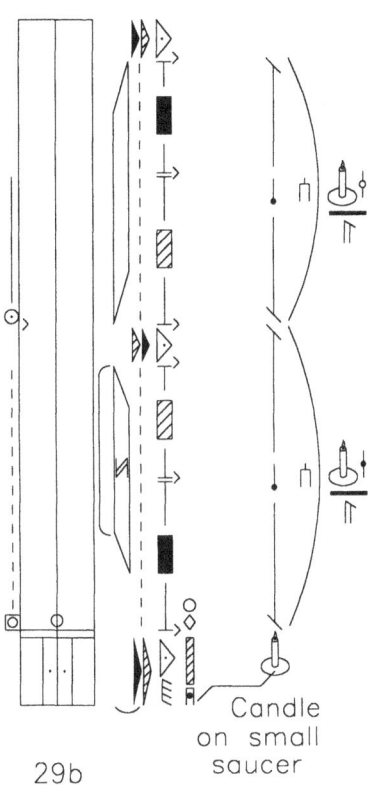

29b

Candle on small saucer

30 Handling a Fan

30.1. A fan, commonly used in Asian dance, is a good example of a prop which has a front and back, an up and down and therefore also right and left sides. In addition a fan may be closed, open, or partially open. In this exploration a more general usage of a fan, as in a ballet variation based on Spanish dance, is covered first. As usage becomes more specific and the manner of manipulation needs to be more exact, the parts of a fan are identified through appropriate signs. These indications should be clearly stated in a glossary at the start of the score. To meet the needs of Asian Labanotators, handling a fan is investigated in greater detail than the other objects explored in this book.

30.2. **Representation of a Fan.** For general purposes it has been common in the past to give a visual representation of a fan; **30a** has been the indication for a fully opened fan, while **30b** represented the closed fan. This method functioned well in dances where the fan was either fully opened or closed. Many fans have a decorated side, this can be identified as in **30c**.

30.3. For more involved usage a symbolic representation is more practical. An abstract drawing of the fan is established, the basic sketch being **30d**. Its open state is shown with the sign for lateral spreading, **30e**, the closed state being **30f**. Orientation of the fan is shown by the direction of its vertical axis, **30g**, combined with the direction of the front or decorated surface, this being identified by a black circle, **30h**, comparable to the sign for the palm which always faces the direction indicated. When the fan is closed, the black dot is still used to show this front side. In **30i** the front surface faces forward. By stating directions for the front surface and the vertical axis (which are at right angles to each other) any orientation for the fan can be shown. Ex. **30j** states that the open fan is upright (vertical axis place high) with the front surface facing backward. These directions are taken from the performer's Standard System of reference, as are the different forms of rotation for the fan. However, such rotations may also be judged from the build of the fan. For this, the Body Key is placed in the fan column, before the rotation sign (see Ex. 30cs). While description of the fan's movements may include rotations, changes are usually given in terms of the new directions faced.

30.4. Ex. **30k**, an excerpt from *Coppélia*,[49] is a typical example of a balletic use of a fan. The dancer is holding the vertical fan in a general way, fanning herself (quick rotary movements of the hand) as she enters. Note the addition of accents at the start of measure 30 and also 32 and 33. Performance of these accents is not stated; usually there is a slightly larger inward rotation with a rise in energy.

Representation of a Fan

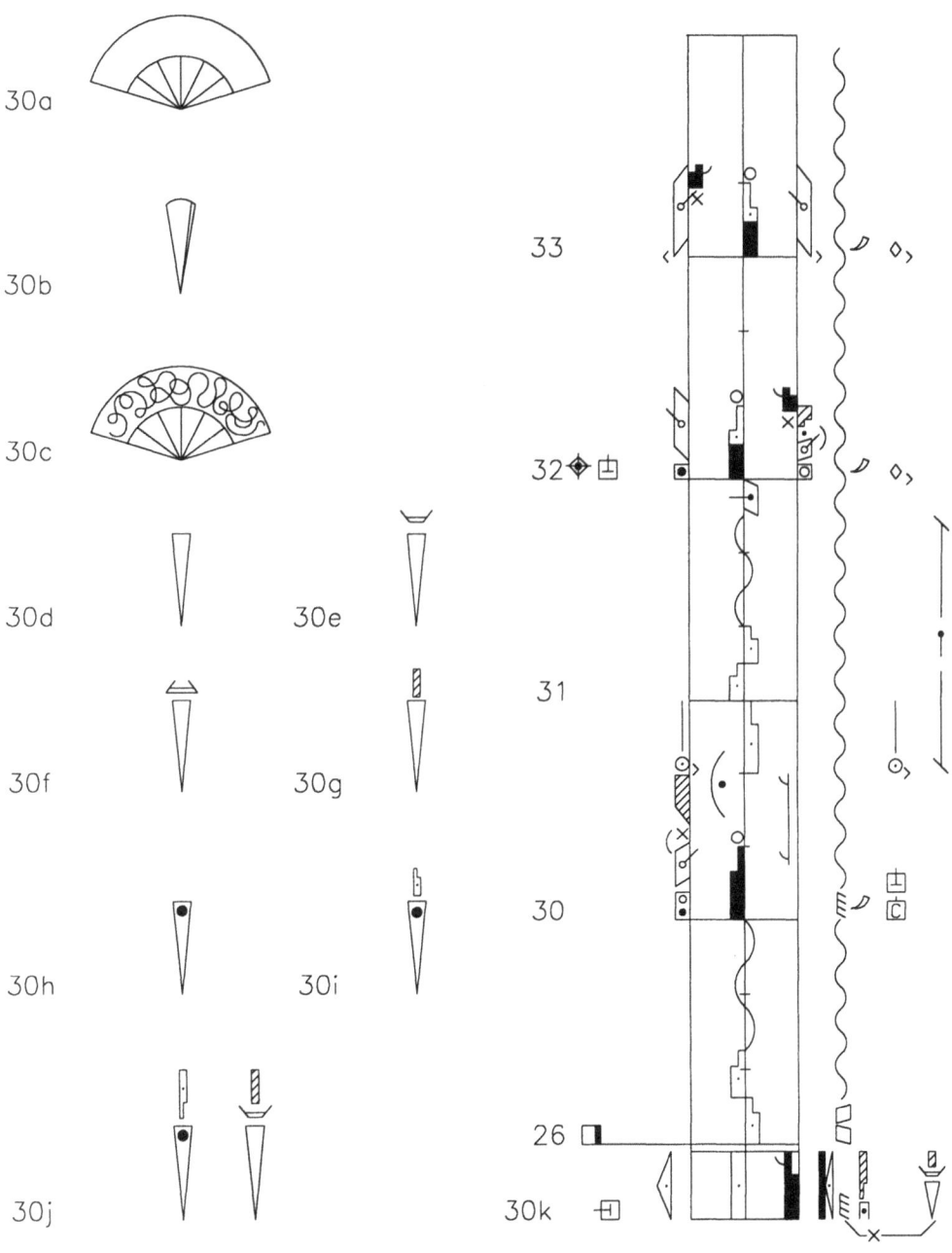

30.5. **Dance with a Fan and Handkerchief.** In this excerpt a slightly more intricate use of the fan is required. Ex. 30l is an example of a dance from China which uses a handkerchief and a fan.[50] No movements are given for the handkerchief, its motion will result from the arm movements. Rotation (twisting) of the wrist (the lower arm) and flexions of the wrist add to the movement description and help clarify the fan movements. The fan is carried along with movements of the arm (an understood body hold) unless a space hold is indicated for it or a new direction for the fan is stated. The arms start hanging straight down, the fan is in the right hand, being held by stretched thumb and little finger together 'grasping' from the left (performer's left), while the other fingers 'grasp' from the right. The result of this grasp is that the axis of the fan is in line with the lower arm.

30.6. In the introductory two measures the fan is held out to the side, facing down. It then points diagonally forward left as the lower arm is raised. At the end of this introduction there is a change in grasp, the little finger releases and joins the other fingers as the hand changes to a position similar to the Japanese 'Hawk's Beak' configuration (see Ex. 30bn for detailed description of this), the vertical line of the fan is now at right angles to the lower arm.

In measure 11 the hand hold reverts to that used at the beginning, but at the end of measure 12 the position similar to the 'Hawk's Beak' grasp is resumed.

Advanced Labanotation

Dance with a Fan and Handkerchief

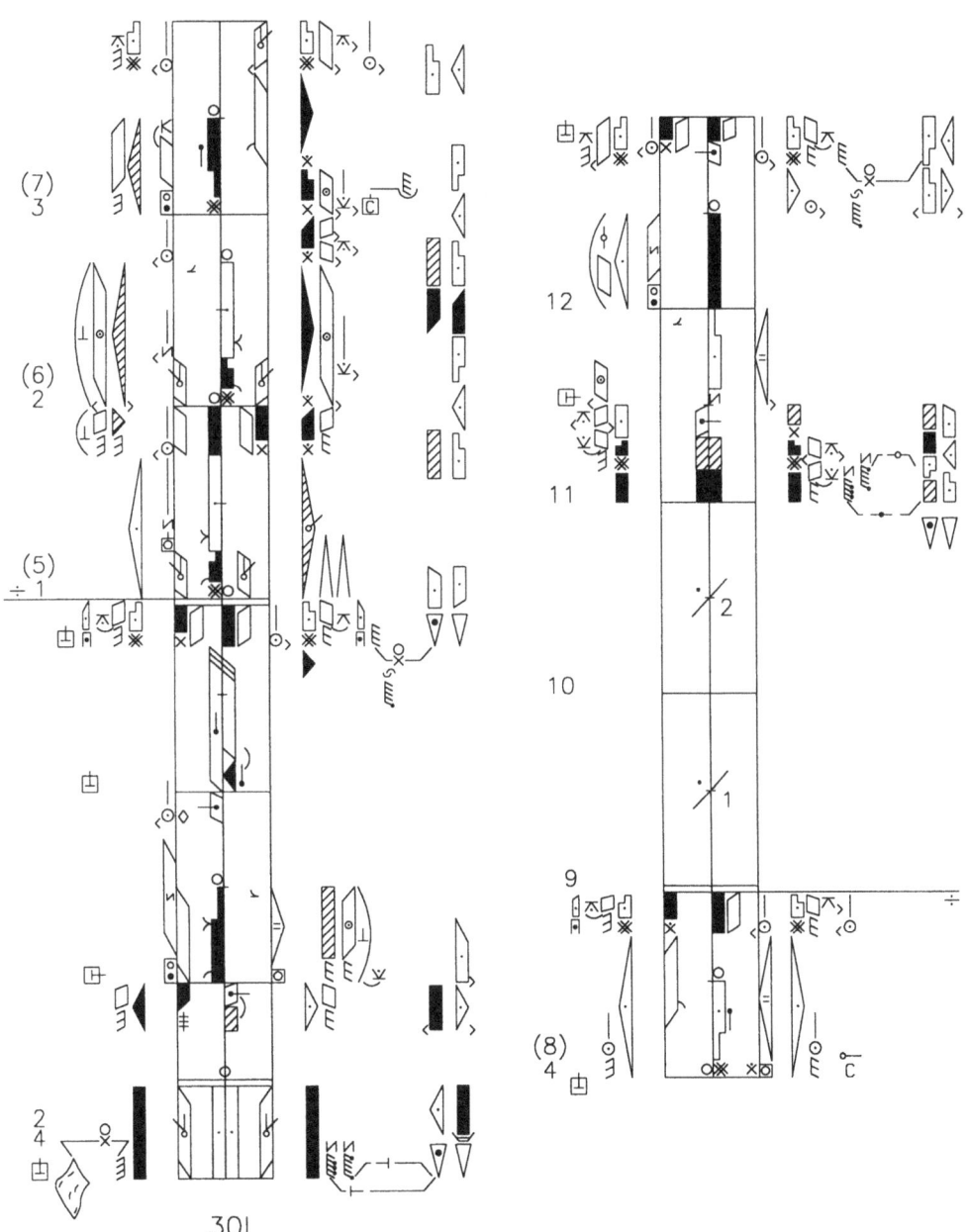

301

30.7. The following more specific information regarding the handling of fans has been contributed by Carl Wolz. Over the years he has studied several different genres of Japanese dance and notated elements of each. Of all the notation problems encountered, he found notating the handling of fans to be the most difficult. The manipulation of these is an important source of movement and a significant element of style. Several different ways of notating fans were tried. The clearest method is presented here. But first a little background information about fans would be helpful.

30.8. Japanese fans of all types are marvels of craftsmanship, having been refined over several centuries. The fan is more than a functional article for keeping cool. It is an important traditional format for painting; both Chinese and Japanese artists have created masterpieces for this shape. Moreover, it was carried by various officials in former days as a sign of rank, and displayed on certain occasions. Today, in Samurai films, one can still see a master-swordsman fend off an attack with a fan before even drawing his sword. In traditional theater forms such as *Noh* and *Bugaku*, fans are used also by musicians and actors. Their most expressive use, however, is in the dance. The Japanese people have long been known for their skills with their hands. This can be seen in many traditional activities such as the tea ceremony, woodcarving, origami, the making of bamboo ware and food preparation. The manipulation skill with fans is in some aspects similar to the use of fingers in baton twirling.

30.9. **The *Sensu*.** In general, fans are the most important properties used in all Japanese dance, and a variety of them can be seen in *Kagura*, folk forms, *Noh* and *Kabuki*. In Kabuki and its related form called *Nihon Buyo*, or *Nichibu*, meaning Japanese dance, the most important type of fan is the folding fan called *sensu*. The *sensu* requires many years of training in order to use it fully both technically and expressively. Ex. **30m** illustrates the open *sensu*; a simple indication of the open *sensu* is given as **30n**, with **30o** the closed *sensu*. Note that this drawing of the closed *sensu* is a simplification of **30p**, which is a more accurate drawing of the closed fan.

The *Sensu*

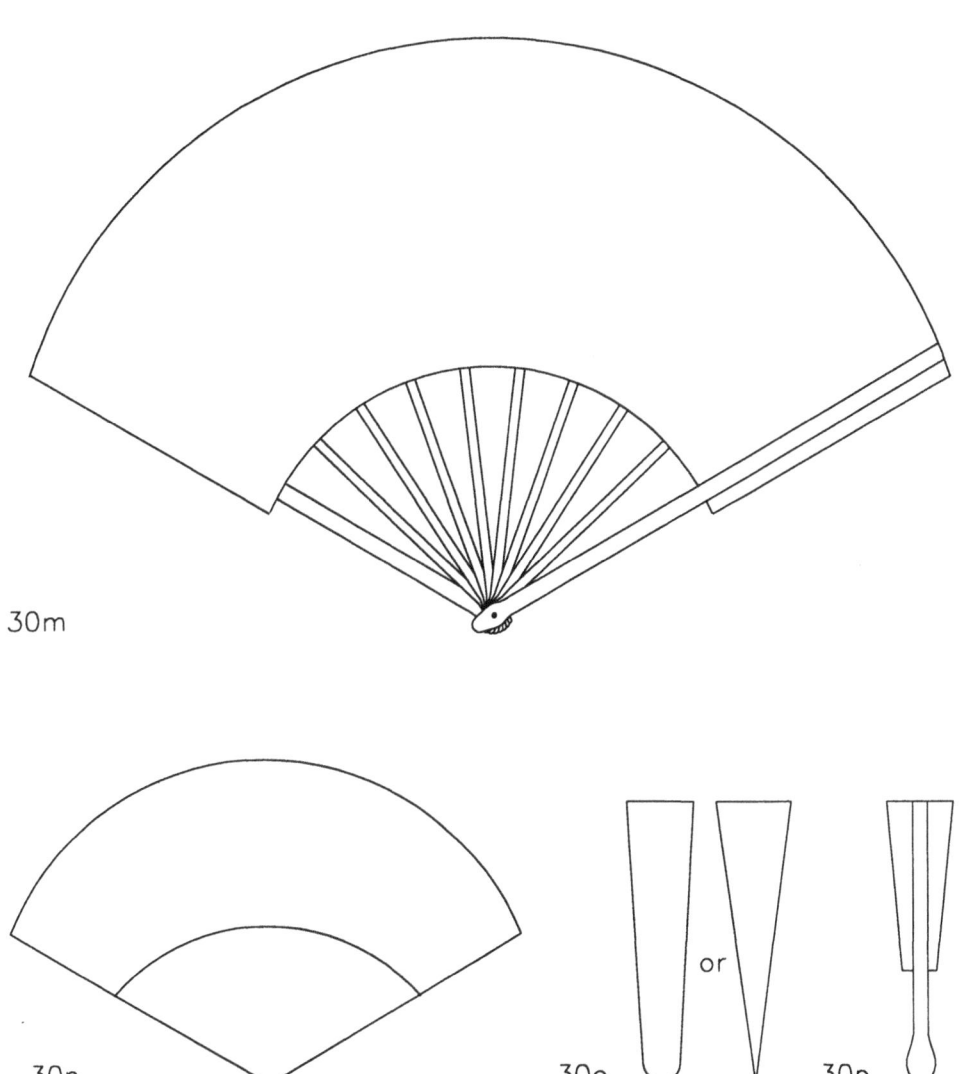

30m

30n

30o

30p

30.10. **Parts of the *Sensu*.** Before discussing the writing methods and symbols, it is necessary for an initial orientation to identify parts of the *sensu*. First let us consider the completely open *sensu*, **30q**. The *sensu* is made of a frame of bamboo ribs held together at one end by a metal pin called *kaname*. The open end of the frame is covered on both sides by paper called *jigami*, or earth paper. The bamboo ribs are called *hone*, meaning bones; however, here they will be referred to as ribs. The largest ribs at each end are called *oyabone*, or parent ribs, and the middle, thinner ribs are called *kobone* or children ribs. There are a total of ten ribs, with nine spaces in between. The *sensu* is considered a family with the paper and the pin holding the parents and the children together.

When holding the *sensu* by the paper corners with both hands in front of you, with the *kaname* hanging down and the paper edge pointing upward, the side facing away from you is called *omote*, or the front or main side; the side facing toward you is called *ura*, or back. The *sensu* is also divided into right and left halves corresponding to the reader's own right and left. Consider it comparable to the hand being upright, open and palm facing forward. This placement is the standard to which all the following examples relate.

30.11. **Points of the *Sensu*.** This orientation, which puts the *sensu* in a plane parallel to the lateral plane of the performer, is used to establish the basic points on the *sensu*. Pins are used to symbolise these points and thus the pins will either be place or side pins of the appropriate level since these points all lie on the lateral plane. The fan points established are read from its Body Cross analysis and therefore will remain constant no matter where the fan is moved. As shown in **30r**, some of the points have a Japanese name; others do not.

30.12. The central symbols are: place high, the top center of the paper, this is called *ten*, or heaven; place middle, the bottom edge of the paper in the center, called *naka*, or middle; and place low, the area of bamboo below the pin, called *chi*, or earth. These points will lie on the vertical axis in the open and closed fan. The side middle pin refers to *saki*, the extreme side corner of the open fan and also corresponds to the end of the *oyabone*. Side high is a point halfway between place high and side middle on the edge of the paper. Side low is at the point where the lower edge of the paper is attached to the *oyabone*. Note that in the movement score these pins are written heavier and slightly larger to distinguish them from relationship pins.

Parts of the *Sensu*

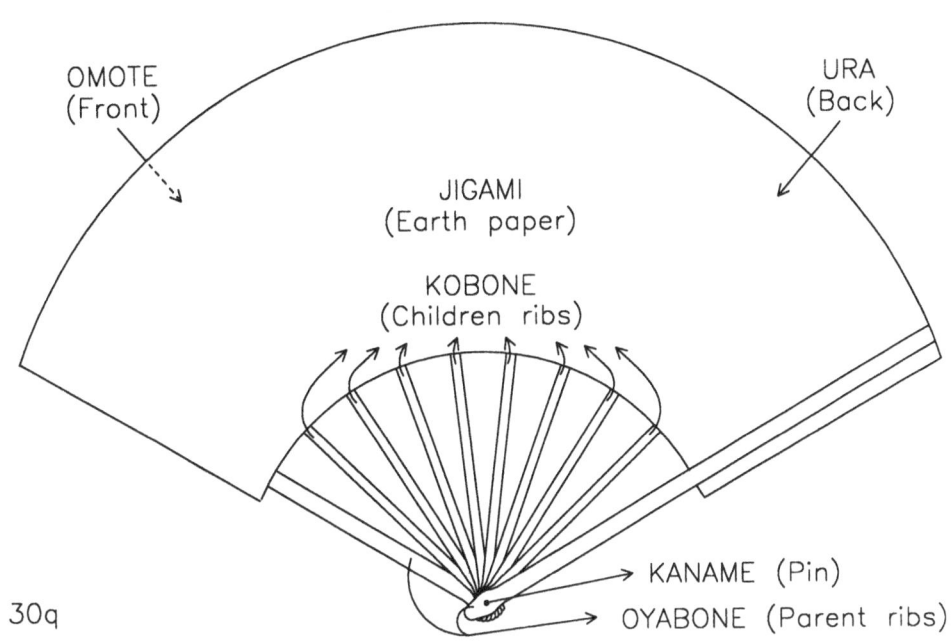

Points of the *Sensu*

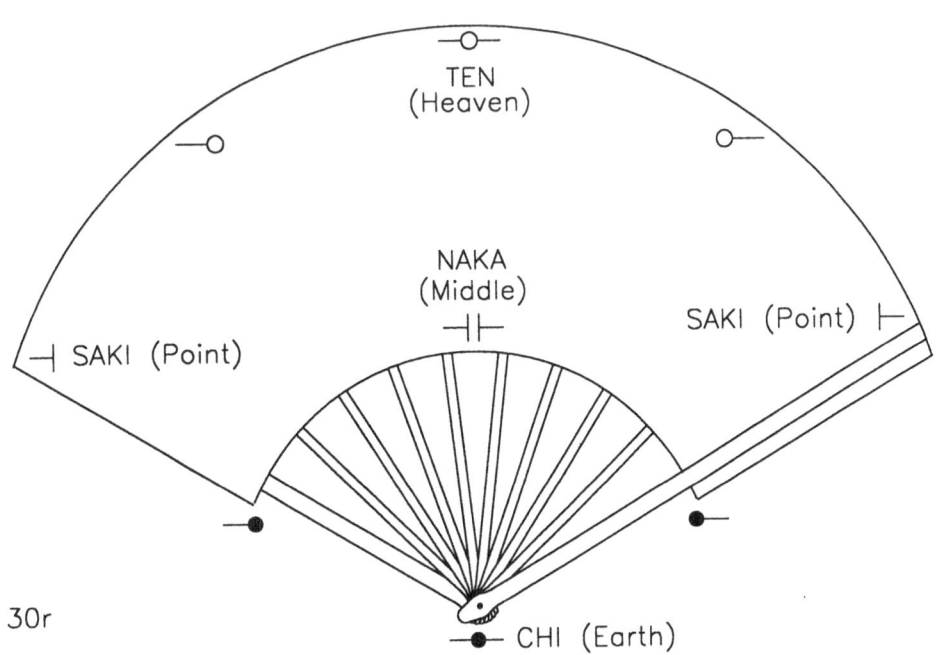

30.13. **Intermediate Points.** It is also possible to write intermediate points by combining two symbols with a dot and a bow, as in **30s**, the point between right side middle and right side low, and **30t**, the point between place high and place middle.

30.14. **Areas of the *Sensu*.** These areas, mostly used for touching, are indicated by area signs combined with pins to represent the section of the sensu around a given point. Some areas are used more in grasping actions. The *chi* and *ten* areas, **30u** and **30v**, for example, are used frequently in the basic holding of the fan, whether open or closed.

30.15. **Intermediate Areas.** It is also possible to write intermediate areas by putting two symbols, connected by a dot and a bow, in an area sign. Note that the dot cannot be omitted, because two pins are used to show an augmented (expanded) area, **30y**. The area between place high and place middle, **30w**, is used for carrying small objects on the fan; the area between right side middle and right side low, **30x**, is a common place for grasping the fan.

30.16. **Augmented Areas.** For augmented areas, the area box, **30y** and **30z**, is comparable to the writing of augmented torso signs; it is used for fans as an augmented area on which carrying an object might occur.

30.17. **Area Surfaces of the *Sensu*.** The general sign for the front, the *omote* side is **30aa** (comparable to the black circle for the palm sign), with **30ab** indicating the back, the *ura* side. When it may be unclear which side of a fan area is being indicated, a tick can be attached to the area sign: **30ac** shows the front or *omote* side of the *ten* area, and **30ad** shows the back or *ura* side of the augmented center of the *sensu*. These extra indications are needed when specific areas are to be stated.

30.18. **The *Kaname* (Metal Pin).** Inside the bottom end of each *oyabone*, near the metal pin called *kaname*, a piece of lead is inserted to give the sensu more weight and a center of gravity nearer the *kaname*. This weight is important in movements where the *sensu* is thrown and caught. Because of the weight factor and because it can be considered a pictogram of the *kaname*, the center of weight sign within a circle has been used to symbolize the *kaname*, shown in **30ae**. Although center of weight for a human is an attribute of the body, rather than a body part that can be used in touching, use of the symbol here seems to fulfil the need.

Intermediate Points

Areas of the *Sensu*

Intermediate Areas

Augmented Areas

30y 30z

Area Surfaces of the *Sensu*

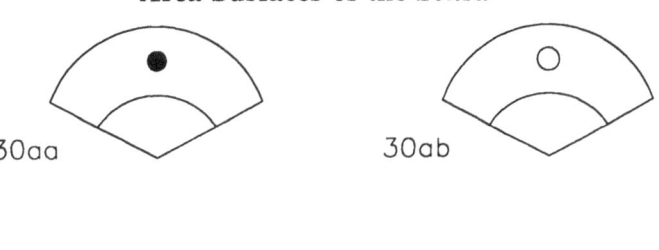

30ac 30ad

The *Kaname* (Metal Pin)

30ae

30.19. Identifying the Ribs (*Oyabones*). The references in **30af** are to the standard orientation of the *sensu* in the lateral plane (see 30.10, 30.11). The outer surface of the *oyabone* ('parent' rib) is called *chichibone*, or Father Rib, and the under surface of the *oyabone* is called *hahabone* or Mother Rib. In order to symbolise individual ribs and their parts, the limb sign is used, **30ag**. The ribs from the right, starting with the *oyabone* (parent rib), are numbered one to five and are identified as being counted from the right by an arrow pointing to the left, indicating the direction toward which the counting takes place. Ex. **30ah** shows the first rib from the right side, the right *oyabone*, **30ai** shows the third rib from the left, the left *shichi-san-bone*.

The third rib from each side is called *shichi-san-bone*, or seven-three rib.[51] It is actually rib number 'eight-three', counting from the opposite *oyabone* (parent rib), but the tradition is to call it 'seven-three' rib. The center ribs, both numbered five, are called *nakabone*, or middle ribs, and are used mostly in grasping.

If it is not important to identify the right or left rib, the arrow is not written: **30aj** indicates either *nakabone*. 'Any rib', as the movement requires, may be indicated by using the ad lib. sign within the limb sign, **30ak**. When the fan is closed and hence all ribs grasped, it is enough to indicate grasping the first rib, **30al**.

Advanced Labanotation

Identifying the Ribs (*Oyabones*)

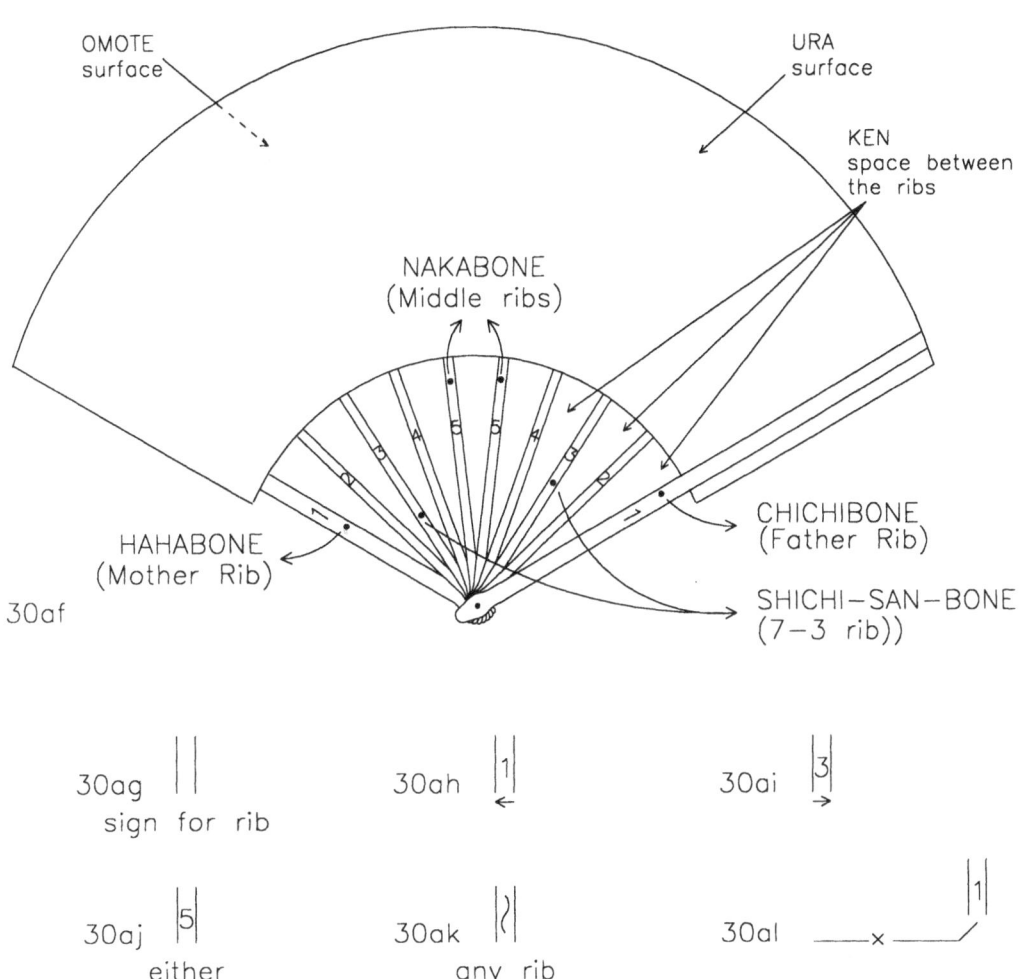

30af

30ag sign for rib

30ah

30ai

30aj either nakabone

30ak any rib

30al

30.20. **Rib Edges.** To specify which side of a rib is being touched or grasped, a tick is added at the right for the right side, **30am**, and a tick placed on the left side to indicate that side, **30an**. These right and left sides are based on the established build of the fan, as described in 30.10.

30.21. **Rib Points.** The point where the rib will be touched or grasped is indicated by the positioning of a sideward tick on the limb sign. Five points are established along the ribs. Each rib point can be designated as being a right or left edge. Ex. **30ao** shows the upper part of the rib just below the paper; **30ap** the point on the rib one quarter-way between the paper and the *kaname*; **30aq** the middle of the rib between the paper and the very bottom; **30ar** the point just above the *kaname* (the pin) and **30as** the part just below the *kaname*. This last part is called *moto*, which means base or source. When writing these points for grasping, the fingers should be centered over the point indicated. The middle point, **30aq**, is used when generally identifying a specific rib, such as **30ah** and **30ai**.

30.22. **Rib Surfaces.** Some Japanese also distinguish between the two sides of the *oyabone*: the outerside is called *chichibone*, or Father Rib, and the innerside is called *hahabone* or Mother Rib. The under (inner) side is shown by a small black circle, **30at**, and the outer by a small white circle, **30au**. However, when in writing it is necessary to distinguish between the father and mother sides of the first rib, it is possible to show this through stating a relationship pin next to the grasping hand.

30.23. **Spaces Between Ribs.** One further concept used in connection with the ribs is the negative space between the ribs called *ken*. Here again, in most cases reference to these can be written with a relationship pin. However, in the interest of creating a comprehensive system, a symbol is offered to provide a direct reference: a dotted line outlining a triangular area shows a space, **30av**. A sideward pointing arrow (indicating the direction from which the counting takes place) and a number inside state which space; **30aw** shows the third space from the right.

The timing of touches and the use of relationship pins in grasping follow standard practice.

Rib Edges

30am ||⊢ = right side   30an ⊣|| = left side

Rib Points

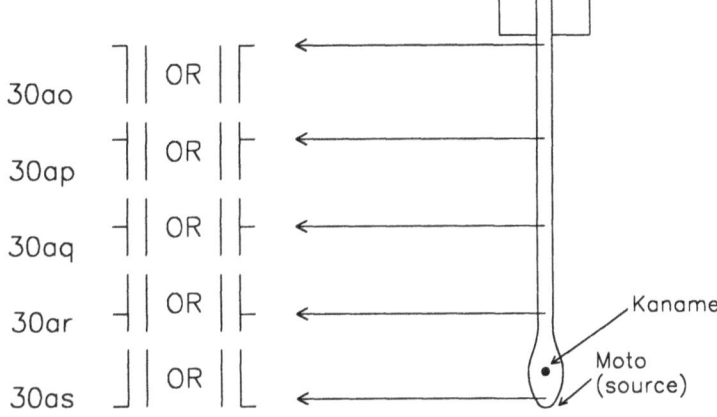

30ao ⊤|| OR ||⊤
30ap ⊣|| OR ||⊢
30aq ─|| OR ||─
30ar ⊥|| OR ||⊥
30as ⌄|| OR ||⌄

Kaname
Moto (source)

Rib Surfaces

30at [•/1]←   30au [○/1]→

Spaces Between Ribs

30av   30aw

30.24. **Movements of the *Sensu*.** The next section deals with writing movements of the *sensu* and is divided into the following categories: fan direction, fan facing, opening and closing, addressing, revolutions. For grasping, the degree of flexion of the hand is sometimes shown because it varies greatly according to the type of grasp or hold.

30.25. **Direction of the *Sensu*.** The direction of the *sensu* is always taken in reference to the *kaname*, the metal pin, even when the point of grasping is not at the *kaname*.[52] This direction, the primary axis, is clear when the *sensu* is closed; when it is open or partially open, the line of direction bisects the angle made by the two *oyabone*, as shown in **30ax, 30ay** and **30az**. Directions are analysed from the Standard Cross related to the performer's front. In some cases, particularly where the performer puts or throws the fan down on the floor, directions may be written from the Constant Cross of Axes.

30.26. **Facing of the *Sensu*.** In group dances, particularly in recent popular theater styles such as *Takarazuka*, the two sides of the *sensu* are different colors, and the switching back and forth to contrast the colors is an important element of the choreography. Moreover, open facing is important in design and expressive content. Many fans are beautifully painted, and some movements are chosen to display these pictures clearly; the raised open fan facing forward is a convention by which the performer gives a blessing to the audience. Some *sensu* are the same on both sides and, while it does not matter which side is showing, it is practical to establish which side is *omote*, front. In the complicated manipulations of the fan and when starting and stopping in writing and reading, it is easy to forget which side is which, thus producing an incorrect result.

The method of identification is to draw or paste a small black circle on the *omote* or front side of the *sensu*. This should be done on the fold where the *oyabone* is attached so that it may also be seen when the *sensu* is fully closed.

30.27. In writing movements of the fan, establishing only the direction of the 'vertical' axis of the fan is usually insufficient, a second direction stating either the 'lateral' or 'sagittal' axis is needed. The preferred method is to write the sagittal axis, the front, which is comparable to writing palm facing in conjunction with arm or hand directions. With this method it is important to establish which is *omote* (the front) and which is *ura* (the back) of the *sensu*.

The symbol to identify the column used for fan facing (see 30bk) is the pictogram of **30ba**, the fan with a black circle inside, comparable to the one used in palm facing. On some occasions it may be useful to use a white circle for the back of the fan, comparable to that used for the back of the hand, **30bb**. It is also possible to show the edges of the fan, **30bc** showing the right edge and **30bd** the left edges, judged from the basic fan direction.

Advanced Labanotation 101

30.28. If the back of the fan or the edges description is used, those symbols are placed in the staff for the fan (see next page for the staff) and thus act as presigns for the direction indications which follow. They remain in effect until canceled by a 'front of the fan' facing symbol, **30ba**. In general, however, the preferred fan facing indication is the black circle, the *omote* or front side of the fan. It is not necessary to repeat this symbol once the column has been initially established except to cancel an alternate analysis.

The end of the closed *sensu*, used for pointing, is called the *saki*, as indicated in **30ax**. Note that, when the fan is open, this point is called *ten*.

For ease of drawing, the fan symbol can come to a point, as indicated in the examples below.

Direction of the *Sensu*

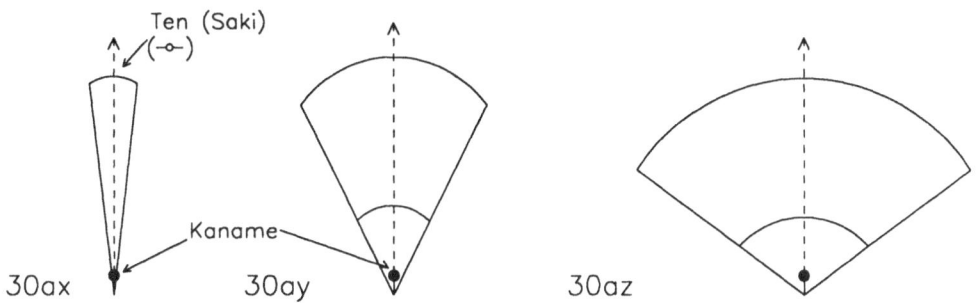

Facing of the *Sensu*

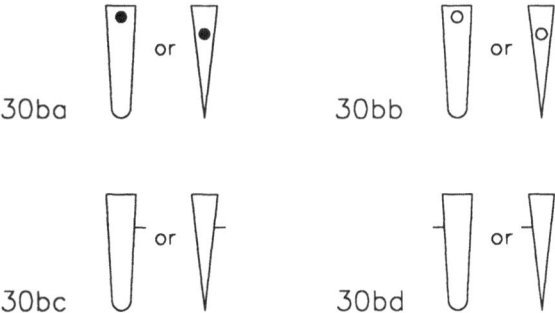

30.29. **Open or Closed State of the *Sensu*.** The folds of the *sensu* are designed so that it can easily be opened and closed to different degrees. The column where its open or closed state is indicated is designated by the sign of o. A double closing symbol, **30be**, is used to represent the *sensu* fully closed; a double spreading symbol, **30bf** is used to represent a fully opened *sensu*. A single spreading symbol with a number inside indicates how many ribs are to be opened, **30bg**. Similarly, a single closing symbol with a number inside indicates how many ribs are to be closed, **30bh**. The *sensu* does not always close its folds in sequence; therefore, a number within the opening or closing symbol, as in **30bg** and **30bh**, actually means the total number of ribs closed, (one may also count spaces) and is not the identifying number of the rib.

30.30. Whether the fan is being opened from left to right is usually clear from the movement context, however, the arrow indicating 'from the left', **30bi**, (as used in identifying the ribs) can show spreading toward the right. Similarly, closing can be shown to be 'from the right', i.e. toward the left, as in **30bj**. Spreading and closing symbols are written in the fan direction column, and are used as pre-signs when the opening results in a new direction (see **30bq**, **30br**). When there is no directional change, the spreading or closing sign is followed by a duration line for timing.

30.31. **Staff for the Fan.** The general rule for notating properties is to place the indication of the prop to the right of the performer's staff. In the case of a fan, the prop column needs to be expanded into a specific staff to indicate the facing directions and movements of the fan. The following placements have been established as being the most practical. The two vertical lines enclose two basic columns, **30bk**. That on the left is used to show the facing direction; next to it on the right is written the direction of the main axis and indications for opening and closing. If any additional movement indications for the fan are needed, they are placed outside the staff on the right, **30bm**.

30.32. Depending on the complexity of the movement, the notator may also need to use columns on the left of the basic fan staff, **30bl**; for convenience these are numbered here. The convention is to place indications of points, areas, etc. touched or grasped by the right hand in column 3, those points grasped by the left hand are placed in column 1. Column 2 may be used when the *sensu* touches another part of the dancer, the floor or another prop. Signs placed in these columns are not movement indications. When frequent touching, grasping and releasing occur, using these extra columns avoids writing additional symbols to indicate clearly what is being released. When two *sensu* are used, a second staff is established at the left of the performer's staff. This staff functions as a mirror image of the fan staff on the right, **30bm**.

Open or Closed State of the *Sensu*

30be ⟋‾⟍ = fully closed   30bf ⟍_⟋ = fully open

30bg ⟍5⟋ = 5 ribs opened   30bh ⟋3⟍ = 3 ribs closed

30bi ⟍5⟋ → = open from the left (toward) the right   30bj ⟋3⟍ ← = closed from the right (toward) the left

Staff for the Fan

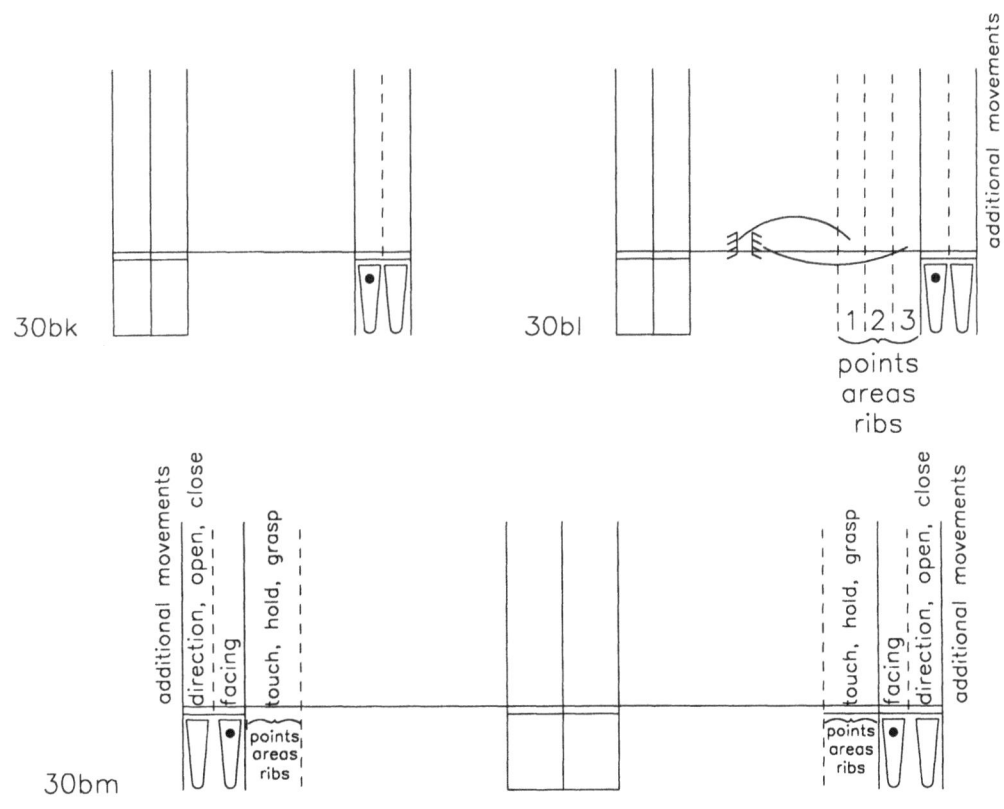

30.33. **Ways of Grasping the *Sensu*.** The following notation examples are all based on published materials by Hanayagi Chiyo.[53] The examples presented here represent only a very small proportion of the positions and movements of the *sensu* used in *Nihon Buyo* and *Kabuki* dance.

30.34. **Grasping the Closed *Sensu*.** The most common position for holding the closed *sensu* is the 'Hawk's Beak' hand, **30bn**. It is applied to several holds, such as the common one given in **30bo**. In the 'Hawk's Beak' hand, the hand is closed but sagittally spread and the tip of the thumb touches the inside of the index finger's third limb section (the 'finger print') when the fan is not between them. In **30bo** the hand grasps the closed fan from diagonally right, the little finger touches the *kaname* and the thumb and index finger touch the left edge of the *oyabone*.

'Hawk's Beak Hand   *Tsune-mochi*: Usual Hold

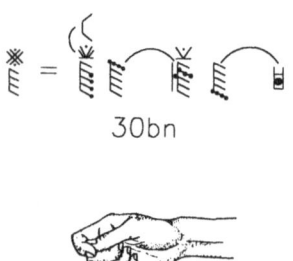

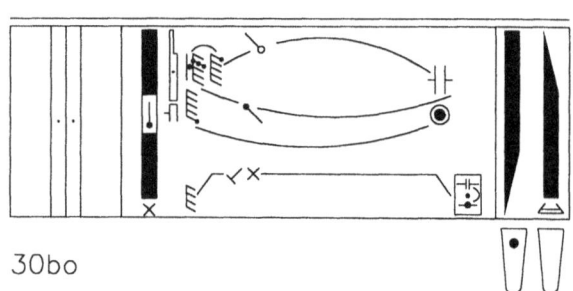

The hold of **30bo**, used with the arm forward middle, expresses *Tsuri*, or fishing; with the arm forward low it shows playing a *Taiko*, a type of drum.

Naka-mochi: Middle Hold

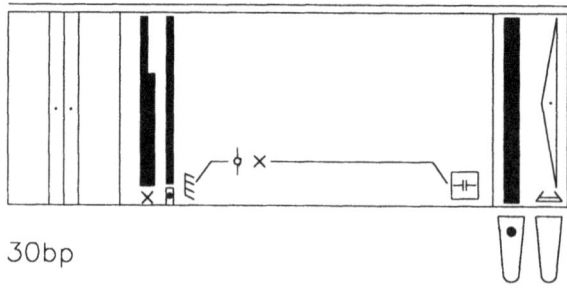

30.35. Grasping a folded fan at the center, **30bp** is called *naka-mochi* (middle hold). With the fan pointing toward the waist, this grasp is used in the pantomiming of *Seppuku* or *Hara Kiri*, the ritual suicide of the *samurai* class.

Saki-mochi: Holding the End (Point Hold)

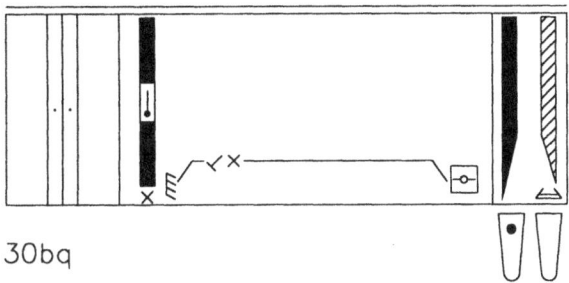

30bq

30.36. In **30bq** the paper end of the closed fan is grasped, this end being diagonally back right high. When shaking the *sensu* right side low with this hold, this basic movement expresses shaking water from a *kasa*, or umbrella.

Ways of Grasping the Open *Sensu*

Nigiri-mochi: Grasping Hold

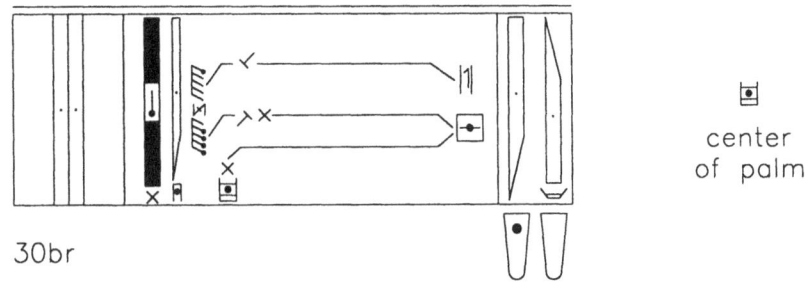

30br

30.37. Ex. **30br** is the basic hold for the open *sensu*. The *chi* area is centered in the palm, the thumb is on the *oyabone*, the fingers grasp from the other side.

Oyabone-mochi: Parent Rib Hold

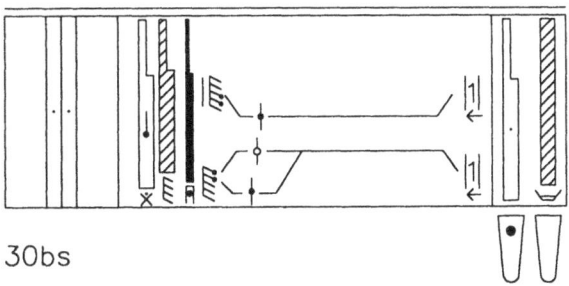

30bs

30.38. Hanayagi Chiyo gives **30bs** as the basic hold; in practice many variations occur, as in closing the *sensu* and for rotating the fan. The hand position helps clarify this finger support of the top of the first rib from the right.

Nakabone-mochi: Middle Rib Hold

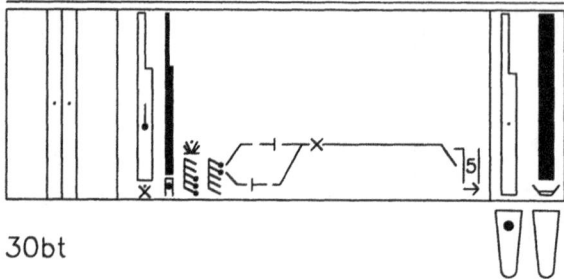

30bt

30.39. When the position of **30bt** is used overhead it can represent another aspect of the *kasa*, or umbrella.

Tsumami-mochi: Pinching Hold

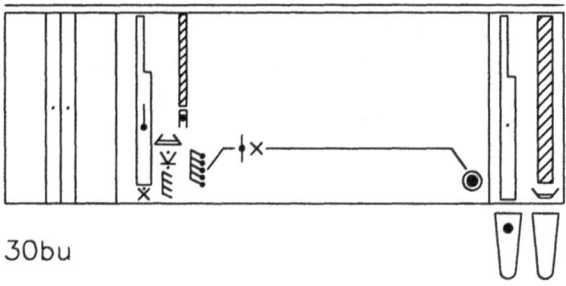

30bu

30.40. The hold of **30bu**, the fingers 'pinching' the *kaname* is usually used when preparing to throw the fan.

Taira-mochi: Flat Hold

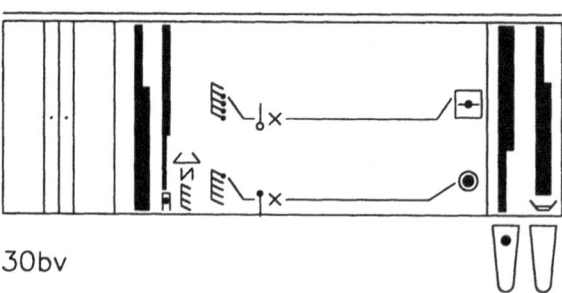

30bv

30.41. When the hold of **30bv** is used by the left hand (not shown here), the fan can represent writing paper.

Opening and Closing the *Sensu*

Akeru: Way of Opening

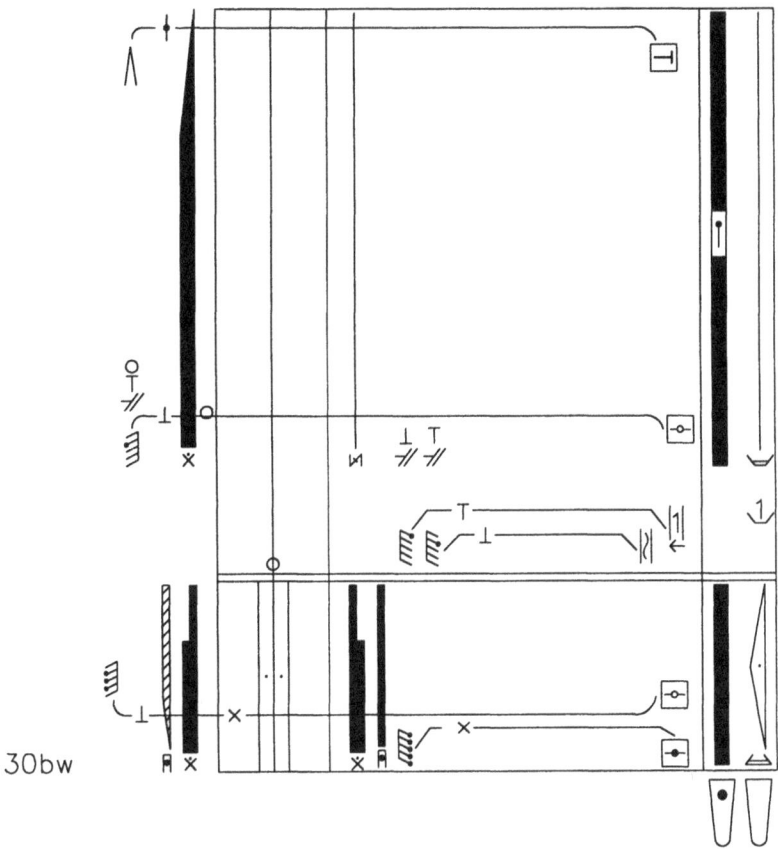

30bw

30.42. Ex. **30bw** shows the correct way to open (*Akeru*) the *sensu*, a way that allows it to be done smoothly. First one space is opened by the right thumb and first finger; then, as these fingers press in opposite directions, the opening occurs as the right arm extends and the left arm moves diagonally across to the right. This whole action is performed smoothly as one movement.

For *Ikken-Ake*, opening one space only, the action must be done with one hand. It is the first action occuring in the above sequence. The *sensu* with one space opened is used to represent a number of things, for example, pouring *sake*, or the plectrum used in playing the *shamisen*, a traditional stringed instrument.

Tojiru: Closing the *Sensu*

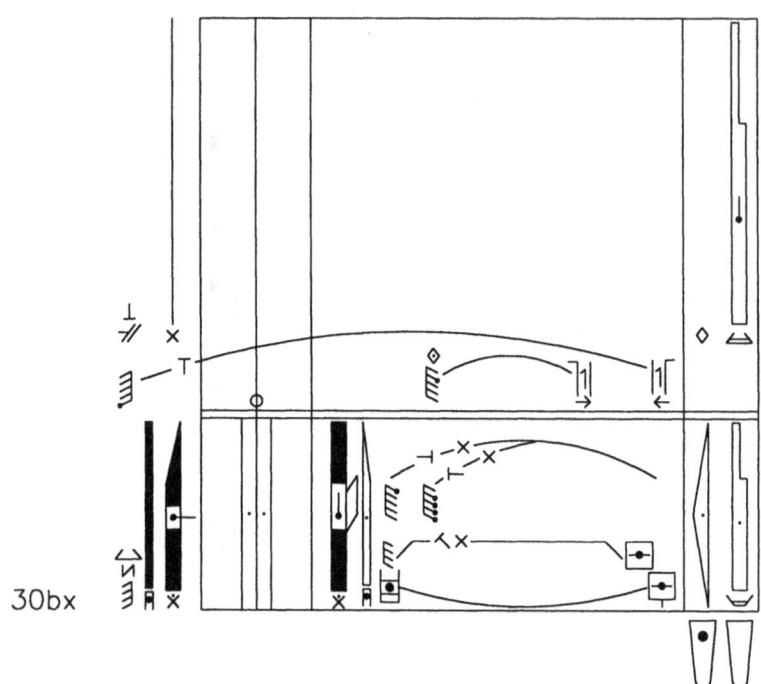

30.43. Ex. **30bx** shows the most basic way to close the *sensu*. Note the placement of the *chi* in the middle of the right palm. While the open *sensu* is pointing forward, facing left, the left little finger, contacting from behind, presses forward on the first rib (counted from the right) thus causing it to close. The right index finger remains where it is, thus aiding in the closing process.

30.44. **Addressing.** In Japanese dance the *sensu* is used in both the closed and open positions to point out things. The part that actually does the pointing is called *saki* (see **30r**) and refers to the very tip of the *oyabone*. In the closed position this is represented by the place high pin. In **30by** the closed fan addresses E, the Emperor.

In the open position, *saki* is represented by the side middle pins; however, addressing is done with only one of these tips at a time. Which one is pointing should be clear from the movement context; in **30bz** person F is being addressed by the right edge of the open fan. The addressing bow is written from the fan direction column in **30by** and extends to the right, or it can extend from the column indicating the part of the fan. Occasionally the place high part, the *ten* of the open *sensu*, will also be used for pointing. The symbol for *saki*, the side middle pin when the fan is open, does not have to be written when it is obvious.

Addressing

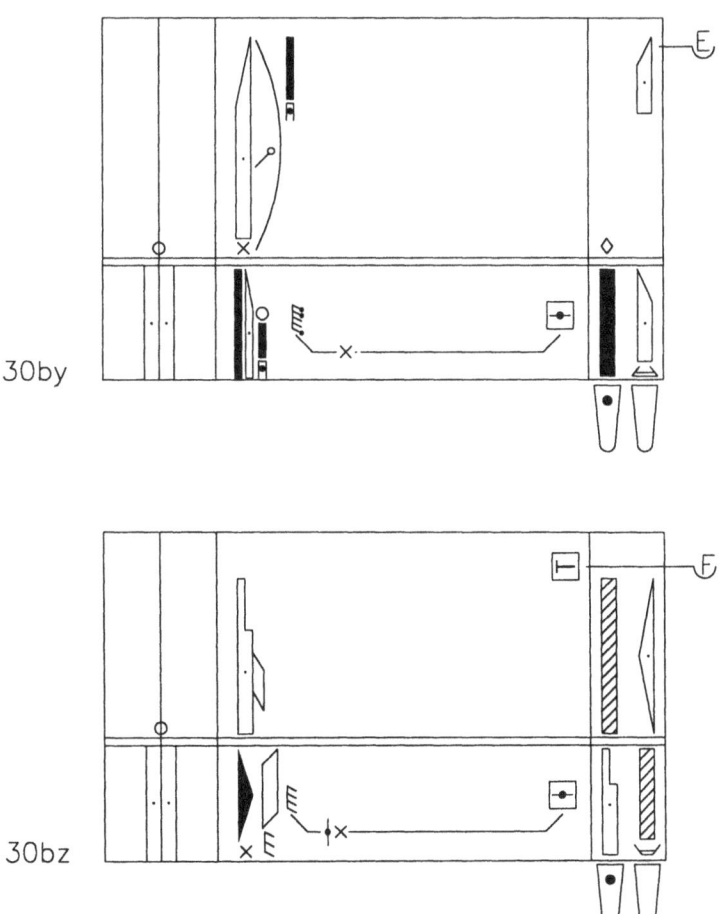

30.45. **Revolutions.** Fans may also revolve around their own three axes. Notating rotations on a vertical axis can usually be avoided, the movement being written by new facing symbols for the *sensu*. Revolutions on the sagittal axis, that is cartwheeling, occur when spinning the *sensu* and throwing it in the air, although the pivot point may not be the physical center of the *sensu*. Revolutions on the lateral axis, that is somersaulting, also occur when throwing the *sensu*. In the technique of throwing the *sensu*, there is an understood spatial displacement upward and slightly backward as the *sensu* is thrown in the air, it is caught as it falls to the original spot from which thrown. There is no displacement sideward or forward. For these revolutions the standard symbols for turning, cartwheeling and somersaulting are used and placed in the fan direction column. If necessary, these signs may also be written outside the fan staff on the right. If the meaning is unclear, the rotation sign may be connected with a small horizontal bow to the fan movement column.

30.46. Ex. **30ca** shows the *Mae-Tonbo*, the Front Somersault. This movement begins with *Tsumami-mochi* (**30bu**) as preparation for a somersaulting action. Note how the fingers are bunched so that the fan is grasped near the ends of the fingers. A slight upward and backward thrust (the minor distal movement, the slight displacement preparation before releasing) sends the fan into the air. It is caught in the same place as it returns.

Mae-Tonbo: **Front Somersault**

30ca

30.47. **Cartwheel Revolution.** *Yoko-Tombo*, which means Cartwheel, is shown in **30cb** as an example to the left. With an inward twist of the arm, the fan is released and then caught again in the same way.

Yoko-Tonbo: **Cartwheel**

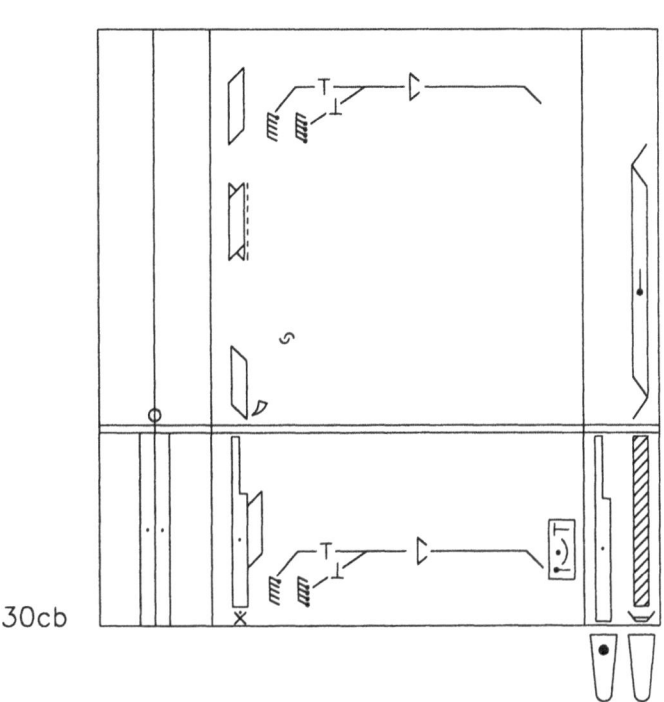

30cb

30.48. **Manipulation of Open** *Sensu*. Known as the *Taira-kazashi-mocchi*, the Flat Lifted Hold, the movement of **30cc** is done with *Taira-mochi* (**30bv**), the flat hold; it is used sometimes near the end of a dance to symbolise a blessing from the performer to the audience. The fan starts facing backward low, the vertical axis forward low. As the arm is raised the fan slowly comes to the vertical and ends facing forward.

Taira-kazashi-mocchi: **Manipulation of Open** *Sensu*

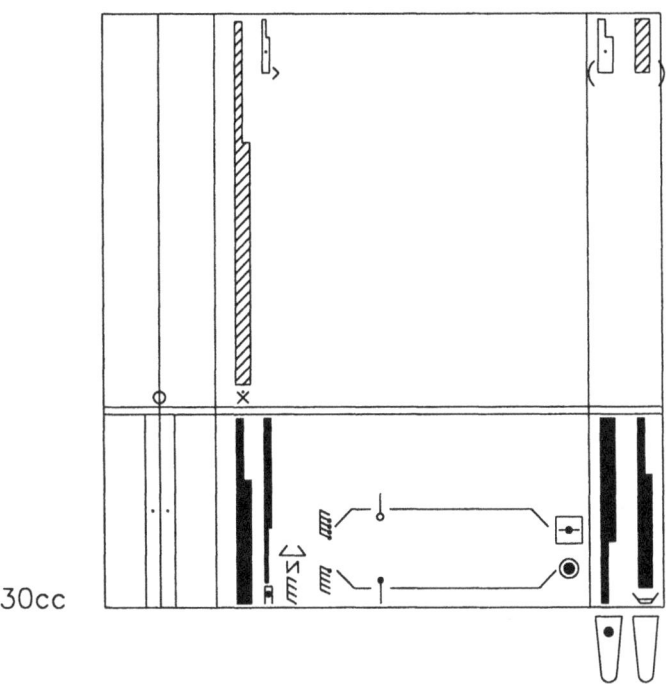

30cc

30.49. *Kaname-gaeshi no kihon* is a Basic Turning of the Pin (Angled Cartwheel), **30cd**. This is a basic but rather difficult movement phrase which occurs when the *sensu* outlines curved figure eight lines in space.

The fan is held at an angle by the thumb and first finger (thumb 'on top') on the first rib to the left, the other fingers lie 'under' the other ribs. (Note that these directions are here being given a relative description, hence the use of quotes for descriptions such as 'under'.) The middle, fourth and little finger bend so as to pass over the first rib as the fan begins to rotate, they then support from 'under' while the thumb releases and the fan is held by the index finger 'above' and the middle finger 'below'. The index and middle finger continue to hold, changing relationship as the fan continues to turn, while the fourth finger bends then stretches to pass around the rib. At the end of the full turn the fan is supported by the middle finger 'above' and the index and fourth finger below. Note the use of the sign of **30ce** for 'other ribs'.

30.50. When manipulating the reverse direction as in **30cf**, the use of the black diamond of **30cg** is needed to indicate that the pin description states the relationship after the movement is completed. This statement can be made in one of the two ways given here. In the score the black diamond has been connected to the backward low pin. After the half return rotation, the index finger is 'above' and the middle and fourth fingers are 'below'. The thumb now moves 'under' as the fan revolves. The fan ends supported by the thumb and index finger while the other three fingers pass to end supporting 'under' the ribs while the thumb is 'above'. A return to the starting position has been achieved.

Advanced Labanotation

Manipulation of Open *Sensu* (continued)

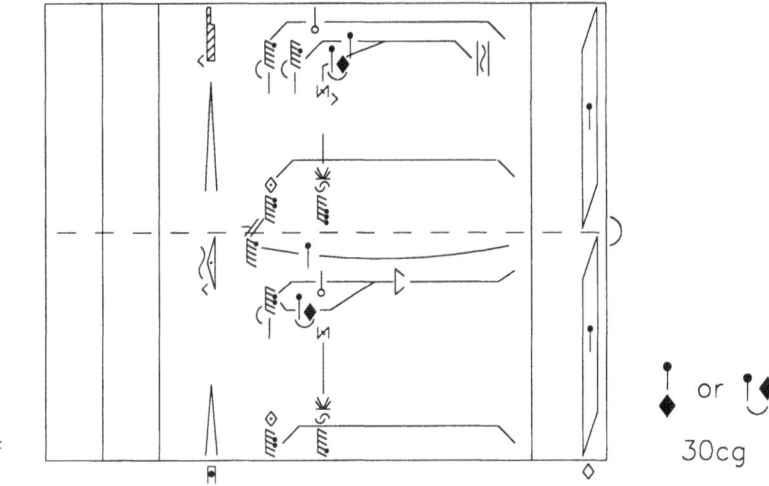

Reverse Rotation

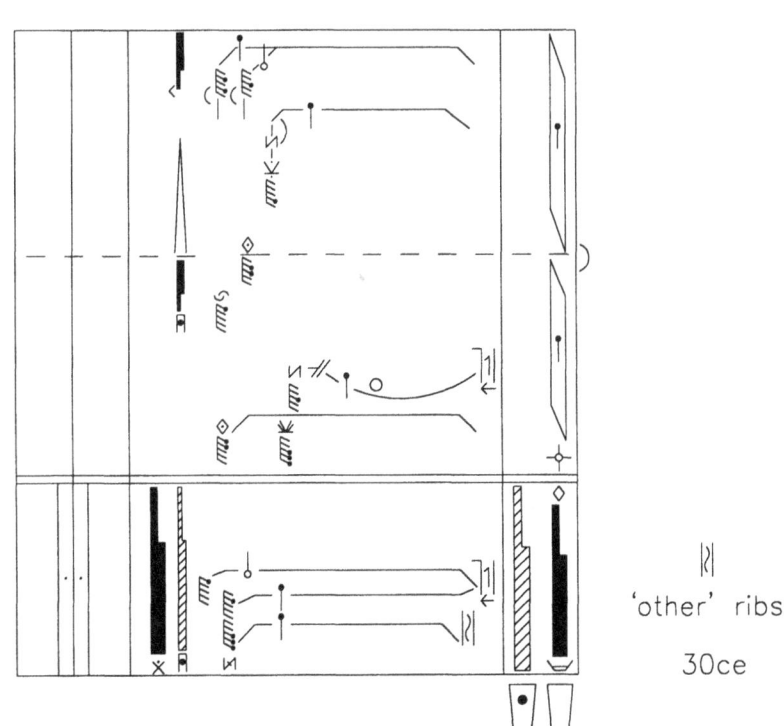

Kaname-gaeshi no kihon

30.51. Lady Senda's Dance.[54] This excerpt from *Ikkaku Sennin* provides the opportunity to see fan movements combined with footwork and body and arm gestures.[55] The aim in presenting this excerpt is to focus on details in handling the fan; therefore certain other features have not been given special attention. The stylistic details given for the footwork in the full score are omitted, focus being on the fan manipulations. However, the full version for the arm positions are included.

Note that in this dance there are changes in meter. The sung accompaniment, giving meaning to the dance, has not been included here.

The 'Hawk's Beak' position is given in **30ch**, its particular abbreviation as used in the score being shown at the left. The abbreviated diagonally low arm position of **30ci** is spelled out fully in **30cj**. The simple sideward position for the arms, **30ck**, should be performed as **30cl**. A back to normal sign within a side horizontal sign indicates a true side middle gesture, **30cm** (see measure 51 in **30cs** and measure 55 in **30ct**). Note the use of the 'Hawk's Beak' finger position in each of **30cj** and **30cl**. When holding the fan, the fan comes between the thumb and index finger. Ex. **30cn** spells out the correct style for the simple walking steps; the feet stay in contact with the ground, as no lifting occurs.

Lady Senda's Dance, **30co**, starts in a low foot-kneel with the fan closed. In the second measure the fan is opened just before she rises to her feet. Opening the fan involves a forward pressure from the right thumb, the right arm ending extended normally forward, while the left fingers press backward, the left elbow contracting before the fingers release and take the 'Hawk's Beak' position as the arm lowers to the diagonal. Note the increase in speed for the steps in measure 4. At the end of this phrase she lowers to the foot-kneel position.

Advanced Labanotation

Lady Senda's Dance

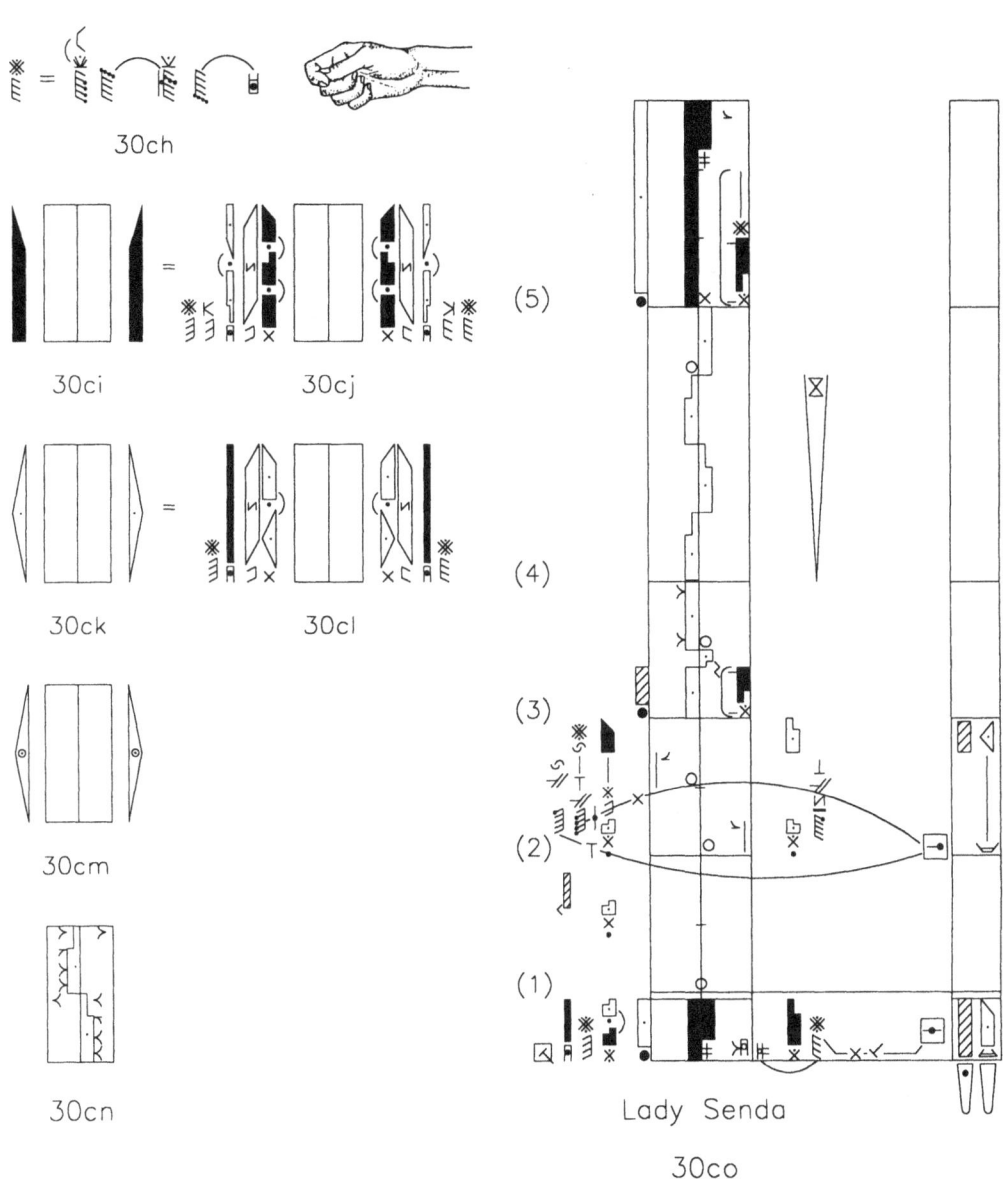

30.52. Ex. **30cp** shows another excerpt from Lady Senda's Dance. Note the indication of increase and decrease in speed modifying the walking steps. She[56] sinks again into a low foot-kneel. The thumb slides to the base, the fan is held by the thumb and finger tips at the *chi*. As her center of weight rises slightly, the right arm makes a curved upward movement, the fan continues to face up while the axis points right diagonal, then rises diagonally before pointing halfway between diagonal left and side left. Her arm returns to forward as she inclines the torso forward. Her torso then comes upright as her arm gestures diagonally upward, the fan axis rising in the same direction before the arm ends diagonal low as she again sinks to the same low foot-kneel, the fan now pointing side left while facing back high. At the end of this phrase her right thumb slides on the fan to the edge of the paper.

Lady Senda's Dance (continued)

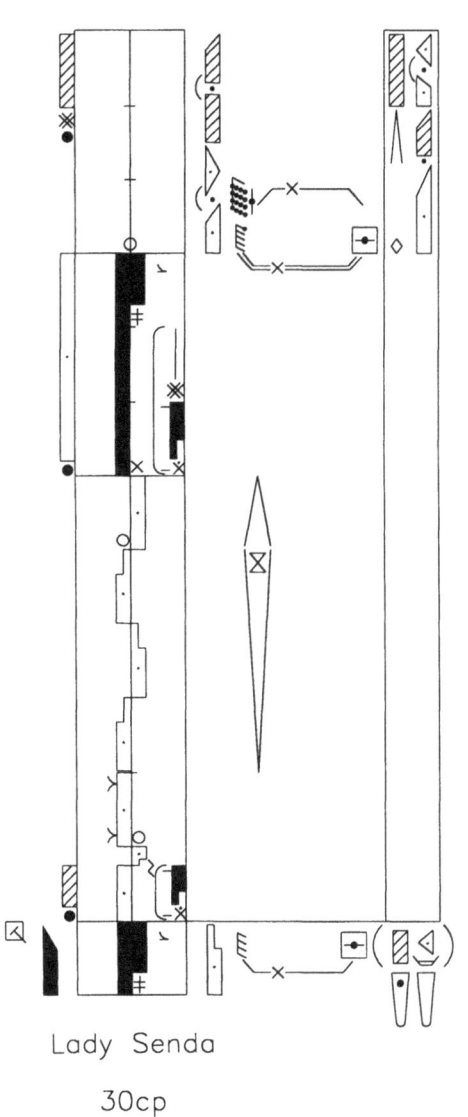

Lady Senda

30cp

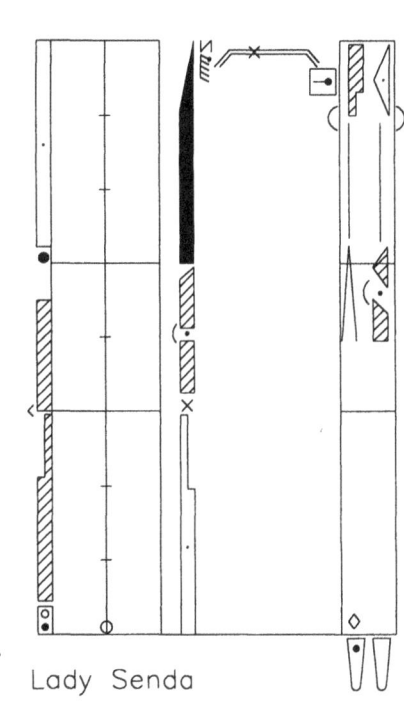

Lady Senda

30.53. Closing the Fan - Lady Senda's Dance. This excerpt, **30cq**, is a continuation from the previous page. It shows the finger tips holding the *chi* from below, the thumb braced on the *oyabone* near the paper. With the fan's axis pointing forward middle and the front directed to the right, her left hand contacts the point between the edge and the middle of the paper section, her left arm being inwardly rotated as it moves to right diagonal low, the palm facing forward. As the left hand presses forward, the right presses downward, thus closing the fan. The right hand changes to grasping the *kaname* with the 'Hawk's Beak' hand position, the left hand releases, also taking the 'Hawk's Beak' hand position; both arms open to the diagonal low position. The axis of the fan is now pointing diagonally while the front faces up.

Closing the Fan - Lady Senda's Dance (continued)

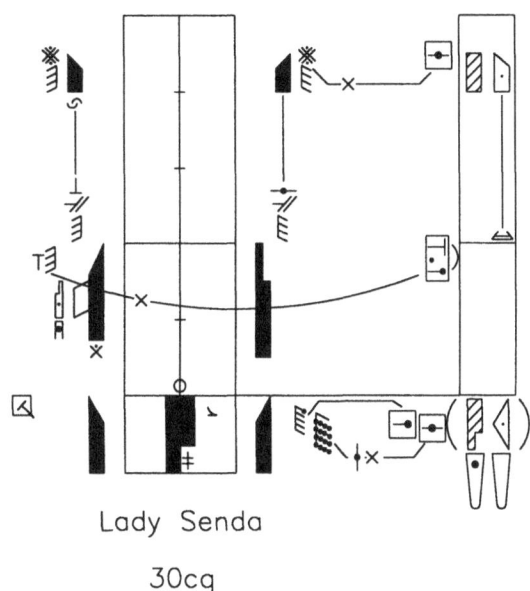

Lady Senda

30cq

30.54. Ex. **30cr** is a slightly later continuation of Lady Senda's Dance. It begins with her standing feet together, with her right arm out to the side, palm down, her left arm in the open diagonally low position, hand in the 'Hawk's Beak' position, the closed fan being held in her right hand. Lady Senda then changes to facing front with a torso 'blind' turn, that is, a turn of the torso to the left with the addition of the secret turn sign indicating the decision to choose a new front. Note use of the 'away' sign to make clear that the torso turn disappears. This torso rotation and secret turn are repeated before she walks forward, makes a half circle to the left and then walks forward again until the $^3/_8$ turn left to end facing front. During the half circle her left hand grasps the fan at the lower part of the paper from above, the thumb being underneath, thus causing the fan to make a forward somersault (performer's point of view) during which the palm of her right hand slides over the base of the fan. Note the spot hold on the supporting grasp for the left hand at the start of this somersault motion, allowing the hand to adjust as needed to retain this grasp. The fan ends facing up and pointing left forward diagonal.

This sequence is followed by opening the fan, achieved through pressure from the right little finger tip which is under the first rib from the left, and the thumb which is diagonally back of the first rib from the right, near the paper. As the thumb presses forward right diagonal, the left hand, which is now touching the fan from below at the same place as before, presses backward and then diagonally right backward, thus causing the fan to open. Its front ends facing right forward diagonal high. The left hand releases and both arms lower to the open low diagonal position. The fan now points to side left, facing forward high, thus bringing the left corner tip of the paper to rest under the right lower arm, just below the elbow. The left hand has resumed the 'Hawk's Beak' position.

Near the end of the sequence shown here, the right arm makes a small detour to arrive slightly flexed in the right high diagonal direction on its way to forward middle, the elbow rotated inward (lifted elbow), the palm ending facing down. The fan is carried along and ends facing down and pointing side left.

Advanced Labanotation

Lady Senda's Dance (continued)

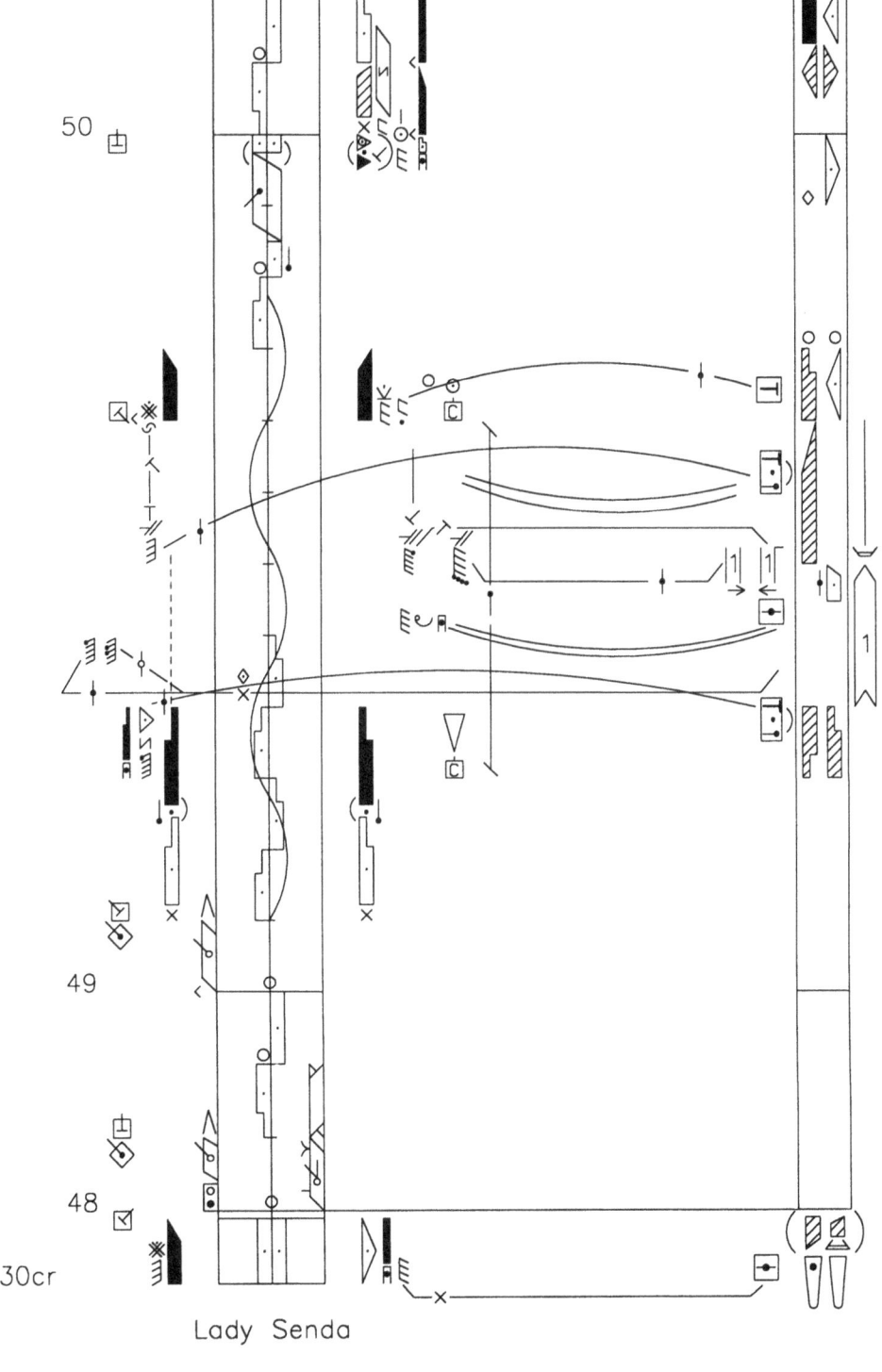

Lady Senda

30.55. Ex. **30cs** is a continuation of Lady Senda's dance. Her forward path ends facing toward diagonal right, an intermediate facing direction brought about by the very slight curved path which occurs during the last two steps. The technique for turning in place with the feet together is not spelled out here. As the feet close at the end of this phrase, the torso has a slight lift, a subtle rise, typical of this style, which requires a more specific description than that given here. The legs return to normal extension (after the slightly bent state typical for this dance style). As the turns in place conclude, the right arm opens, the hand grasp on the fan changes to finger tips and thumb holding at the base section in preparation for the rotation of the fan around its vertical axis. The fan ends facing up, pointing halfway to diagonally backward high.

As the arm rises right forward diagonally high, elbow rotated in, the fan makes an arc-like movement, ending facing and pointing diagonally at an intermediate situation, just past pointing up and facing between left diagonal middle and low.

A quarter twist of the torso to the left and the inward rotation of the right leg lead to the decision to take downstage left as the new Front (a secret turn). Halfway through the half circle walk, the thumb slips along the first rib as the fan rotates again to its left and the arm lowers to the open diagonal low position. The fan is now facing forward high and pointing left side, the paper near the fan edge now being under the lower arm, a similar placement to that in Ex. 30cr. After the turns in place on both feet, there is again the very slight rise in the torso and in the legs.

Lady Senda's Dance (continued)

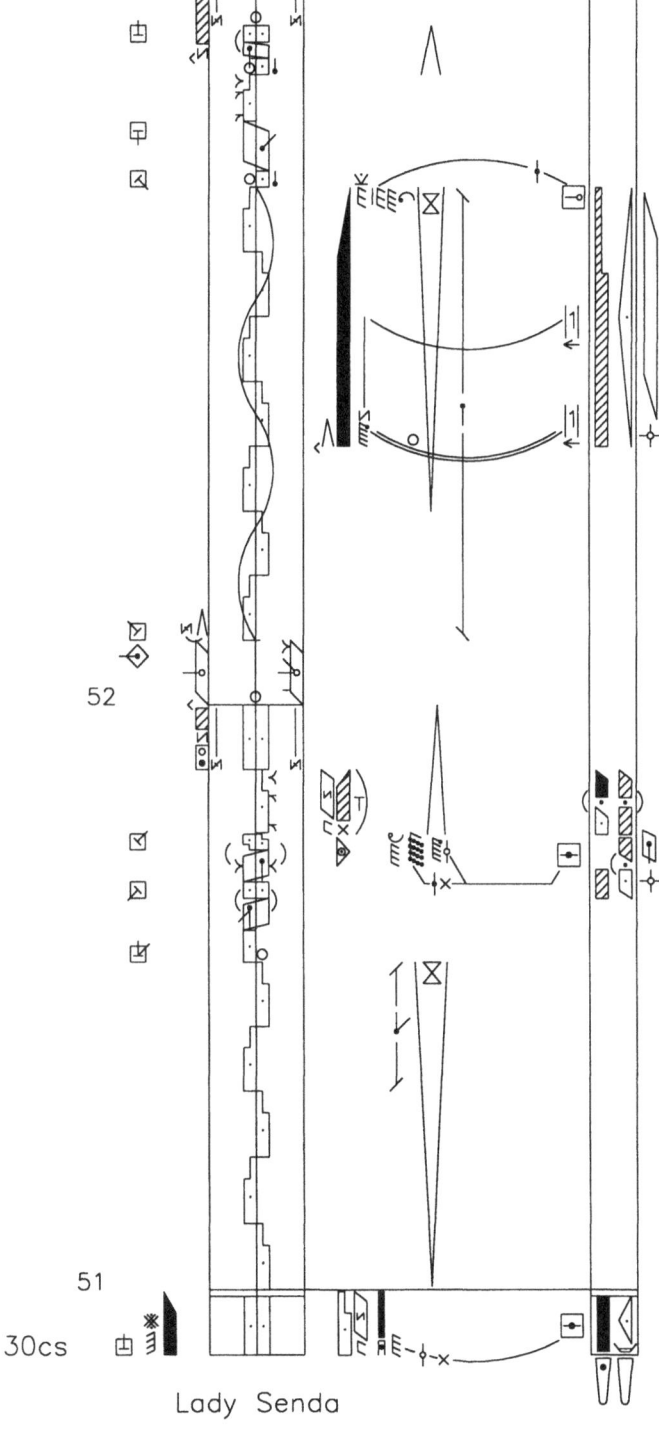

Lady Senda

30.56. This section of Lady Senda's Dance, **30ct**, is a continuation of **30cs** and concludes these excerpts from this source.

During the right arm movement of measure 53, the fan is carried along, its relationship to the hand is retained (an understood body hold). The torso and inward leg rotation to the left result in a new choice of Front (a blind turn).

During the swivel turn on both feet in measure 54, the right arm rises to forward middle, palm down, the fan now facing left side high and pointing left side low.

As the arm opens to normal side middle (see **30cm**) the palm faces forward, the fingers change their grasp, and the fan tip makes a $5/8$ horizontal circle to the right, ending facing between left forward diagonal high and place high. The arm then rises diagonally in an arc to forward horizontal, palm down, at which point the fan is facing down, pointing to side left. It maintains this side direction (space hold) while the arm makes a forward sagittal path, moving down, then close to the body before returning to forward middle. The palm ends facing side low.

During this arm movement, the fan faces backward middle and then ends facing up, the left point of the fan touching under the lower arm. During this action the fan has, in fact, made a half forward somersault from the person's Standard Cross (not shown in the notation).

This sequence ends in a simple manner. Two backward steps end with feet together, the arms having opened out sideward before lowering to the familiar low open diagonal position.

Advanced Labanotation

Lady Senda's Dance (concluded)

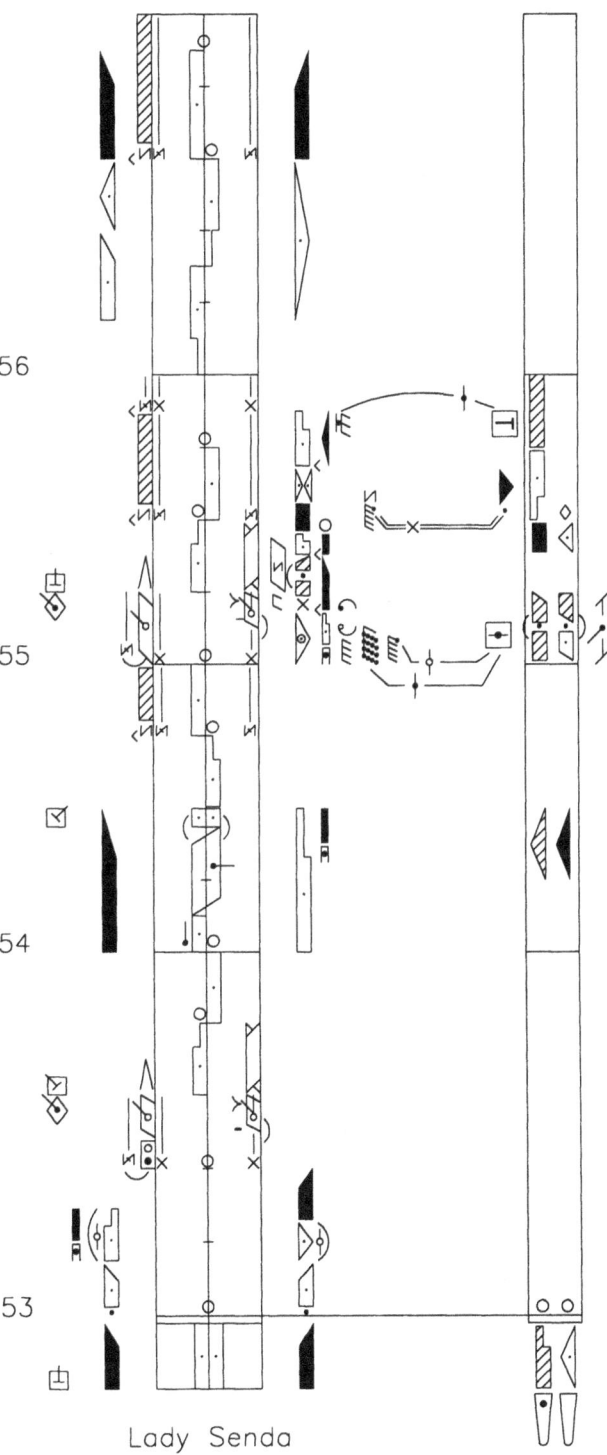

Lady Senda

31 Handling a Long Ribbon

31.1. Long ribbons are visually effective and are a popular prop in certain Chinese dances and in Rhythmic Gymnastics. The visual patterns the ribbon makes often need to be described as well as the general arm patterns and other accompanying steps and body movements. As with handling most properties, the details of wrist flexion and rotation (twisting) are not spelled out, unless the effect depends on them.

31.2. For the Red Ribbon Dance,[57] a small representation of the ribbon is given, as in **31a**; the factual particulars, the dimensions, are set forth in **31b**. Note that the ribbon is narrower where it is attached to the stick. The stick is held at the base in the right hand. A few typical movement patterns are given here.

31.3. Ex. **31c** starts with the right arm forward. The lower arm then describes backward somersault paths in the areas of left side middle, forward middle, right side middle and then forward middle, during which the ribbon makes a three-dimensional figure eight pattern, illustrated through design drawing.[58] The design drawing itself indicates the three surfaces on which the design is traced; these are shown next to the appropriate parts of the pattern. In the dance this pattern is repeated as the dancer runs forward.

31.4. At the end of the leaping run of **31d** (which is similar to **31c**), the left leg extends forward, 'piercing', so to speak, the circle made by the ribbon. The relationship of the left leg to the design is shown by the 'through' pin placed in the dotted bow connected to the design. The ribbon, manipulated by the lower arm, makes a $3/4$ circular design on the front (forward middle) surface. The size of this pattern should be large, as shown in the addition bracket on the right.

31.5. In **31e** the dancer holds the ribbon out to the side, quickly fluttering it down and up as, with quick steps, she revolves on a straight path, traveling forward.

31.6. During the repeated two-step turn pattern of **31f** the dancer travels on a $1\,1/4$ clockwise circular path spiralling in. On each turn the arm makes an overhead half circle arc, which results in an inward spiralling shape for the ribbon. To distinguish the dancer's path from prop indications, the body-as-a-whole sign has been added here.[59]

Handling a Long Ribbon

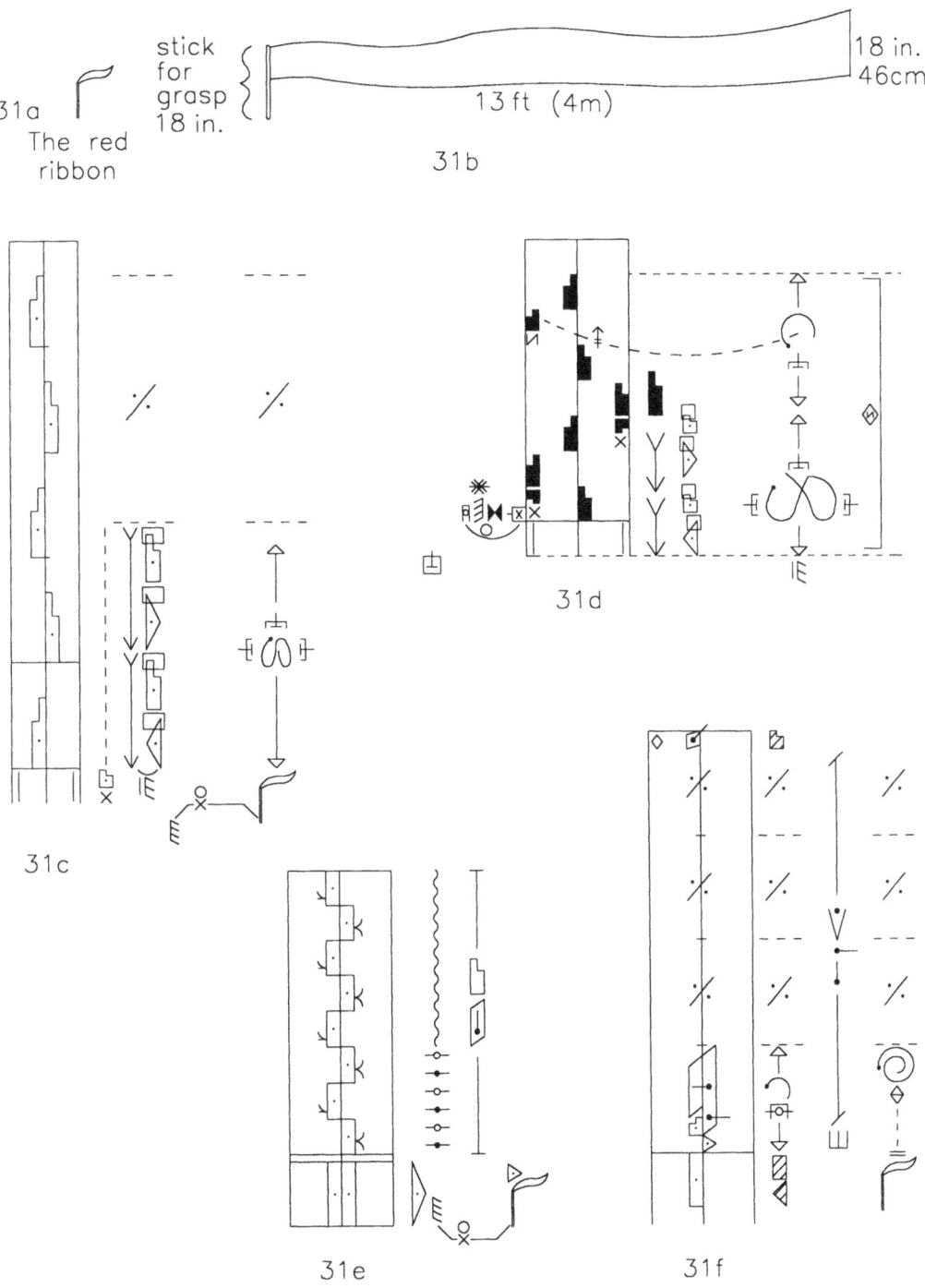

32 Folding a Large Cloth

32.1. A large piece of material may need to be folded in a particular way for choreographic reasons as well as practical concerns, so that it can be easily unfolded later in the dance. One such example, **32a**,[60] which reveals details needed to handle such a cloth, comes from Doris Humphrey's *Day on Earth*. The cloth is two yards by three yards (two metres by three metres) and is made of China silk. At the start of this excerpt the cloth is folded in half and lying on a box with the folded side resting on the floor. This fold, indicated by a dotted line, is on the downstage side of the cloth; that side of the cloth is, therefore, identified with side and place low symbols, as shown in **32b**. The designations for the parts of the cloth are drawn as seen from above. Note that this identification of the parts is based on the cloth's initial position; even though the cloth's orientation will change, the 'names' of the parts will remain the same. In addition to the corners, the center (middle level) and the centers of the side edges, six more intermediate places are marked as **a**, **b**, **c**, **d**, **e**, and **f**.

32.2. For our purposes here the original timing has been condensed. Our focus is on how the cloth is handled. In the column for the prop, sometimes only a section of the cloth is shown, illustrating the important places to be grasped, **32c**. In measure 119 dancer L grasps the low level downstage corners. As she turns to face downstage, she lifts the cloth up and the cloth makes a resultant upward path, **32d**. After a step to the left, as shown in the floorplan of **32e**, with arms spread wide she flexes her wrists backward, rotates her arms outward, and then contracts them, bringing her elbows above the edge of the cloth and in front of it, **32f**.

32.3. With the elbows now supporting the points a and b from in front, **32g**, they move outward to the side as the lower arms close in, moving in opposition, thus causing lateral closing of the cloth, **32h**.

Advanced Labanotation

Folding a Large Cloth

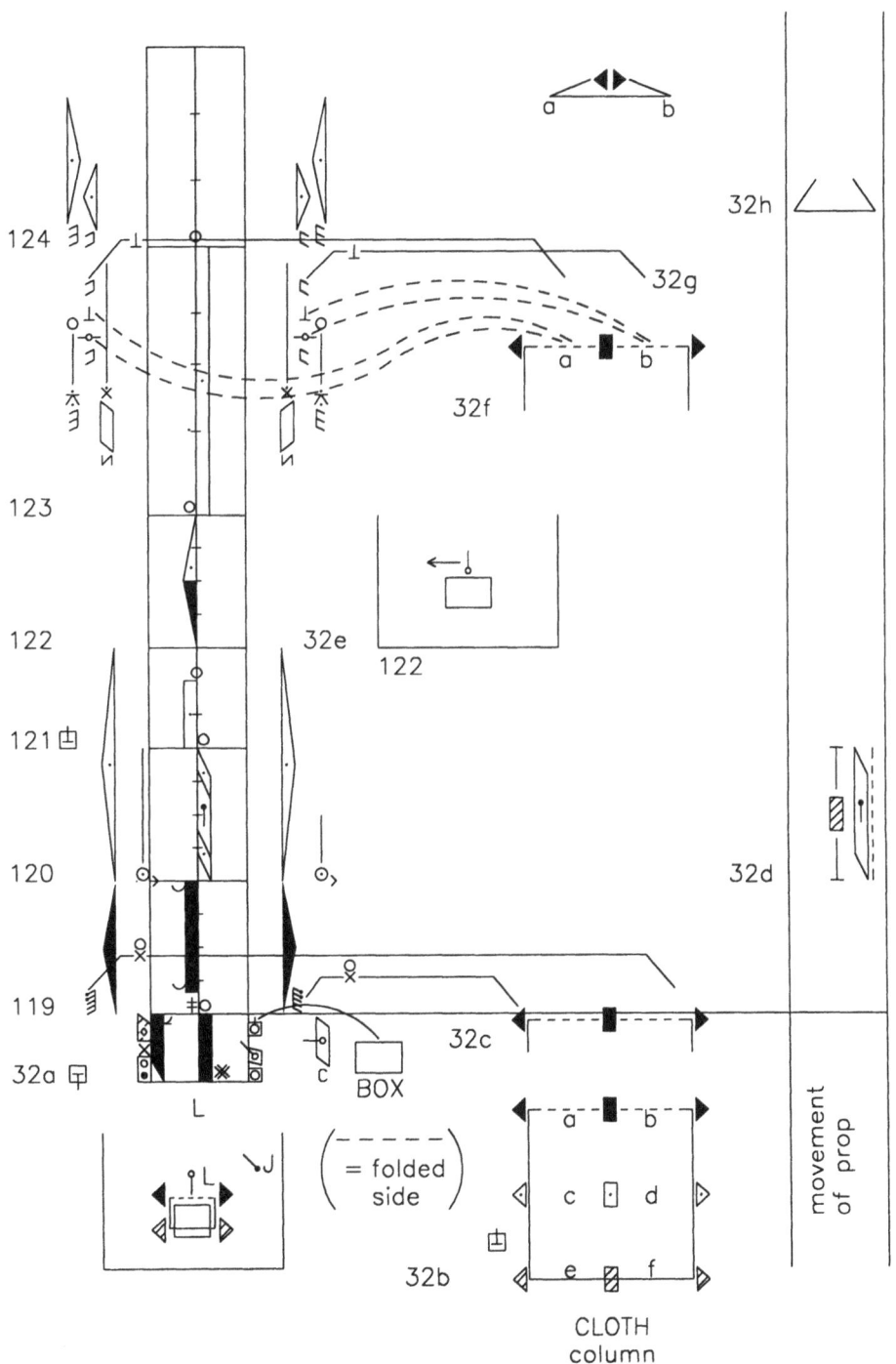

Handling of Objects, Props

32.4. As she takes a long step backward, dancer L's right hand grasps the two corners, **32i**, and the left hand then grasps the center of the edge, **32j**. The cloth is extended sagittally forward, **32k**. Points **a** and **b** are now together. As the arms change direction, moving to the sides, the cloth is given a quarter turn to the right, **32l**, to end as in **32m**.

32.5. L takes a step to the right in measure 128 and bends her knees as her left foot closes in place. Then, with the torso leaning backward and the arms bending and brought slightly backward, the cloth rests on the front of the torso, **32n**. This allows the hands to be freed so that they can come together near the front of the waist. Note use of the dotted line in **32o** to indicate where the next fold will come. From the movement it is clear that the fold comes in the center, where the waist is.

Folding a Large Cloth (continued)

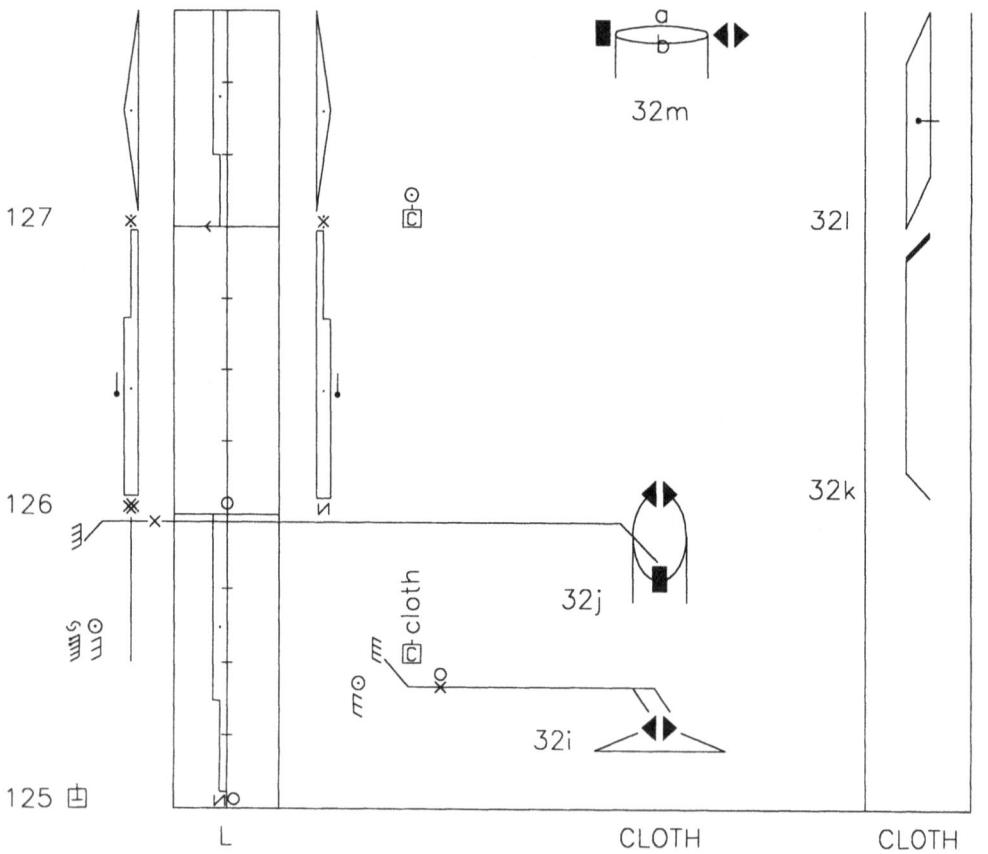

Advanced Labanotation

Folding a Large Cloth (continued)

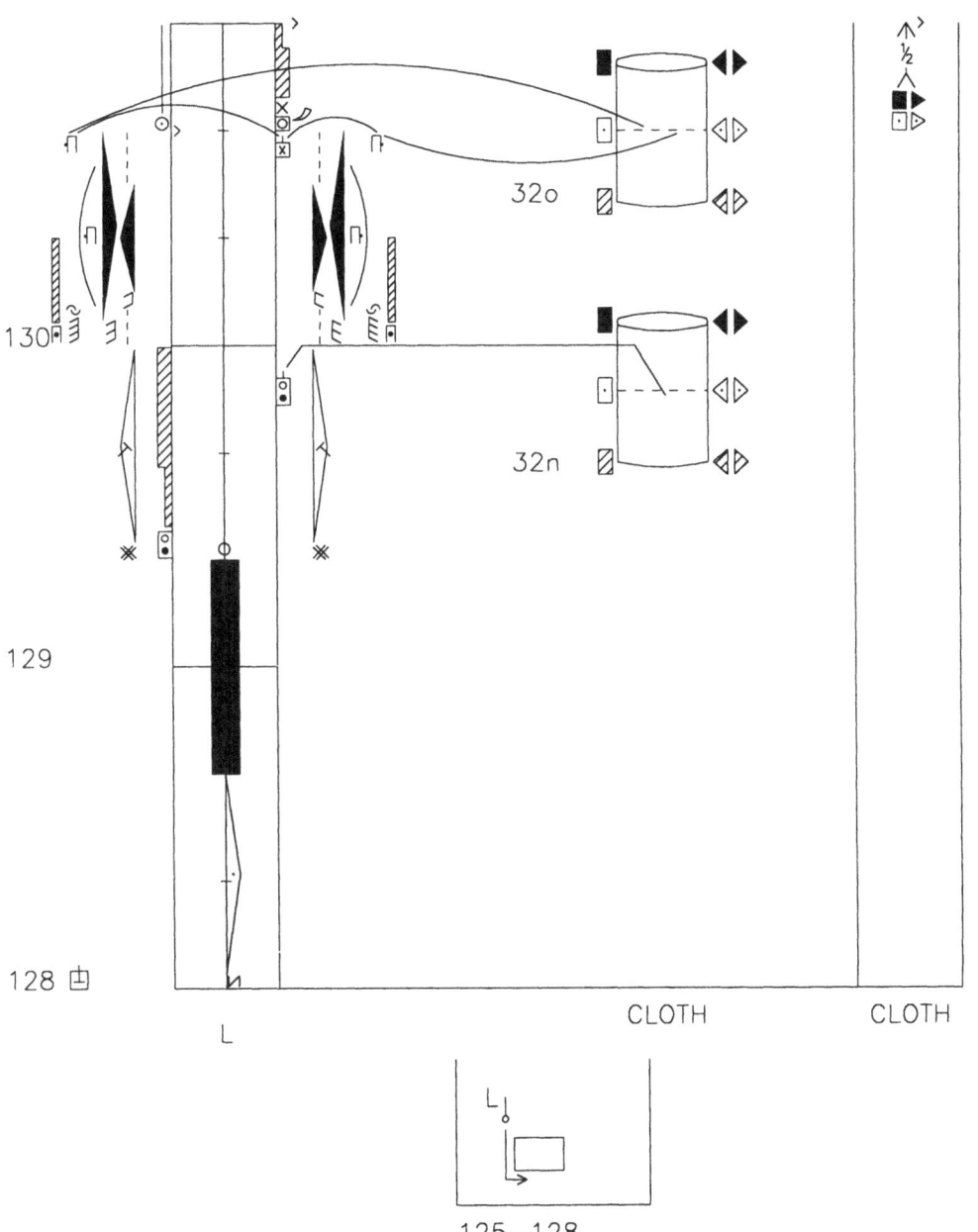

32.6. As the chest bends forward the little finger edges slide out to the edges of the cloth, making the crease that is needed, **32p**. In the prop column the $1/2$ forward somersault path results in the low corners and edges meeting the high ones, **32q**. The hands now grasp the middle level edges and center.

32.7. The steps to the right and diagonally forward in measure 132, are reflected in the floorplan of **32r** below on this page. An accented forward high arm movement, begun with the elbows, leaves the new center part, **c,d**, behind as the two new corners being grasped in measure 133 move forward high with the arms, **32s**. With the fold (**c,d** edge) near the chest, the left hand grasps the middle level corners just before the right arm bends and the hand grasps the new **c,d** corner, **32t**. The arms then both move forward high, causing the prop to make a $1/4$ turn to the left, **32u**. As the dancer kneels she flicks the cloth so the lower edge touches near the stage right end of the box (as she faces it) and the rest lowers, **32v**. An aerial view of the cloth on the box is shown in **32w**. Having released the cloth, she grasps the edges of the box and slides her right leg backward, as she lowers her torso forward onto the cloth, her head turned to the right.

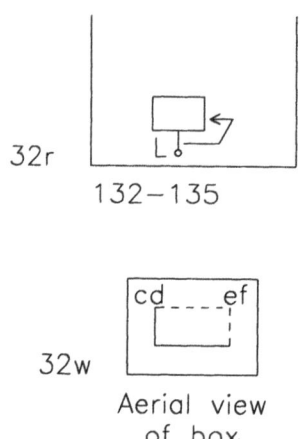

32r

132–135

32w

Aerial view of box

Folding a Large Cloth (concluded)

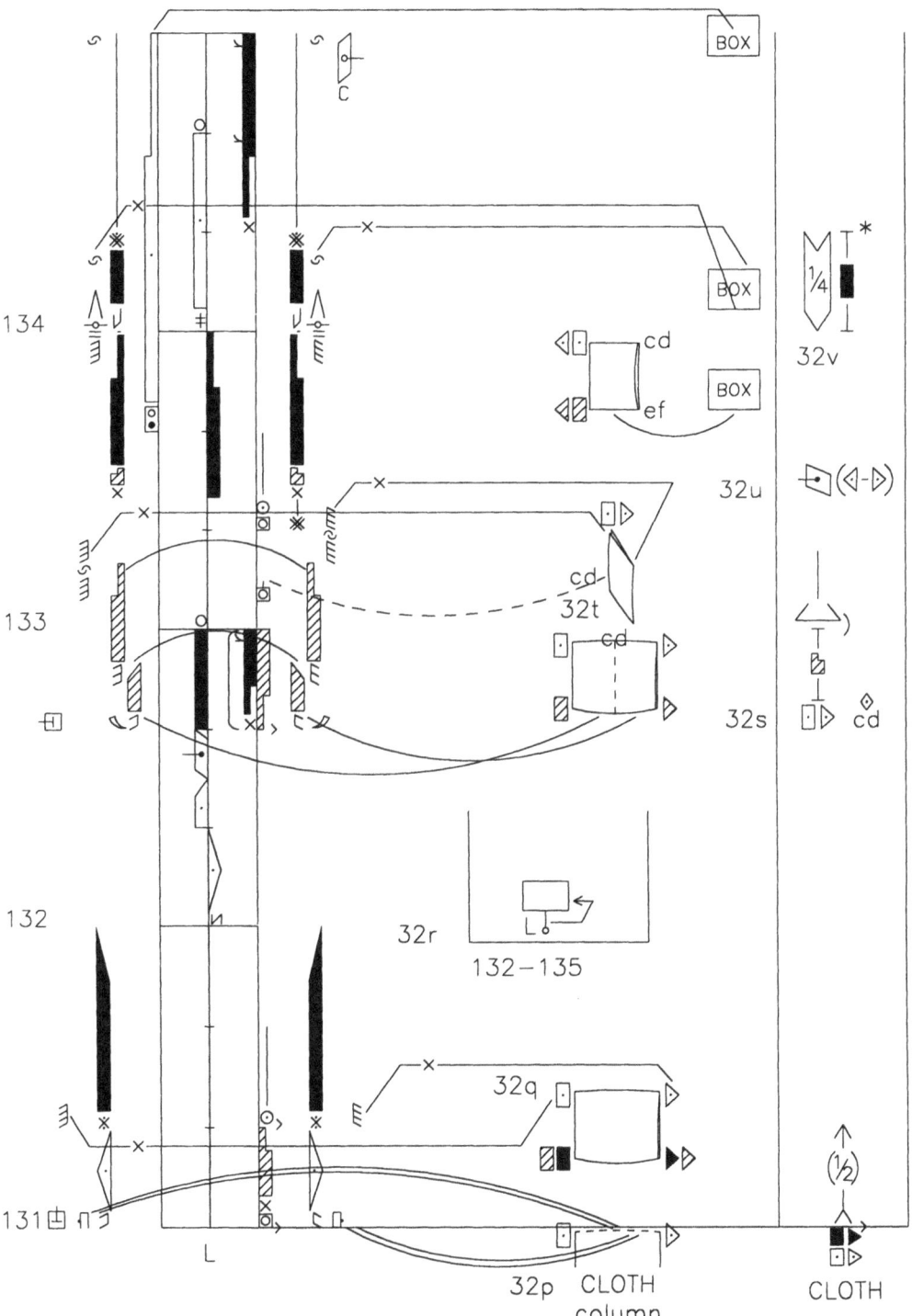

33 Handling a Blanket

33.1. In this pantomime sequence, **33a**, a girl enters carrying a folded, rolled up blanket. Note that the signs for folding and the lateral closing indications have been combined here into one sign. She then places the blanket on the floor and spreads it out. For this spreading, no specific movements have been given for the arms, instead indications for the blanket are shown: unfolding, spreading laterally and sagittally, ending with three-dimensional extension. Note the sign for 'a shape' (the diamond with a horizontal line through it), which is followed by a pictorial drawing of the desired shape.

33.2. Stepping forward on her left knee onto the blanket, and continuing with two more steps, she ends to the left of the middle of the blanket. She then does a $1/4$ roll to her left onto her right side. Grasping the side edge of the blanket, she gathers it in across her body as she performs a $1/2$ roll to her left onto her left side. From there she grasps the other side edge of the blanket with her left hand, gathering it up to cover herself as she rolls to her right onto her back. Note use of the gathering indication first for the right arm, then for the left in this section.

33.3. As though with a new idea, she throws off the part of the blanket in her left hand, then throws off the part in her right hand. Grasping the corners of the blanket behind her, she pulls it over her head as she sits up, then wraps it around her body as she bends her torso forward. With arms extended forward, still holding the ends of the blanket, she walks forward on her hips, pulling the blanket with her, until she is no longer on the blanket. She then passes through kneeling to end lying prone, the blanket completely covering her. Note use of the small horizontal staple near the end to indicate an extra support column for the hands.

Advanced Labanotation

Handling a Blanket

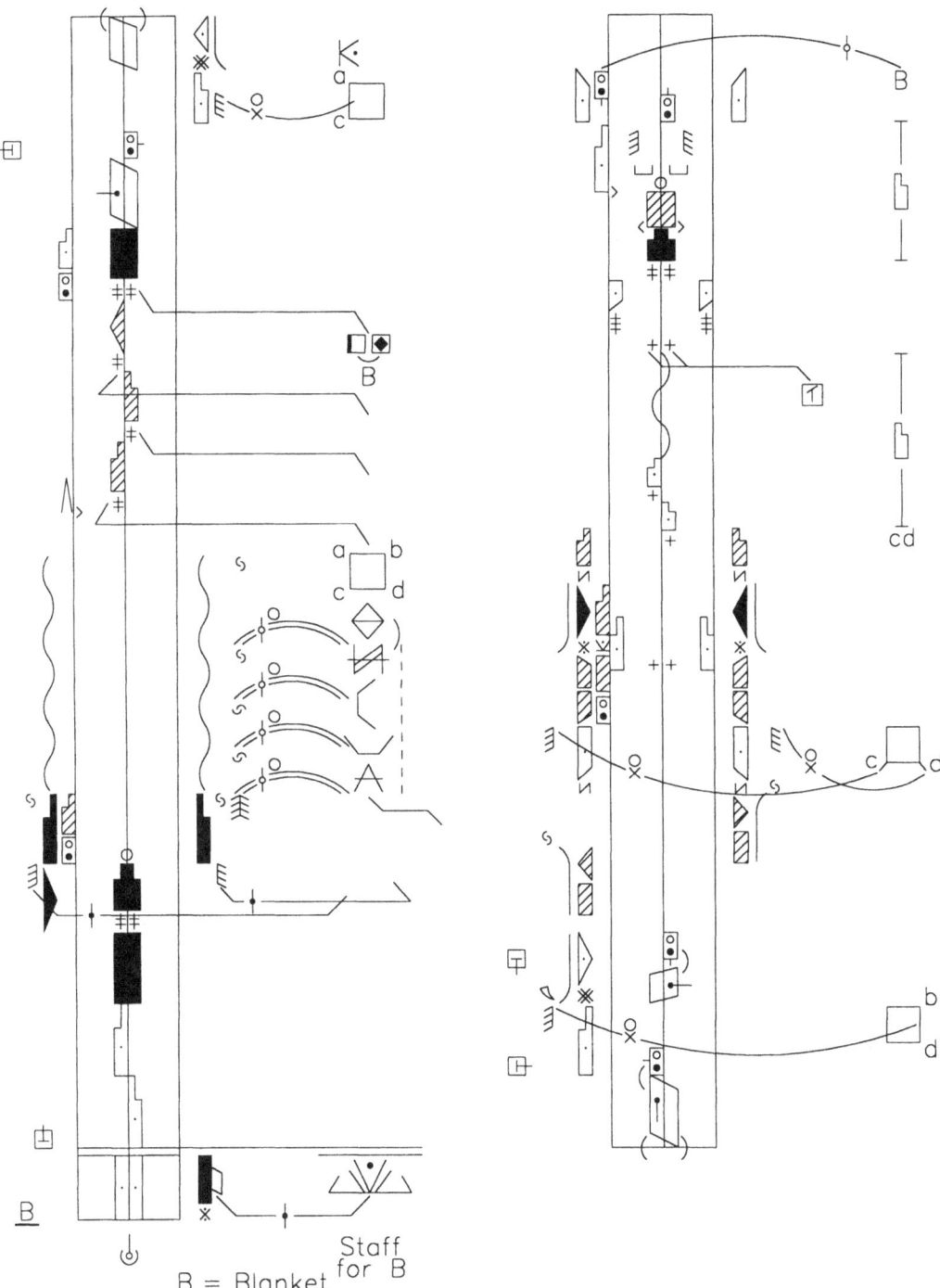

33a

PART III CLOTHING

34 Hat, Belt, Handkerchief, Sleeve, Pocket

34.1. **Hat.** Wearing a hat can be written as in **34a**, in which the supporting bow clearly indicates that the hat is supporting on the head, or as in **34b**, which may be spatially more practical. It is generally assumed that the hat is resting on the top of the head, thus the detail given in **34b** can be omitted. If the head were supporting on the hat the body configuration would doubtlessly reveal this fact.

34.2. The sequence of **34c** starts with the hat resting on a table. It is picked up by the brim and carried to the head, being turned $^1/_2$ to the left on the way. Once on the head, it is then tapped twice on the crown. Note the important detail that the brim is grasped from above, thus facilitating the turning of the hat during the movement to the head.

34.3. A gallant gesture with hat in hand is shown in **34d**. The movement of the right arm is described as usual through direction symbols while the path followed by the hat is indicated through design drawing.

34.4. **Belt.** A belt (or girdle) shown in **34e** is grasping the waist. The supporting part is actually the waist, but it is the belt which is doing the grasping. In **34f** a belt is worn. The front of the belt is grasped between the thumb and index finger, the thumb grasping from behind, the index finger from in front.

34.5. **Handkerchief.** A handkerchief (as distinct from the larger kerchief or scarf, which is worn on the head) may be held and waved for ornamental purposes; in such cases it is often grasped with three fingers in the center, the rest of the material falling into folds, **34g**. It may be used functionally, as in **34h**, where it is used to blot the brow, shown by the action of the hand and the contact of the handkerchief with the brow. Note the abbreviated form of the effort sign for dabbing.

34.6. Placing a handkerchief in a pocket is shown in **34i**. The left thumb and index finger open the edge of the pocket (note the forward sagittal opening indicated for the pocket) and the right hand moves to above the pocket, stretches, lowers, as it places the handkerchief inside, then releases and rises.

Advanced Labanotation

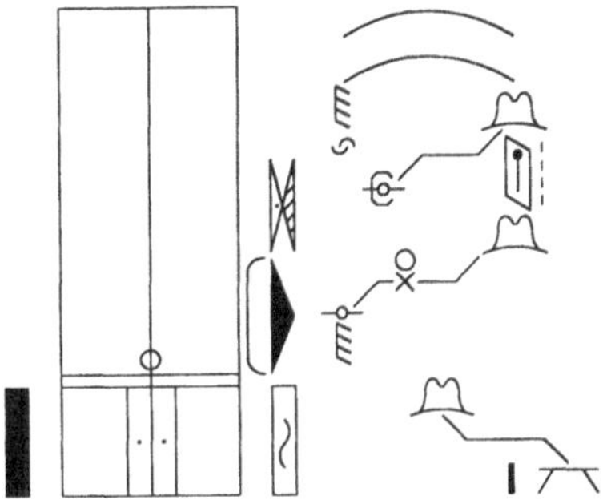

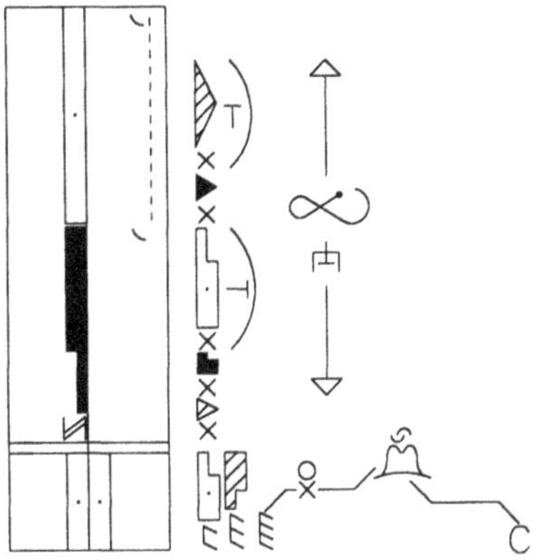

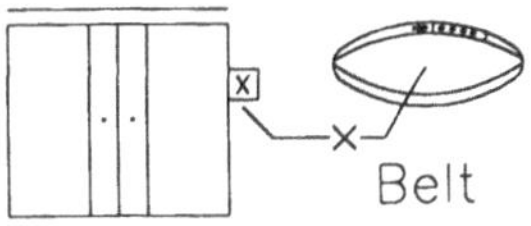

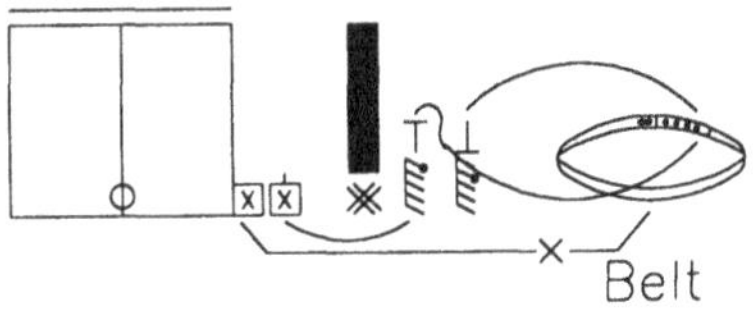

Hat

Belt

Handkerchief

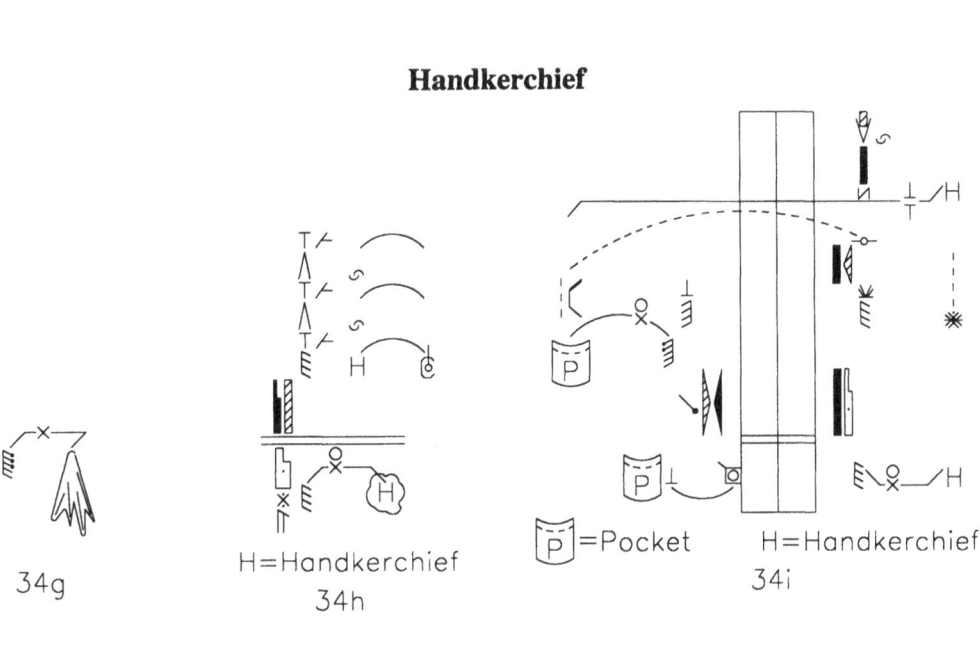

34.7. **Reading Example - a Hat.** The following excerpt has been taken from the Mexican dance *Jarabe Tapatio*, better known as *The Mexican Hat Dance*.[61] Only a section of the woman's part is given here. The man wears a *sombrero*, the large Mexican hat with a very wide brim. In the glossary to this dance 'H' is given for the hat with 'HB' representing the hat brim.

34.8. At the start of this excerpt, **34j**, the woman is circling around her partner (indicated by P within the circling sign) while he throws his hat down, near her feet. She then picks up her skirt and circles around the hat as, with her left leg crossed diagonally behind the right, she taps the brim with the toe of her left shoe. Note the use here of a column to represent the brim of the hat. For the next phrase of eight measures her right foot steps onto the brim as does the left, each foot touching first and then, with a tiny spring, landing on the brim, the right foot diagonally forward, the left backward, gradually making a full circle around the brim. During this pattern the man has a step circling clockwise around the woman.

34.9. In measures 125-126 the woman steps onto the floor, kicks her right leg in an arc above the hat and then kneels to pick it up. Placing it on her head she grasps the brim on either side and then embarks on a toe-heel step.

Advanced Labanotation

Reading Example - a Hat

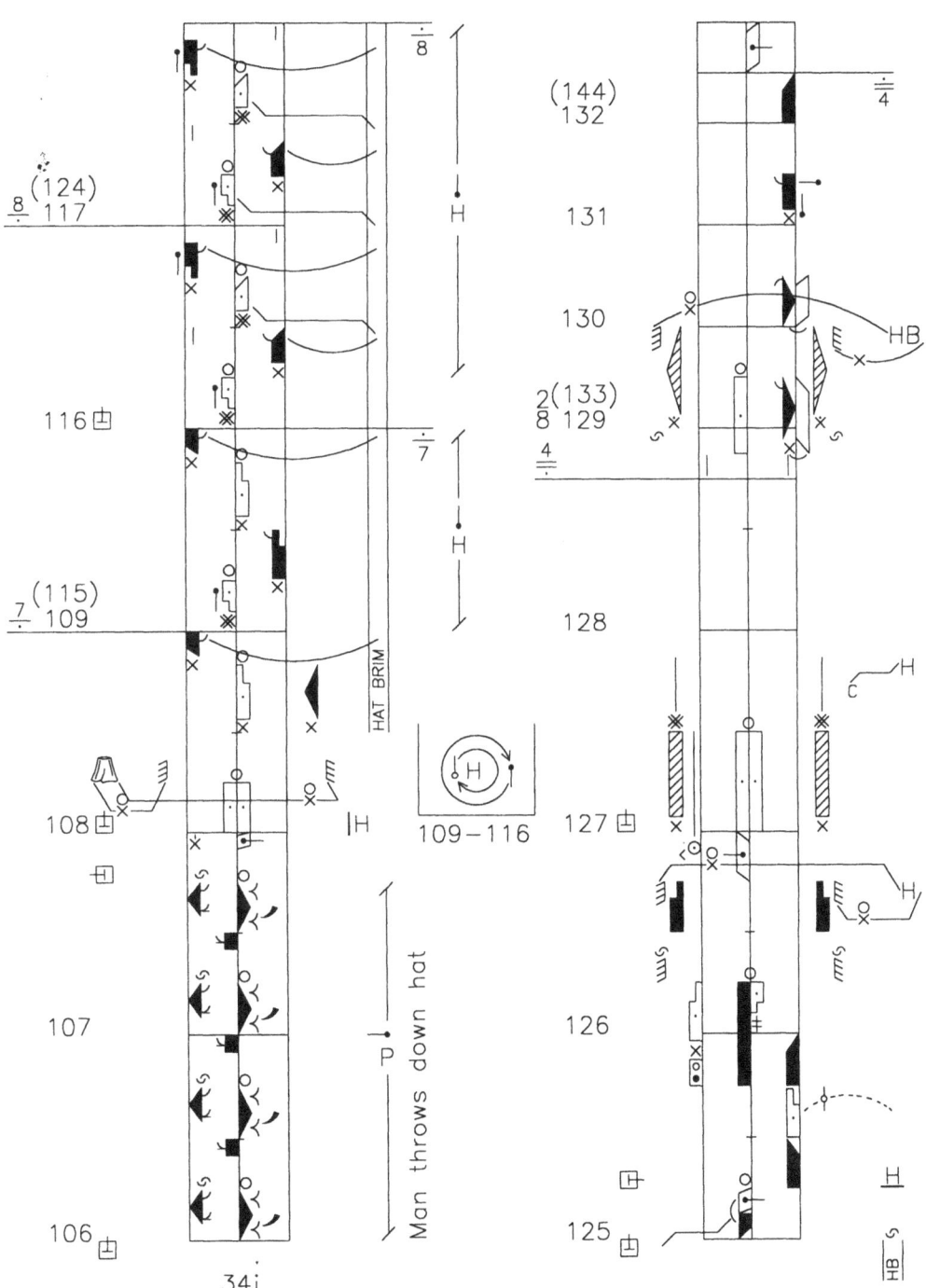

34j

34.10. **Reading Example - a Handkerchief.** For this excerpt from a *Girl's Russian Dance*,[62] **34k** shows the glossary indication given for holding the handkerchief, i.e. between the 3rd knuckles of the index and middle fingers. Not notated here is the fact that the dancer starts with the handkerchief tucked into the top of her skirt at the left side. The handkerchief is not brought out until the end of measure 20, at which point it is taken out by the right hand in preparation for the 'brushing' movement.

34.11. After the series of low kicking steps, the last of which is shown in measures 20-21 of **34l**, she leans over her extended right leg, flicks (shown by the compact effort sign) the handkerchief across her right instep, then sweeps the lower leg diagonally backward as she brings her right arm across to the left side. During the three stamps that follow, the arms make an inward circular movement ending with the back of the hands on the hips. The handkerchief remains in the right hand. It also remains there when the arms gesture sideward, palms up as she travels backward with steps on her heels.

34.12. A repeat of the low kicking step then occurs on the other side (not notated here), leading into the leg extension and sweep across the instep as before, but now on the left side. This is shown in **34m**, the handkerchief indicated as being taken by the left hand just before the new measure. As this is a continuation of the same dance, the hold sign written above the right hand column serves as a reminder that the handkerchief is still in that hand.

34.13. During the lilting step in place in **34n**, with the handkerchief now in the right hand, the arms wave from side to side causing the handkerchief to wave also. In **34o**, with the handkerchief still in the right hand, the final bow is given with a gracious gesture of the right arm. The handkerchief flicks as the arm is raised and flicks again at the end of the gesture down.

Advanced Labanotation

Reading Example - a Handkerchief

34k   H = Handkerchief

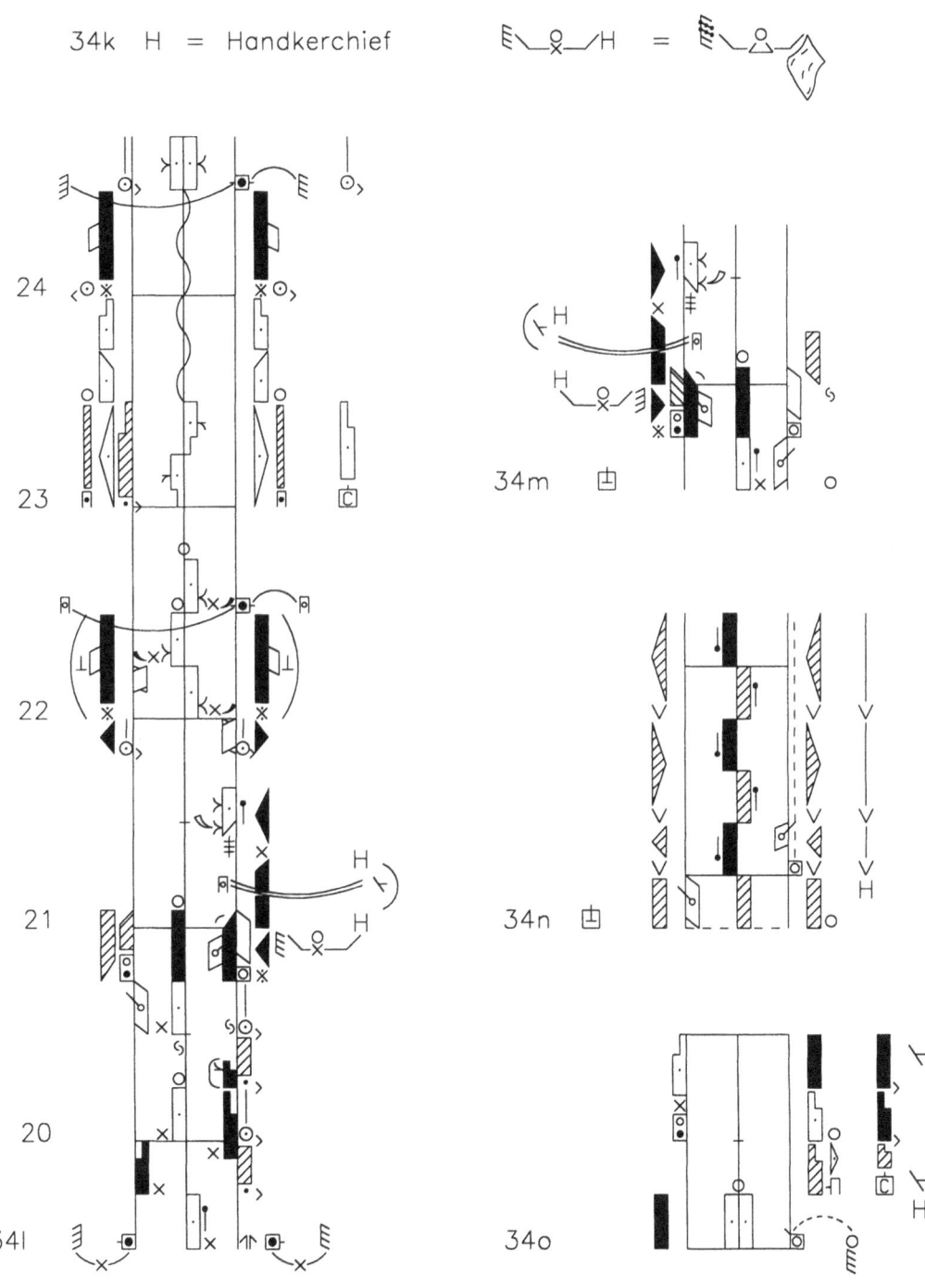

34.14. **Sleeve.** Placing an arm in a sleeve may occur in the process of getting dressed. When an everyday action is enough the instructions can be given in words; it is only when timing is important or when stylized movements need to be recorded that the action needs to be spelled out. In **34p**, while the left hand holds the coat, the right arm slides through the sleeve, leading with the finger tips.

34.15. The hands may be inserted into the lower part of the opposite sleeve, as when needing to keep them warm, or as part of an official bow. An example of this is shown in **34q**.

34.16. **Pocket.** A hand may be put into a pocket or an object may be put in or taken out. The next examples are a modification of the notation in the score of *The Green Table*,[63] more detail being given here than was necessary in the original score. At the start of **34r** the drawings of the pistol and the pocket are identified. The starting position is with the arms folded, sailor style, and the pistol in the left jacket pocket. The left elbow then draws back so that the right hand can open up the pocket on that side, the right hand grasping the edge and moving it slightly forward (shown by the pin). The pistol is then grasped by the left hand, the lower arm raised slightly to take it out before the arm lowers. In the last movement the arm extends forward, the torso tilting rather far forward, the head being excluded as the dancer is looking at his 'opposite number', marked here as 'P'.

34.17. The second example here, **34s**, comes from the reprise of the *Gentlemen in Black* scene near the end of the ballet. Here we see the pistol in the left hand, the arm held up. The thumb and middle finger of the right hand then open the pocket, grasping the edge and moving it slightly forward. This allows the left hand to place the pistol inside the pocket by moving the lower arm to it. The left hand then releases the pistol, followed by the right releasing the pocket.

Sleeve

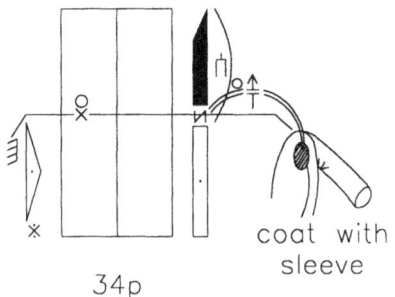
34p

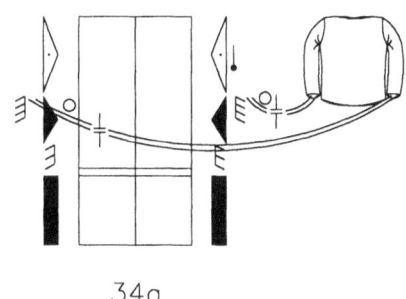
34q

Pocket

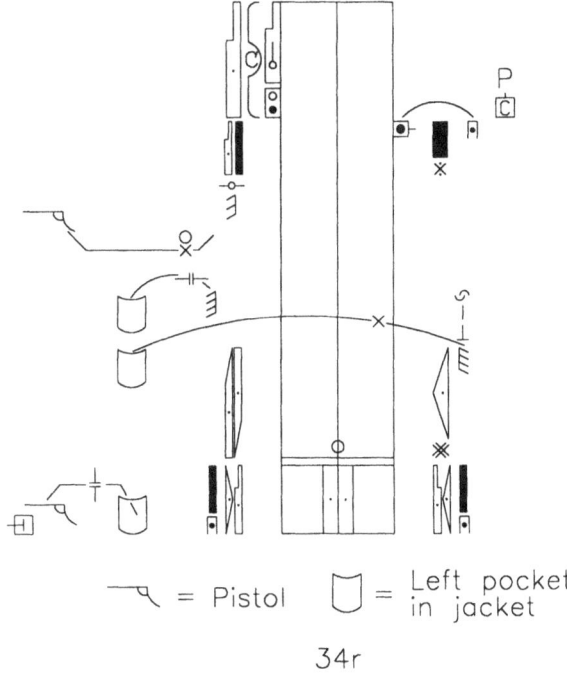

⌐ = Pistol   ⌂ = Left pocket in jacket

34r

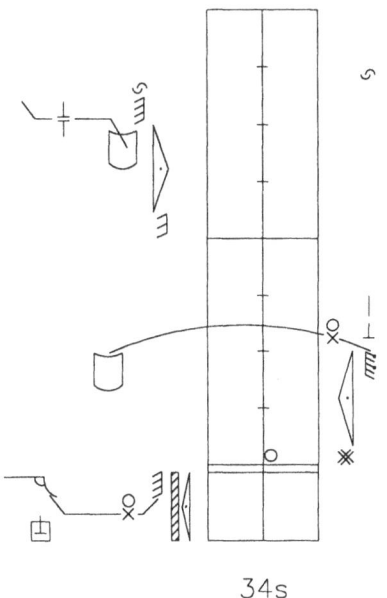
34s

35 Handling a Scarf

35.1. A scarf or kerchief is often waved in Balkan folk dances where the leader of an open circle often improvises appropriate patterns. For such usage the object is usually held in the fingers by one corner thus allowing the rest of the scarf to be seen. In **35a**[64] as the dancer progresses diagonally the scarf circles clockwise in the air. Here the hand action is also written since, as the hand displaces in a circular pattern, each sideward displacement is accented.

35.2. Details of a long scarf are given in **35b**.[65] Where this scarf is held is indicated by a line connecting two dots. This scarf is shown to be held up in **35c** as the dancer prepares to make her entrance. Where the hands grasp on the scarf is indicated, making clear that there is a longer piece of material beyond the right hand's grasp.

35.3. In **35d** the right hand has to 'creep' along the scarf in order to hold it more at the center. In performance this action, which occurs during other movements, should not be observed by the audience. This fact, the unawareness of the audience, is not included here. The scarf is held by the last two fingers against the base of the palm while the first three fingers extend and grasp a little further along. By contracting after they grasp, the scarf is moved slightly to the right. During this action the last two fingers and palm have released; they then grasp at the new location while the first three fingers release in order to move further along and to repeat this whole pattern.

35.4. The action of 'stuffing' a scarf into the belt is shown in **35e**. The left hand grasps the left side of the belt and the slight sideward displacement opens the belt. The right hand, which is grasping the center of the scarf, goes inside the belt, taking the scarf with it. The left hand lets go of the belt and then grasps the end of the scarf which is pulled down as the arm stretches downward. The middle of the scarf is now inside the belt.

Advanced Labanotation

Handling a Scarf

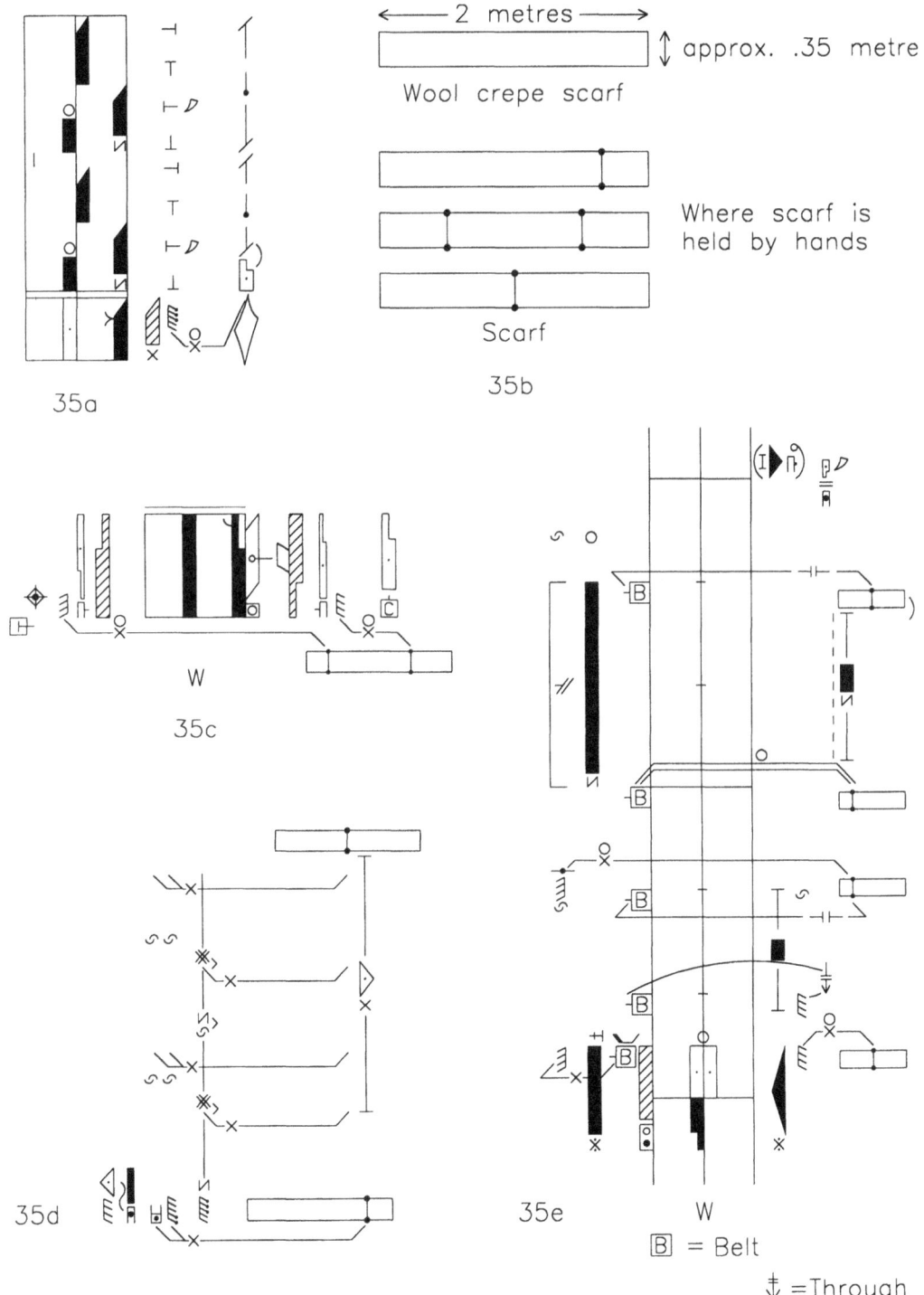

35b: Wool crepe scarf, 2 metres × approx. .35 metre

Where scarf is held by hands

Scarf

B = Belt
⇕ = Through

35.5. In **35f**, after a curved, throwing gesture with the right arm, the woman (W) releases the scarf which is then shown to be grasping (encircling) the neck (throat) of the soldier named Z. He grasps the scarf at his throat as he rises and arches backward.

35.6 In **35g** a scarf is grasped near either end. The right arm then makes a circular movement passing behind the head so that the scarf is then touching the back of the neck. A similar movement for the left arm winds the scarf completely around the neck.

35.7. A long scarf (veil) rests loosely high on the person's shoulders in **35h**, the center part touching the back of the neck. Touching the veil from in front, the performer makes a small upward movement of the hands (a shift). As a result the veil drops along the back until it is caught at the elbows.

Advanced Labanotation

Handling a Scarf (continued)

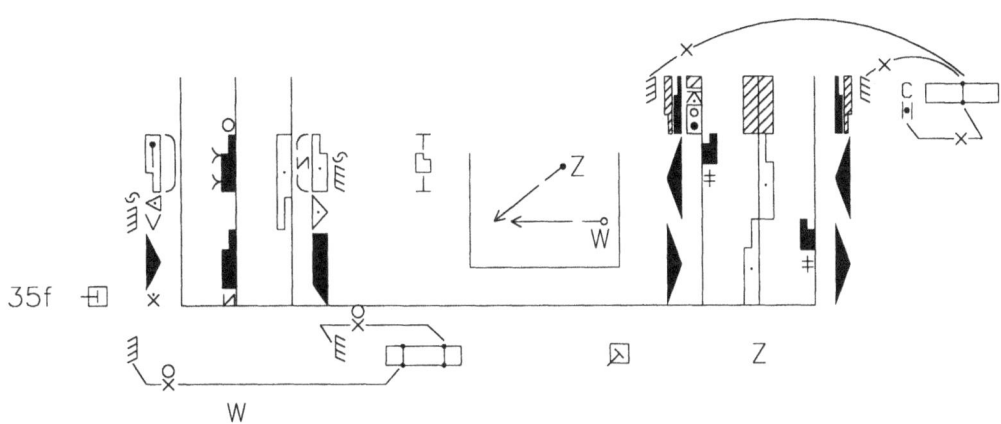

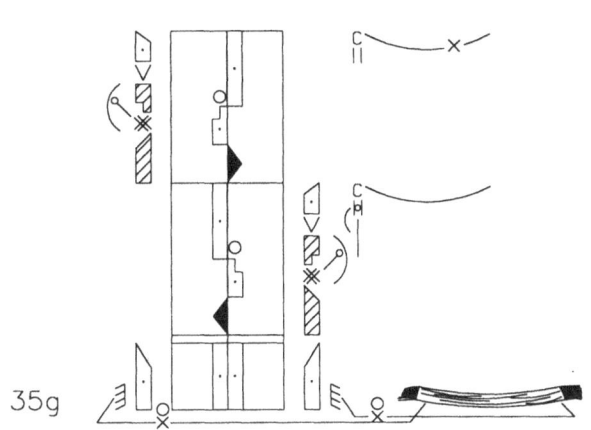

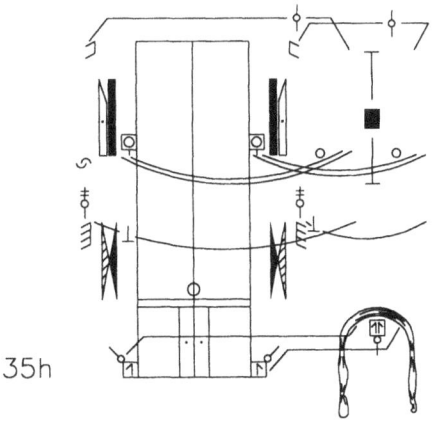

36 Handling a Veil

36.1. In **36a**[66] a veil (marked 'v') is carried in front of the performer. It is then lifted up before being placed on the ground as the performer kneels.

36.2. Ex. **36b** is an excerpt from Nijinsky's *L'Après-midi d'un Faune*.[67] The faun picks up the last 'veil', which is larger, like a dress. As the faun kneels, facing stage left but with chest twisted to the right, he leans over to pick up the dress at the top edge, near the ends. He rises, then as he steps forward slips his left lower arm under the dress closer to the center, and then slips his right lower arm under the dress in a similar way. As he rises and lifts his arms, the dress slips onto his elbows.

Handling a Veil

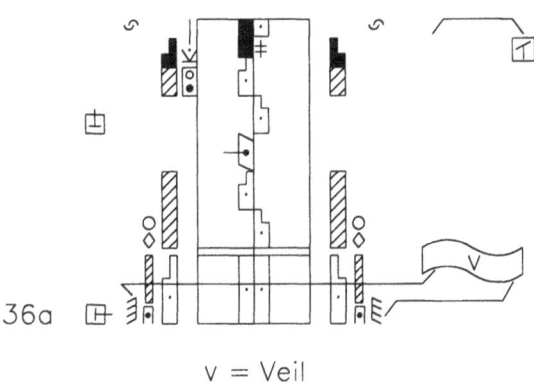

36a

v = Veil

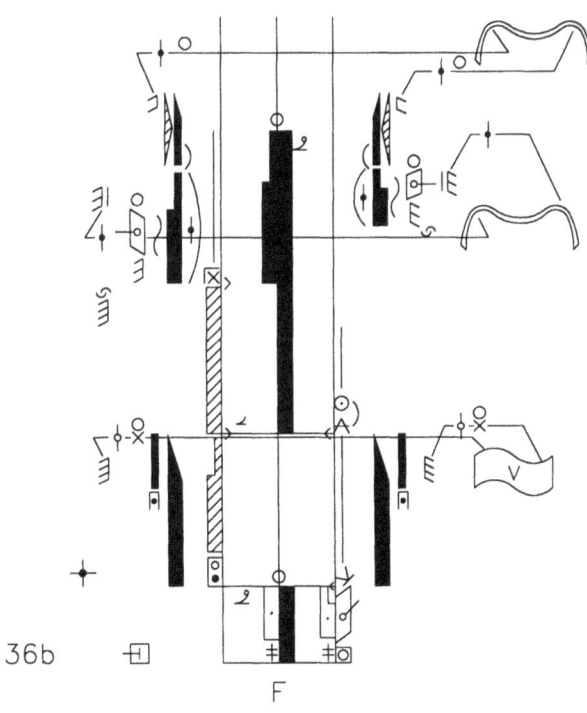

36b

F

36.3. The parts of the veil are given in **36c** below for this next notated sequence, also from *L'Après-midi d'un Faune*. Ex. **36d** shows how the ends relate to the right shoulder at the start. The drawings of **36e** and **36f** show that the two ends are tied above the shoulder. The detail of **36g** (see endnote 67), taken out of context here, describes the position with the right and left hands grasping the top of the veil near the edge. The right hand is up, the palm facing forward; the stretched thumb is under and in front, making a fold at the top of the veil as it grasps; the stretched fingers 'grasp' (sagittal closing against the thumb) from behind. The directions for the thumb 'grasping' the top of the veil result in its making a fold at the top of the veil. The left hand grasps in the same manner, close to the right hand. Note use here of the sagittal closing in to express the grasping between stretched fingers and thumb. The part of the veil grasped is shown on the sketch of the veil.

36.4. In **36h** the leading nymph (N5) takes off the first veil. It is draped so that the two ends meet at the right shoulder, the center part being under the left arm. Grasping the corners, the left hand grasps the part in front, this will be the right upper edge of the veil. The right hand grasps the part nearest the back which will become the left upper edge. Small quick backward and forward displacements undo the velcro holding the ends together. As the right hand releases, the veils slips down. The right hand then grasps near the right end of the veil, the left hand releasing. The grasp of the right hand is as described in **36g**; the left hand grasps in the same manner, sliding along the fold in the veil as the arms open. The nymph then carries her arms to the right side and, with a sideward motion of the hands, drops the veil.

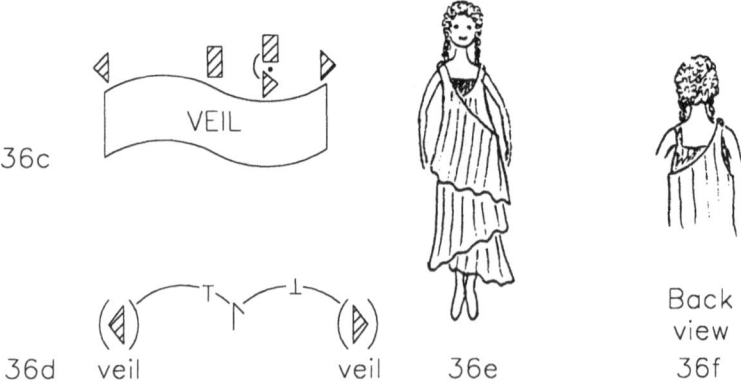

Advanced Labanotation

Handling a Veil

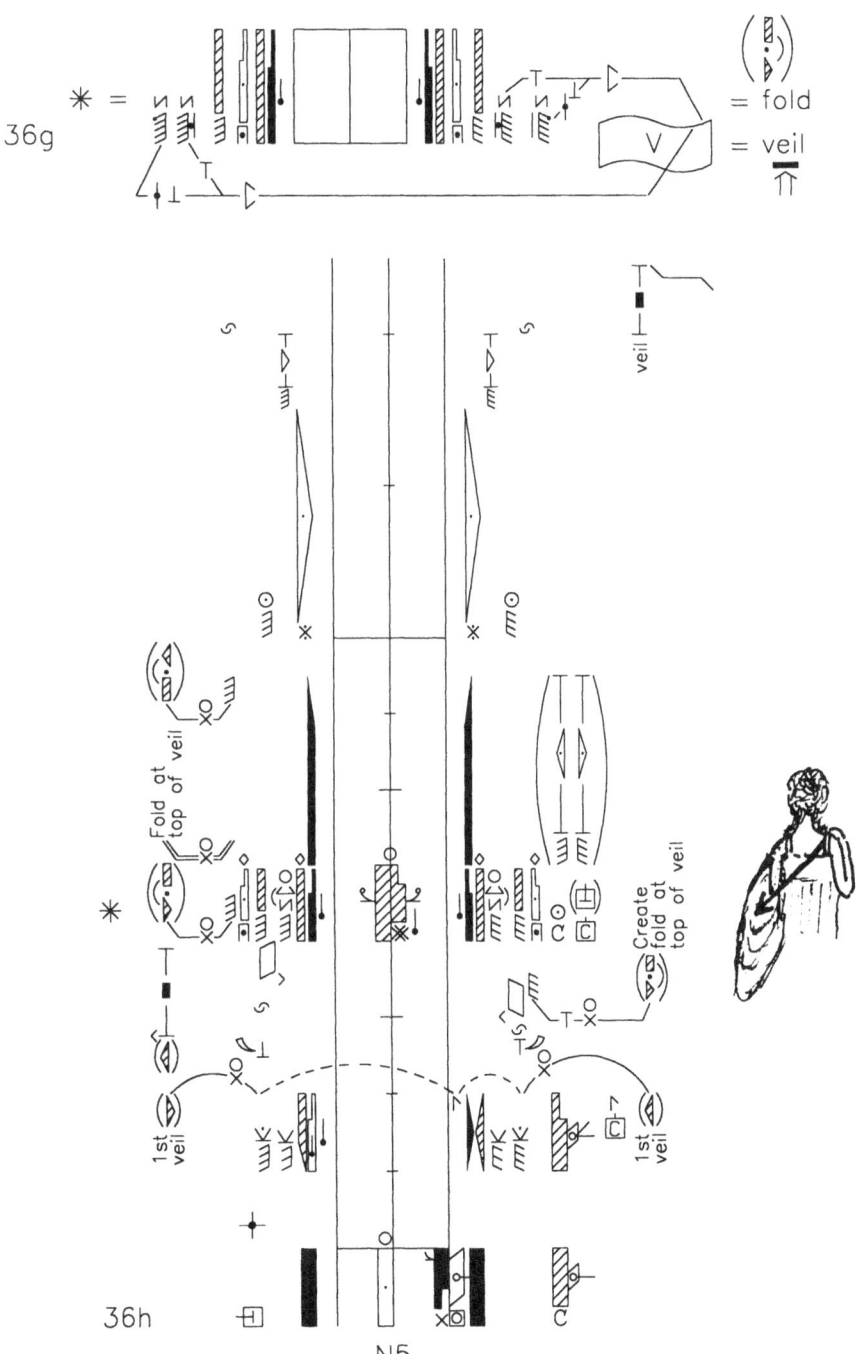

37 Handling a Skirt

37.1. In many dances the girl holds or manipulates her skirt. The skirt may be represented through a drawing, as in **37a**, or the word may be used, often in an abbreviation, **37b**. A column to the right of the staff can be designated for the skirt, **37c**. For particular needs the skirt column can alternatively be placed on the left of the main staff. However, for ease in indicating the grasp and subsequent movements, a column for the skirt can be placed on either side of the staff, **37d**.

37.2. Where on the object grasping occurs can be shown pictorially, as mentioned in Section 4. In **37e** the upper sides of the skirt are held; in **37f** it is the lower edges. When such visual representation is not possible, a small direction symbol in brackets is used to designate the part of the skirt. The forward middle part is designated in **37g**, while in **37h** it is the right forward low diagonal part. Note that these direction symbols are small and placed in parentheses. If it does not matter where the skirt is grasped, the ad lib. sign can be used next to the skirt, as in **37i**. Alternately, indicating the skirt by 'sk', as in **37j**, eliminates any suggestion as to where it is being held.

37.3. Generally, holding the skirt is shown with the hand grasping, as in the previous examples. This usually means the thumbs grasp from in front, the fingers from behind.[68] In some cases grasping is specifically with thumb and index finger, as in **37k**, or it may be index and middle finger, **37l**. Note the optional use here of the double bow at start, coming from the fingers, joining into a single bow and then separating at the finish, next to the skirt. Such use can be further specified by adding whether the thumb grasps from in front, indicated in **37m**, or from behind, as in **37n**.

37.4. A couple are dancing right shoulder to right shoulder, circling around each other with linked right elbows in **37o**.[69] At the start the girl is holding her skirt with her left thumb and middle finger. With a swaying step (note the slight swaying of the inverted pelvis[70] from side to side) she folds the skirt in front of her body and then opens it out to the side.

Handling a Skirt

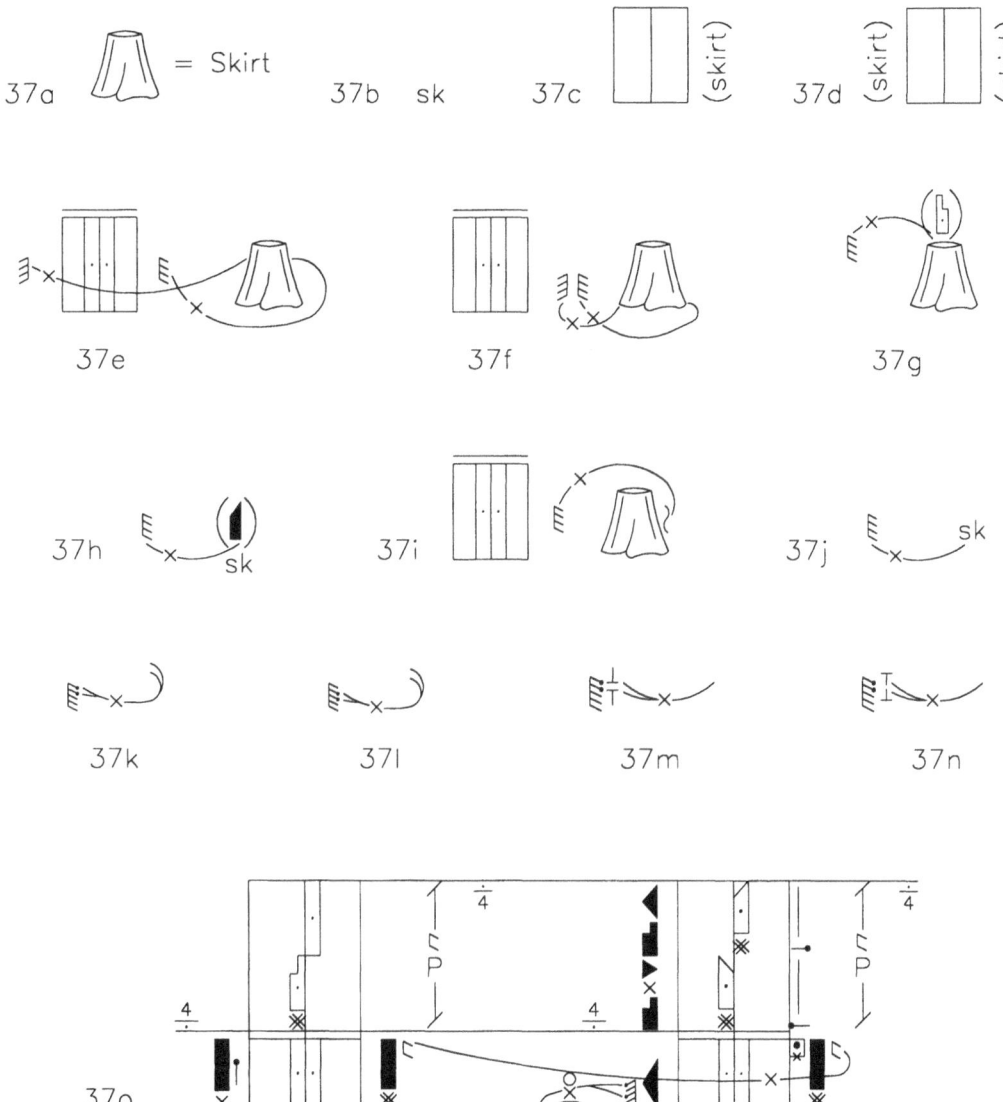

37.5. A similar gesture with the skirt is made in **37p**[71] as the woman walks diagonally away from person M (who is on her left), flicking her skirt in a circular manner on each step. This movement is indicated through design drawing, the movement starting with a slight accent. An incomplete circle is shown; because she is traveling, this becomes possible, so the circle need not be completed. Note that her face is looking toward M, not actually at him, but her eyes are looking at him ('out of the corner of her eye'). While she keeps looking toward M, her sidewards glances (eye movements) are looking him 'up and down'.

37.6. After leaning over and grasping the lower front part of the skirt (on either side), the dancer in **37q** then extends her arms forward and, arching backward, performs forward mincing steps, exposing her ankles.

37.7. Not actually touching the skirt is shown in **37r**.[72] Here the arms are very bent so that the hands start near the waist line, hands pointing down and the palms in front of the skirt. As the arms extend downward, a gliding addressing is shown in relation to the skirt. It is as though she is smoothing it. This action could also be written with gliding nearness, as in **37s**.

Advanced Labanotation

Handling a Skirt

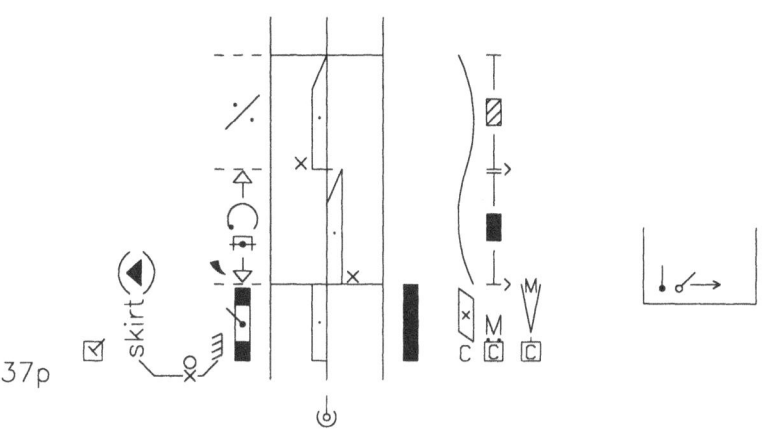

37p

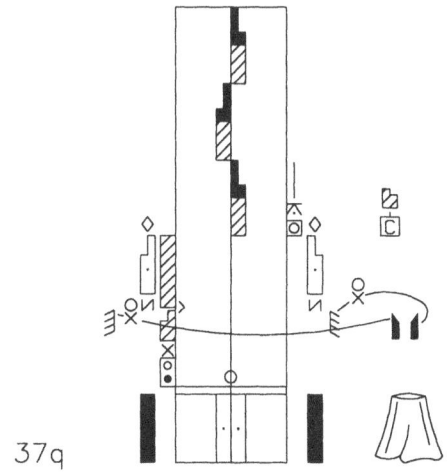

37q

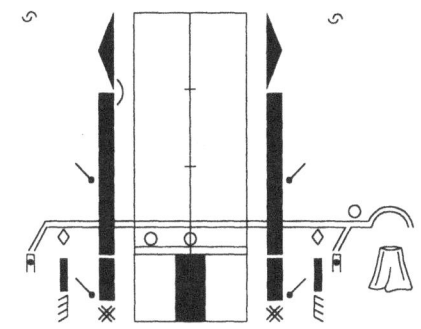

37r

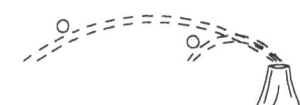

37s

38 Handling Long Sleeves

38.1. Long sleeves feature in several Asian dance forms. In some cases a stick is held within the sleeve; this provides an aid to controlling the path of the sleeve and where it should fall. In notations of long sleeve dances emphasis is mainly on the movements of the arms and in particular the wrists which produce a flicking action to give motion to the sleeves. If these are followed carefully the sleeve should react correctly.

38.2. For the Chinese *Long Sleeve Dance*[73] explored here, instructions are given on the length of the sleeve, judged from the finger tips; also given are six inch divisions labelled for identification, this example being for the left hand, **38a**.

38.3. Coming from in front of the pelvis, the first movement in **38b** is of the right arm making an outward circular movement to the side, led by the back of the wrist. At the end of this gesture the wrist unfolds with an accent, giving the sleeve a flip which causes it to move. The aim of the left arm gesture, which follows, is to flip the left sleeve across the right shoulder with part B touching. To produce this movement, as the lower arm moves diagonal back high with the little finger edge leading, a quick inward twist of the hand causes part B of the sleeve to rest on the right shoulder. As the left elbow lowers to the side, parts C and D of the sleeve slide across the right shoulder. During this movement the torso makes a slight circular movement ending forward with a slight contraction on the right side.

38.4. Overlapping sequential movements then follow for the left arm - before one sequence has finished the next has started. The forward movements are led by the outer side of the lower arm, the downward ones by the inner side. This phrase ends with the left arm making an outward arc, coming from near the left shoulder, out to the left, led by the back (outside) of the wrist and concluding with the same flip as performed by the right wrist in count 1. Ex. **38c**, starts with both arms performing the lateral half circle (similar to the end of **38b**), crossing the arms and then continuing with overlapping gestures forward low, the torso being inclined forward and rounded.

Advanced Labanotation

Handling Long Sleeves

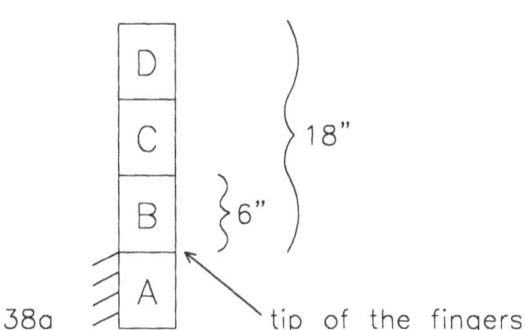

38a

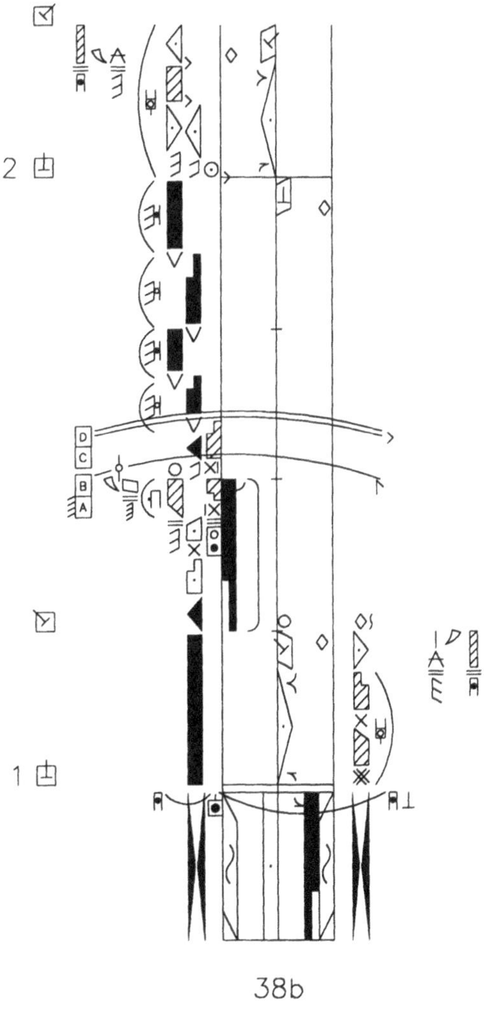

38b

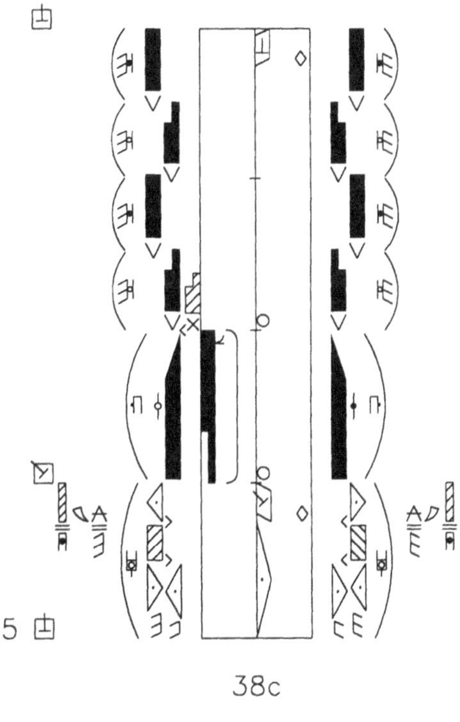

38c

38.5. Continuing with the Chinese *Long Sleeve Dance*, parallel lateral arm circles occur in **38d**. An interesting feature here is the slight twist of the torso on each sideward step, which produces the need to describe the arm circles from the Constant Cross of Axes because the arms do not follow this twist. The arms and sleeves remain on the same plane, making cartwheel circles to the left, the arms slightly bent as they cross the body, and normally extended when on the open side.

38.6. This section, **38e**,[74] features sagittal arm circles. The Stance Key is required because of the twist in the chest. This twist has resulted from the space hold for the front of the chest-plus-waist during the turn to face downstage right. The sequence progresses toward the right-front Constant direction. The previous position for the arms is shown at the start. The left arm moves down and to back low from where it performs a full forward sagittal circle, led first by the outside of the wrist, then by the inside and ending with a flick as the wrist unfolds. At the same time the right lower arm moves up and then forward at the end of which there is a flick of the wrist. The whole arm then moves across the front, and as the elbow is raised and the lower arm moves diagonally backward left, section B of that sleeve passes under the left arm pit. The right arm continues with a sagittal gesture up and forward, as at the start; then both arms describe forward sagittal circles, the left arm ending forward low, the right arm back middle. From there each moves to backward low and makes a full backward sagittal circle in a windmill fashion, aided by the twists in the chest. These features end with a pose in which the back of the right hand touches the back of the waist, and the palm of the left hand touches the waist at the front.

Handling Long Sleeves (continued)

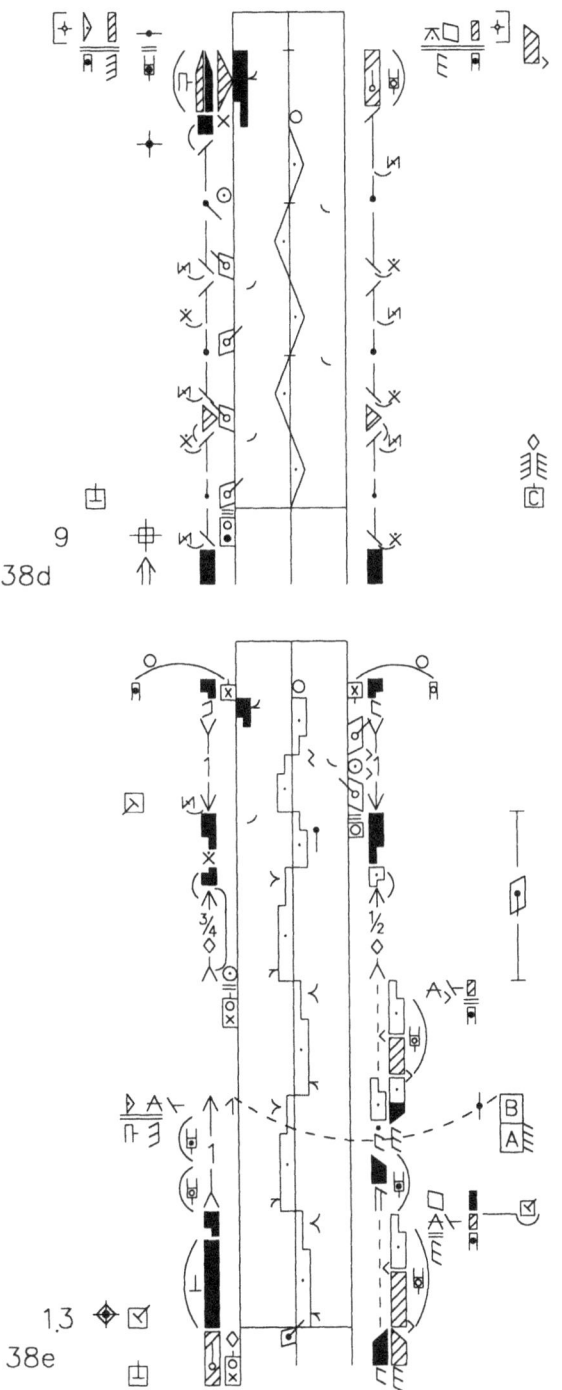

39 Using a False Leg, a Crutch

39.1. **Using a False Leg.** A third leg was used for a character dance in the 1842 ballet *La Jolie Fille de Gand* choreographed by Albert. More recently Paul Taylor used this device, and also a four-legged performer, in his 1989 ballet *Minikin Fair*. It is from this latter that these examples come.[75]

39.2. An enlarged staff is used to accommodate the extra leg for the man, **39a**. This staff is designated by a symbol for the shaft of the false leg and the foot, **39b**. As with a walking stick, the leg is either supporting, i.e. taking some weight of the body, or it is a gesture, **39c**. In a similar way an extra staff is placed on the left as well as the right for the four-legged women, **39d**.

39.3. It is, of course, the right arm which manipulates the leg under the costume. For the woman, both arms must be used. This prop may be thought of as an extra body part and not just a prop.

39.4. The entrance of dancer T is shown in **39e**. The right hand holding the top of the leg is given in the starting position. Although the false foot has no articulation, it can touch on the heel and roll to the whole foot, as occurs in **39e**. Note here the torso inclusion in the forward leg gestures; the movement of the leg causes the torso to incline slightly in the opposite direction.

39.5. In **39f** a lifted gesture for the false leg is followed by a simultaneous step on it and a gesture of the right leg. The small springs in **39g** in which the false leg is also in the air are assisted by the right arm contracting a little more and then resuming a single degree of contraction when the false leg is supporting. Note at the start of **39g** the relationship of the false leg to the feet, shown by the meeting line.

39.6. All legs in the air occurs at the start of **39h**. Landing is on the right leg before springing up to land on both feet with an accent, the false leg hitting the floor as a gesture at the same time; another spring up and again an accent on the landing.

Using a False Leg

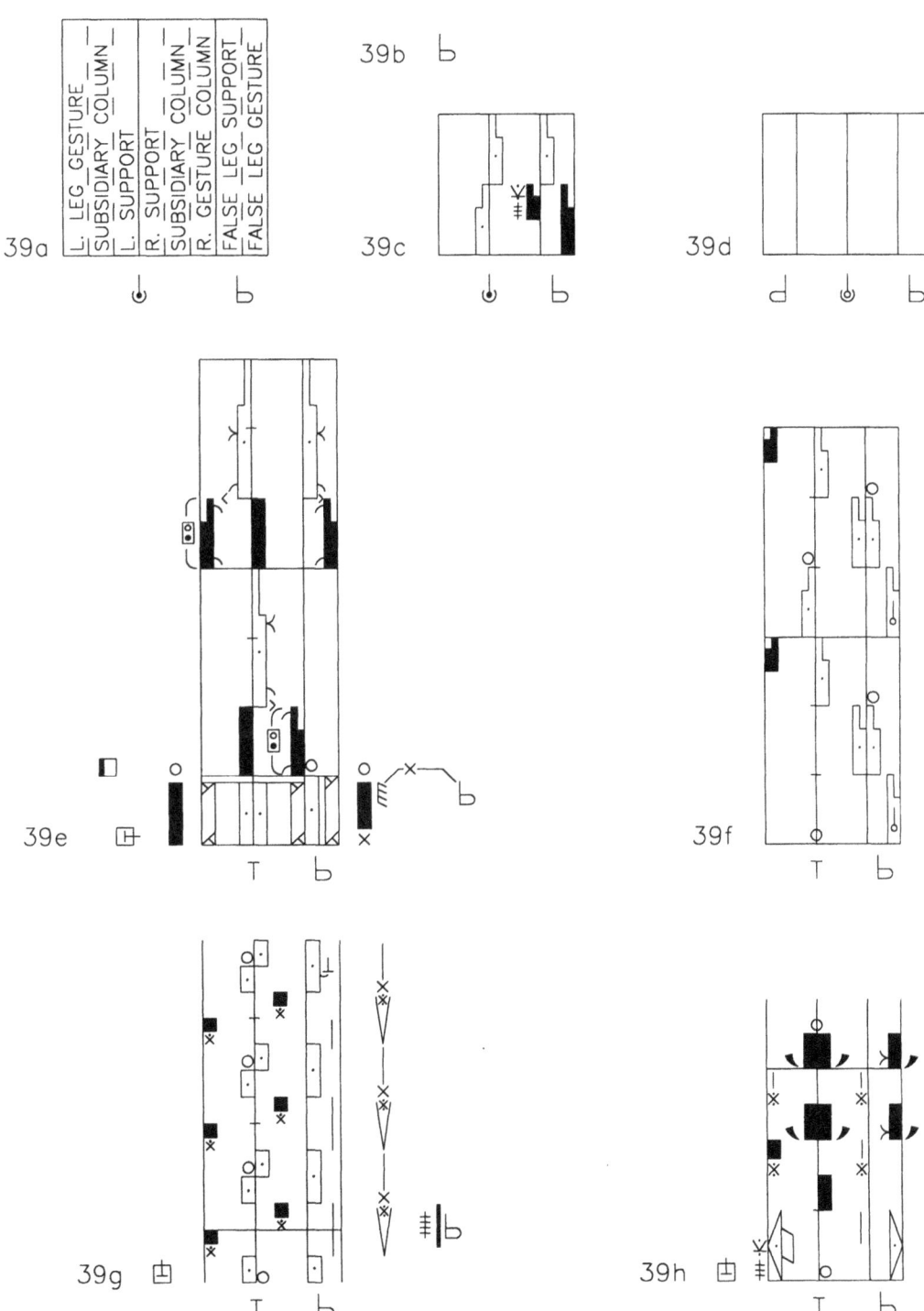

39.7. The leg rotation pattern of **39i** produces traveling to the right side. For this the right arm is down, slightly flexed and placed at the side of the body. The relationship of the false leg to the two feet is to place the false leg to the right of the feet.

39.8. The legs swings in **39j** become higher in the second measure, while the upper body twists in opposition, the head being excluded from this twist. Design drawing is used in **39k** to clarify the idea of the false leg movement, the design being a circle 'drawn' on the floor. During this circle the right leg passes above the false leg, and during the spring the backward left leg gesture passes above the false leg; thus the false leg passes beneath both legs. To assist this maneuver the right lower arm twists inward, then outward.

39.9. A *cabriole* (heel click) occurs in **39l**. Both legs are parallel and the torso leans into the opposite direction; there is no spring with this as weight is retained on the left leg. The quicker repeat of this *cabriole* is with both legs to the left side, weight being maintained on the prop.

39.10. A larger circular gesture with the false leg is given in **39m**. Again design drawing is used to clarify the sequence in which the false leg starts with a counterclockwise curve 'drawn on the floor', followed by a lateral circle 'drawn on the surface in front' (a cartwheel path to the right); this leads into a clockwise circle, which passes under the left leg and then under the right during the spring in the air. In the notation the relationship is shown as the legs being above the prop, which, of course, produces the same result.

39.11. Both hands are holding the false leg in **39n**. As the torso leans forward, the head remaining upright, not being included, support is taken on the left leg and the false leg. Both legs go into a sideward split leap while weight remains on the false leg. On the landing on the right leg there is a quick $1/2$ turn to the left followed by three quick steps completing another $1/2$ turn. During this, the false leg makes a lateral half circle arc to the left, the lower arms moving in the forward high area and then down to accomplish this pattern, which, in the ballet, is repeatedly performed traveling in a circle.

Using a False Leg (continued)

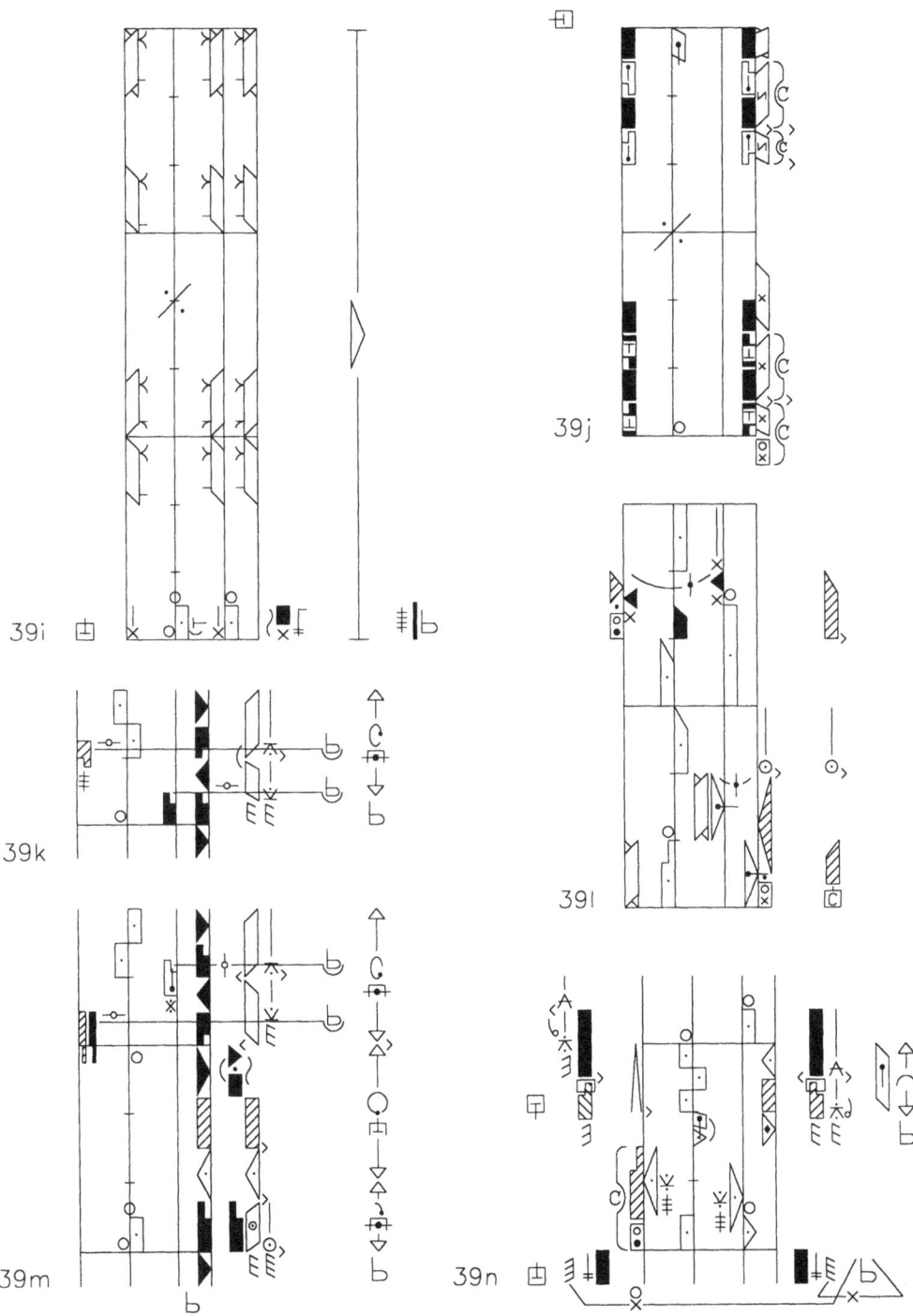

39.12. **Using a Crutch.** An important difference between using a false leg as for a three-legged dance character and using a crutch, is that much body weight is placed on the crutch; it has a functional use and is not being used for a special effect. In **39o** the crutch is given a column outside the staff; the drawing representing it is given to indicate how it is held. At the start the crutch is resting on the floor. The right leg is clearly the injured member, being held immobile. Note use of the column to the left of the staff for the center of weight. To begin a step, the crutch is moved forward, then, as it takes weight, the center of weight travels forward leading into the forward step on the left foot; as a result the crutch becomes vertical. Released from the floor, the crutch again is moved forward prior to taking weight again.

39.13. The next example, **39p**, makes use of a support column for the crutch, the right support column with the additional dotted line being identified as the crutch column. Before the crutch 'steps' forward, it is understood that it will advance into that direction, in the same way that a leg moves forward prior to a forward step. Once the crutch 'step' is completed, the left leg steps forward. When weight is centered on the left foot, the crutch is shown to be released in order to prepare for the next step. It is more direct to indicate what happens to the crutch rather than indicate movements for the right arm.

39.14. **Using Two Crutches.** The staples below the staff in **39q** designate the inner subsidiary columns to be additional support columns for the two crutches. Both crutches are moved forward at the same time to take weight, the forward movement of the center of weight soon following. As with the legs, the crutches contact the floor at the start of their forward 'step', and by the end of the symbol they are in place. Once the body weight is fully supported by the crutches, the feet can release and take weight between the crutches, i.e. in place. The whole pattern then repeats. The forward traveling for the center of weight continues into the forward weightbearing of the crutches. If the feet were shown to be supporting (stepping) forward, they would be beyond the base of the crutches. This is possible; it depends on how much weight the legs are able to take and for what duration.

Advanced Labanotation

Using a Crutch ## Using Two Crutches

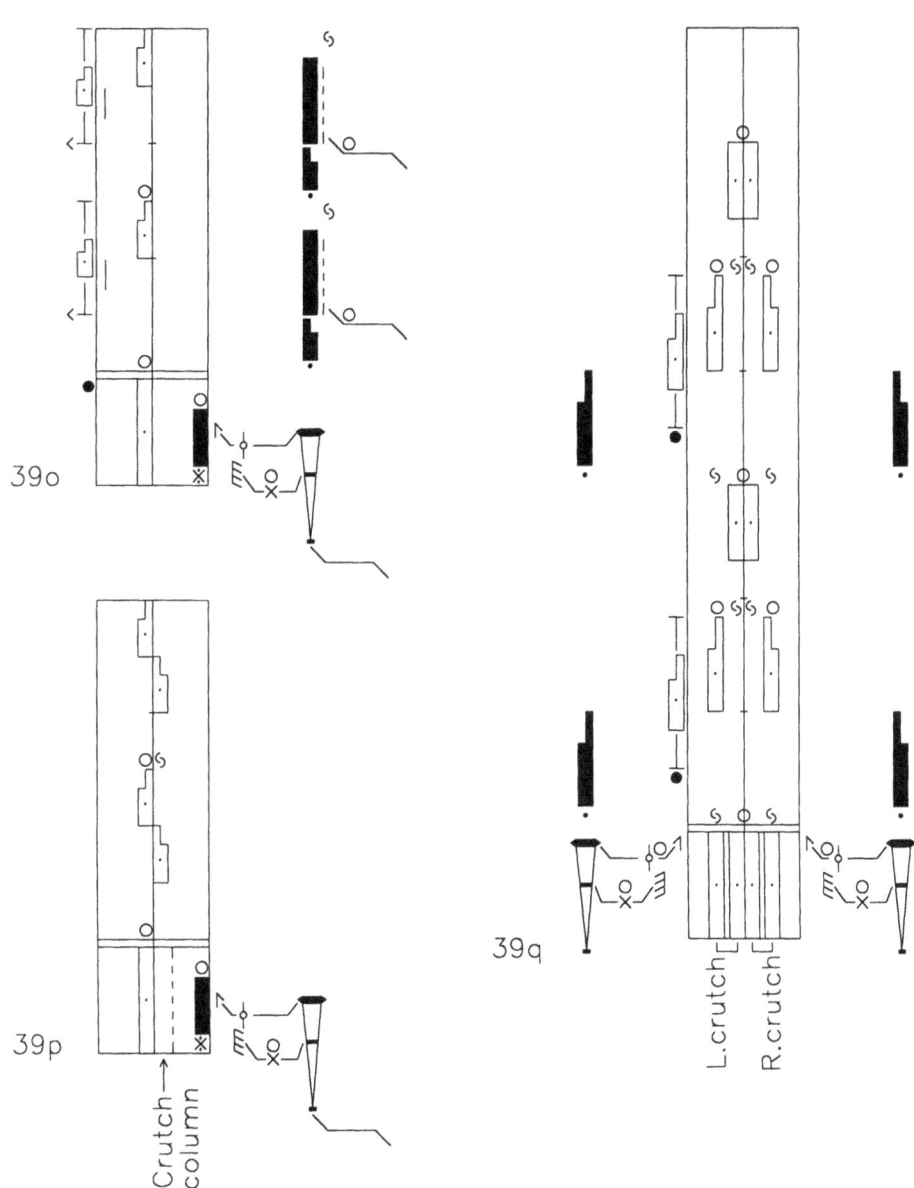

39o

39p

Crutch column

39q

L.crutch R.crutch

PART IV STAGE PROPERTIES

40 Using a Chair

40.1. While a chair, like most pieces of furniture, is usually a stage prop, it is often used choreographically for dance, and also in circus routines and other settings where it is used to display skill or to express a dramatic idea.

40.2. In the example below, **40a**, parts of the chair have not been given indications; the drawings of the chair visually represent its position, the horizontal line under the chair indicating the floor. The thick horizontal line indicates the performer's relationship with the chair, showing that it is in front. The right hand touches the back of the chair and remains there while the right foot is placed on the seat. The diagonal arm gesture causes the chair to tilt, and then, when the hand lets go, the chair falls backward to the floor.

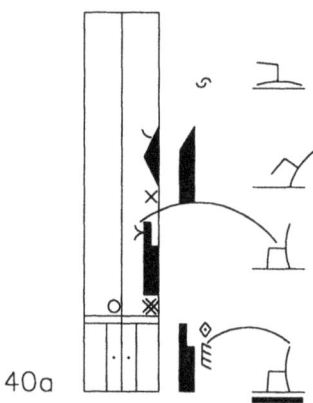

40a

40.3. **Reading Study Using a Chair.** In the reading study of **40b**,[76] given here in Motif Description, the person's relationship to the chair progresses from the first awareness of it to various manipulations and involvements to finally discarding it. Movements in the center of the staff are for the body-as-a-whole. Note that in phrases 6 and 7 it is the body-as-a-whole which gestures toward and away from the chair, but without traveling.

Advanced Labanotation

Reading Study Using a Chair

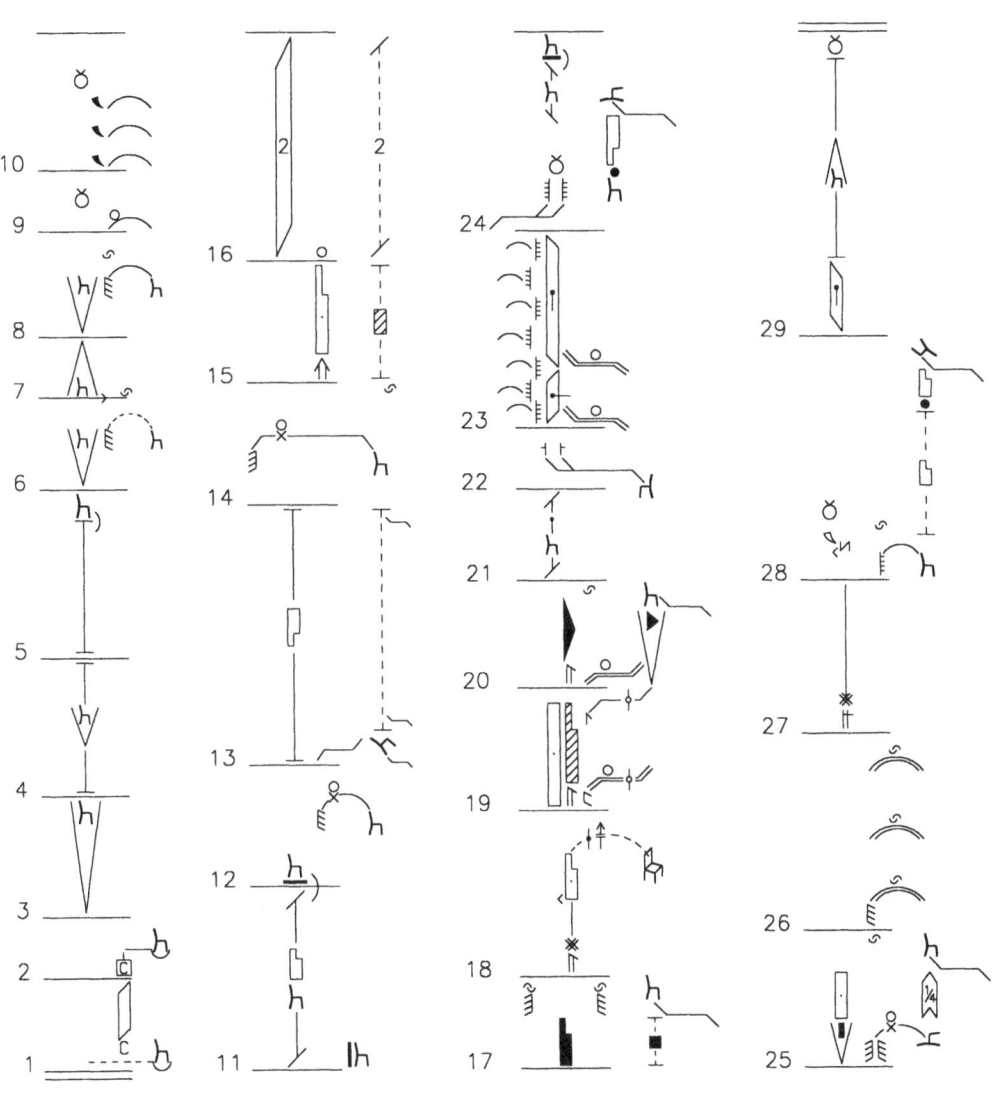

40b

40.4. **Reading Example - Chair, Pillow.**[77] The legend at the start of excerpt **40c** identifies the chair, the front of the chair seat, the chair as focal point for orientation, the pillow, and the pillow on the chair.

40.5. The piece begins with the performer sitting on the chair, the pillow on her lap. The pillow is then placed on the floor in front of the performer who stands up, then sits down, then again stands up as though uncertain what to do. She walks to and fro before picking up the pillow and then stepping onto the chair only to step down on the floor again in the next count.

40.6. Turning to face the chair, she places the pillow on it and then turns to sit down on the pillow. She extends her lower legs forward and then stands up, twisting at the same time to the left to pick up the pillow by the corner. She then drops the pillow to her left so that it is in a forward diagonal relationship to the chair.

40.7. After a lunge forward to stage right she again turns left to face the chair, this time almost crouching as she grasps the front edge of the chair in both hands, her arms forward, very bent. But she then lets go, lifts her arms up before twisting to the right to pick up the pillow in her right hand. The phrase ends with a low step to the side - is she about to throw the pillow? Our excerpt ends here.

Advanced Labanotation

Reading Example - Chair, Pillow

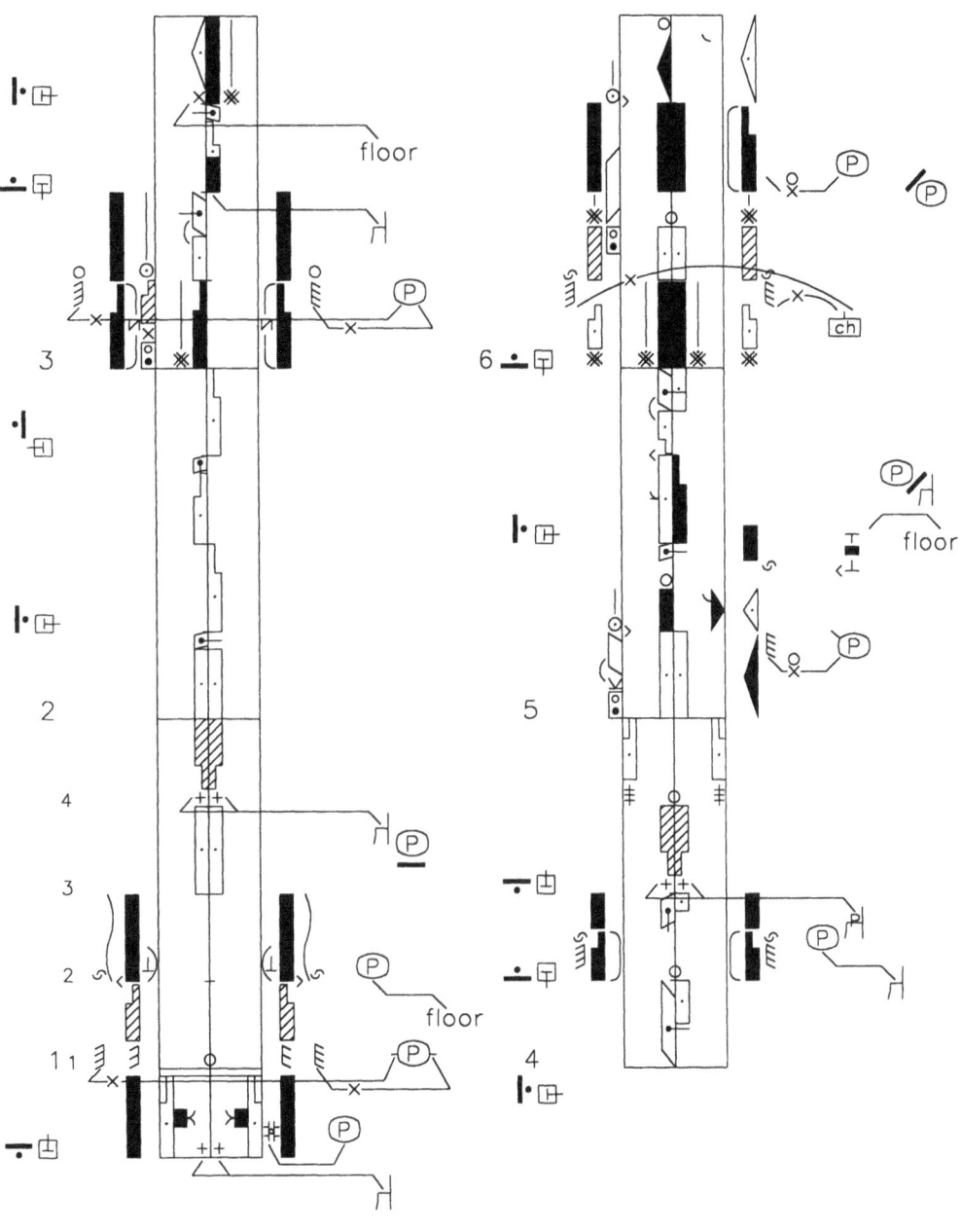

40c

⌐ = chair   • = ⌐   Ⓟ = pillow

[ch] = front of chair seat   ꟼ| = pillow on chair

41 A Table

41.1. **Contacting, Resting on a Table.** When sitting at or standing next to a table, the arms may be contacting, grasping the table, or arms or body may be leaning on the table. The following examples,[78] taken from the latest score of *The Green Table*, show movements and positions of the dancers from the opening scene, 'The Gentlemen in Black'.

41.2. Because contact or support refers so often to the table, the special usage was adopted to have the contact bow extending beyond the staff to mean a relationship to the table, rather than to the floor. In **41a** dancer 'a', who is in a low support, has his left lower arm and his right elbow both placing some weight on the table. If such a convention were not in effect, contact with the table would here be written as in **41b**, a modification of the notation in the actual score. The left hand grasps the edge of the table, while the sideward tilt of the chest-plus-waist causes the right elbow to take some weight. In a busy score, it can be seen that repetition each time of the sign for the table would be cumbersome. Giving the prop its own column, beyond the body column, makes it immediately clear if one starts to read in the middle of a score, even without having read the introductory instructions.

41.3. Dancer 'k' in **41c** is also in a low support, leaning to the right and placing weight on the right side of his waist since he is leaning to the right. His right elbow takes weight and the weight of his head rests on his right hand which is grasping his chin.

41.4. **Supporting on a Table.** As discussions become heated in this scene, one man springs onto the table, **41d**. Placing weight on his hands as preparation, he lands on the table with knees very bent, then makes two threatening lunges at his opponent before springing off the table onto the floor. Here supporting both on the table top and on the floor has been spelled out.

41.5. Another gentleman takes a leap onto the table, **41e**. He stays in a low level support while brushing his left leg along the table top; his left hand takes some weight to help balance while his right arm makes a threatening gesture. He then springs sideward landing on the floor.

Advanced Labanotation 173

Contacting, Resting on a Table

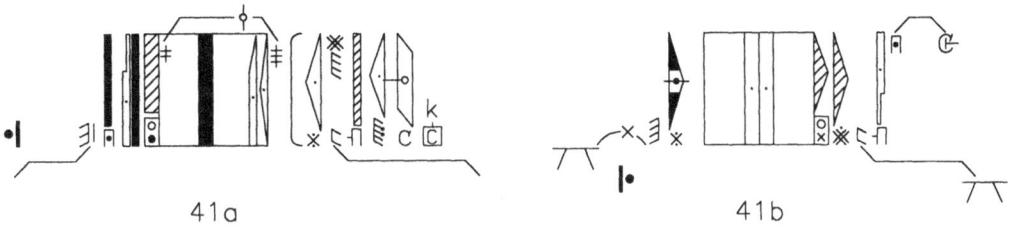

Supporting on a Table

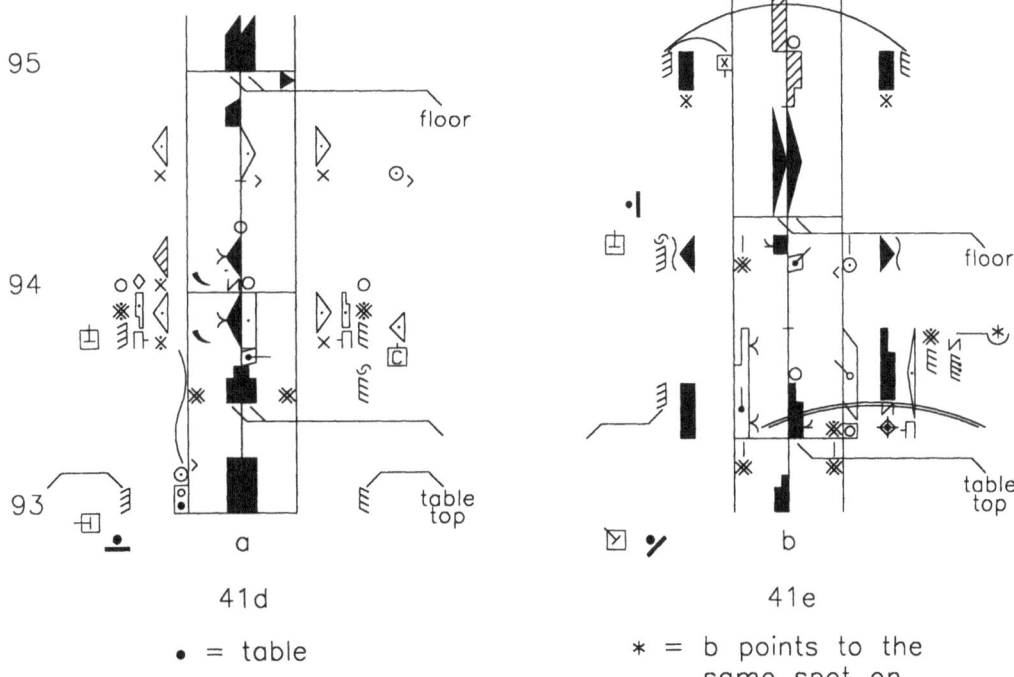

• = table

* = b points to the same spot on the table as a.

174 *Handling of Objects, Props*

41.6. Reading Example - Manipulating a Table. In the following reading sequence, **41f,**[79] a table is being handled. At the start, the table is in front of the performer. Identification of the parts of the table is given. The top surface of the table is identified as S (for surface). The edge nearest the person is marked E, the opposite edge is F; the nearest corners are marked **a** and **b**, those farther away are **c** and **d**; the four legs are given numbers. For this example, more than one way of showing the changes for the table is given: I, the movements of the performer; II, where the parts of the table are grasped; III, movements for the table itself; IV, where the top surface, S, and the edge E are facing; V, pictorial drawings of the table in which the underside is shaded.

41.7. Grasping the nearest corners, the performer's arms move forward low, tilting the table away from him. The right hand then grasps the nearest leg (leg 2) and leans and steps forward as the table completes a $1/4$ forward somersault. On count 4 he steps back, comes upright and releases his hands before grasping the two nearest legs, 1 and 2. Leaning the torso forward again, he makes the table complete the next $1/4$ somersault, resulting in the top surface being on the floor.

41.8. Reaching across his body, the performer grasps leg 2 with his left hand, 4 with his right. On count 8 and 9 he steps and leans to the left, raising the table in a $1/4$ cartwheel to the left so that the top surface is now facing right side middle. On count 10, 11 and 12 he grasps the corners that are nearest (**c** and **d**) and again steps to the left, while he tips ($1/4$ cartwheel) the table back to its upright position at the end of 12.

41.9. Grasping opposite corners (**d** and **a**), with a push the performer turns the table $1/4$ to the right. He lets go and then, grasping either side of the table top (E and F), he lifts the table up.

41.10. From these five choices of description it can be seen that the changes for the table could be understood solely by the rotations indicated in column III. It could also be worked out from where the two surfaces S and E, which are at right angles to each other, face at each point (as in column IV). The movements of the person fill in the manner of achieving this sequence in turning the table, but by themselves do not give any immediate message as to what should happen. The information in column II in conjunction with the movement of the person is an important clarification. The pictorial drawings, V, give an immediate message but may not always be easy to draw. Combining these with the indications for the legs and corners is an added help. In Knust's original notation the information of III and V were not given.

Advanced Labanotation

Reading Example - Manipulating a Table

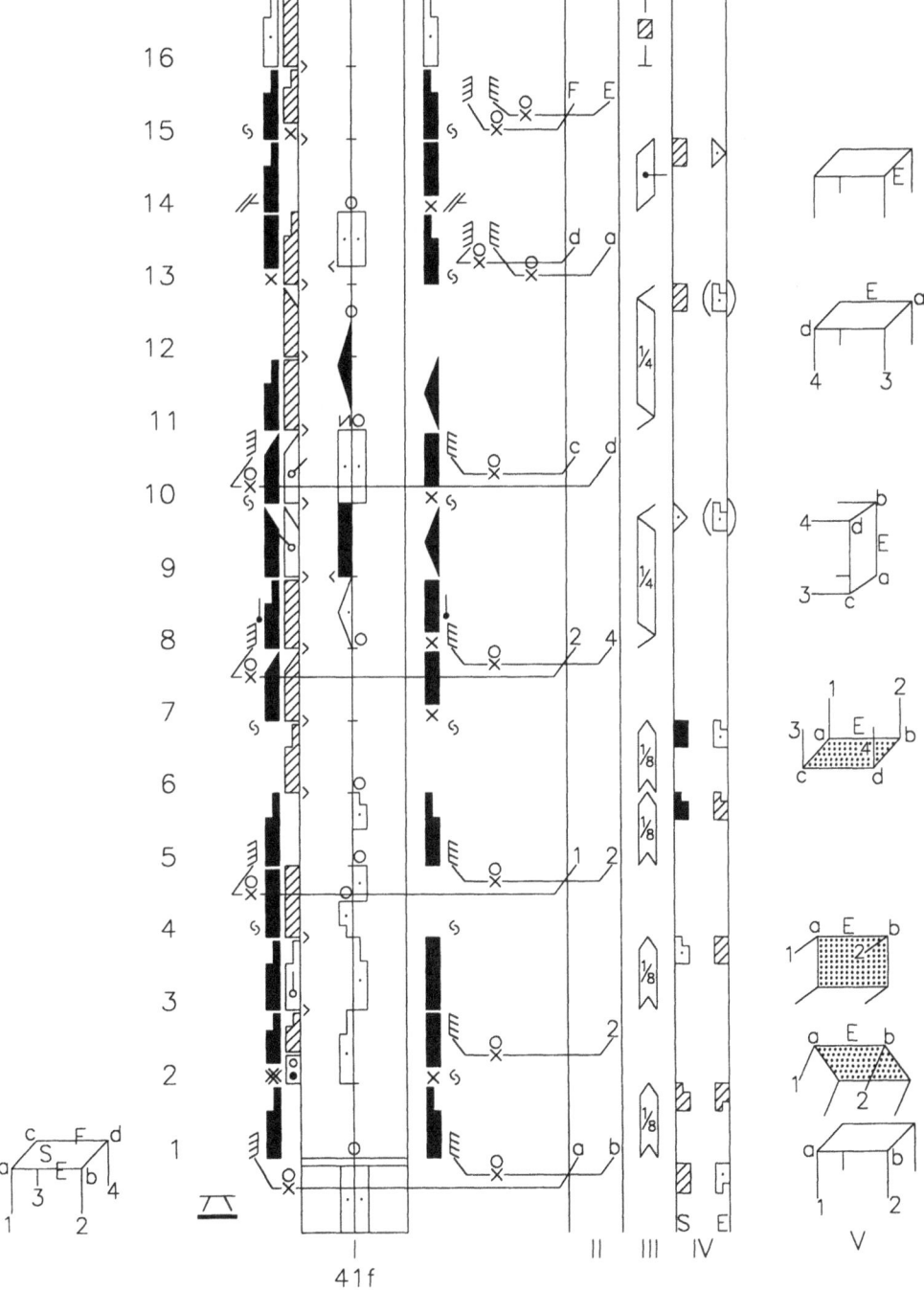

41f

42 A Rug

42.1. Stepping onto a rug is shown in **42a**: the left foot steps forward onto the rug and the right foot joins it. It is not necessary to repeat the indication for supporting on the rug, as stepping in place must automatically mean also on the rug. The long backward step is off the rug and onto the floor, as shown by the T in a box representing *terra*. In **42b** the third step is off the rug, onto the floor, the floor being understood because this supporting bow extends beyond the prop column. Another way of showing that the prop is no longer a supporting surface is shown in **42c** by use of the release sign in the prop column.

42.2. Once both feet are shown supporting on the prop, it is understood that subsequent steps are performed on the object until the release sign or indication of a different surface is shown. This is illustrated in **42d**: both feet start on the rug, and the steps side to side remain on the rug. During the jump backward, the release in the prop column makes quite clear that landing will be on the floor and no longer on the rug.

42.3. Ex. **42e** shows a similar example but the *assemblé* spring is still on the rug. In the sequence of **42f** it is easy to see when a spring lands off the prop and when it lands on it.

A Rug

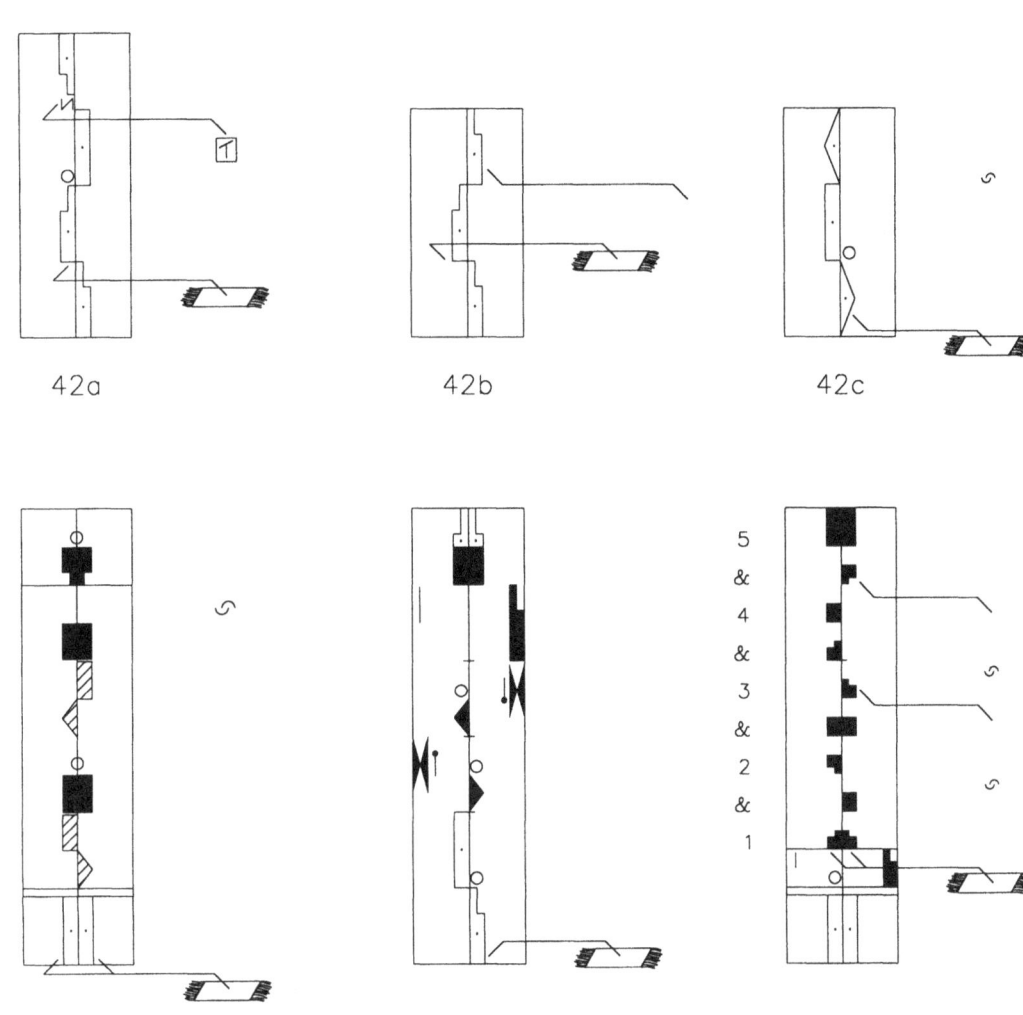

43 A Barre

43.1. Using a horizontal bar fixed to the wall for training exercises is familiar to much of Western dance. Notations of particular dance techniques cover barre[80] exercises as do forms of gymnastics. In classical ballet the hand rests on (does not grasp) the top of the barre. The starting position of **43a** shows a familiar placement of the left hand on the barre. Note that no level is given for the left arm, since level will depend on the height of the barre and the height of the person. In such exercises, the barre is the focal point; hence the indication at the start, the focal point being at the performer's left.

43.2. When a barre exercise travels the hand may need also to move in the same direction. In **43a** no special indication is given concerning the hand on the barre. A sliding action is shown in **43b** as the steps carry the body forward.

43.3. Ex. **43c** starts with both hands grasping the barre (here indicated with the word 'barre'). The exercise involves lowering completely to the floor with the feet together, then, while remaining low, stepping to the side and closing before rising to normal standing. The exercise is then to be repeated to the other side. Note that here a spot hold is used for the hands, as they should not move.

43.4. A familiar example of placing weight on the barre occurs in stretching exercises. Facing the barre in **43d**, illustrated in **43e**, the performer's right leg rests on the barre at the right side. As she moves the center of weight sideward (shown as a path for the center of weight), weight is taken on the right leg and, at the end, the ankle becomes a major support; this is comparable to standing in a wide second position. Because no distance is given for the path of the center of weight, the distance is known by the angle made between the left leg and the horizontal surface of the floor. This is shown through use of an angling sign, here indicating three increments, i.e. a 45° angle. (For angling see <u>Advanced Labanotation</u> *Kneeling, Sitting, Lying*, Part 7.)

43.5. Hanging over a bar, or, as in the illustration of **43f**, a gate, weight is placed on the lower part of the front of the pelvis. In this example only the position reached is shown.

43.6. In contrast **43g** shows the movement into sitting on the right parallel bar. From standing between the parallel bars, the performer lifts up, supporting on both hands. The legs swing forward, then backward with pelvis inclusion, and then swing higher forward and over to the right. The center of weight travels to the right, the hips support on the right bar, and the lower legs swinging backward on the outside of the bar.

A Barre

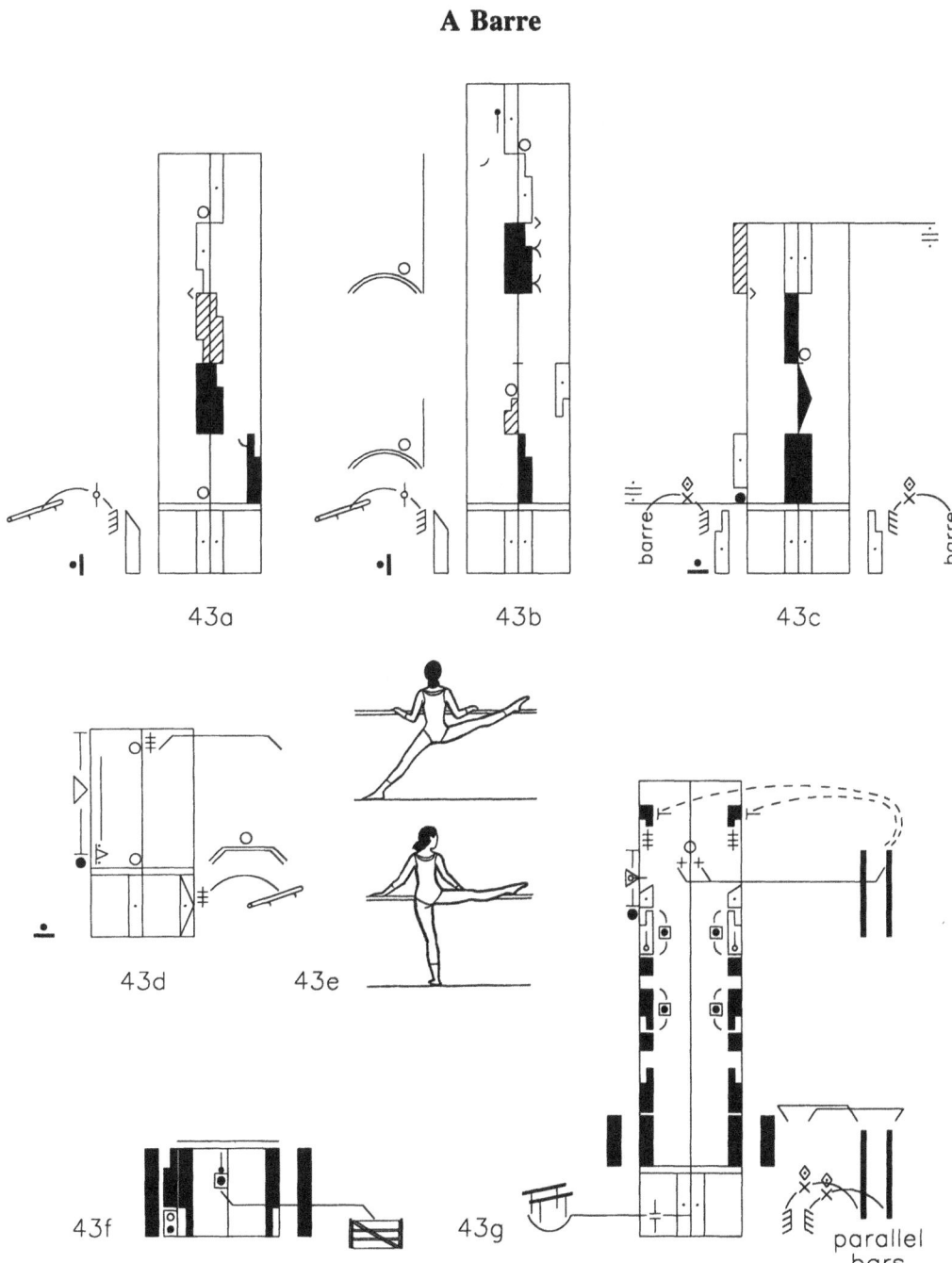

44 A Wall

44.1. In the following examples the wall is represented by a W in a box, **44a**. Leaning against a wall may involve partial weight being placed on the hands, as in **44b**, illustrated in **44c**. A greater degree of leaning will mean that the hands become a major support, **44d**, illustrated in **44e**. In terms of weight placement this is comparable to a large 4th position on the feet. Note in this example the use of the unit ankles-to-chest to describe the body angle, also the use of small horizontal staples to state that the Inner Subsidiary Columns (the ISC) on each side are also to be support columns. (See the <u>Advanced Labanotation</u> issue on Center of Weight for the use of ISC.)

44.2. Movement into such partial supporting on a wall is given in **44f**, which begins facing the wall. Here there is a falling forward (center of weight forward high) while at the same time the torso leans forward high. The arms start slightly bent and then, as weight is taken, they break the fall by contracting much more.

44.3. Falling backward against a wall is shown in **44g**. Here again one arm contacts the wall and helps to break the fall. The right arm does not become a major support, as weightbearing is taken by the back of the torso. If the performer were standing closer to the wall, the torso might not become a major support but take some weight, as in **44h**.

44.4. Sliding down a wall is shown in **44i**. The person starts close to the wall with his back touching it, **44j**. As he bends his legs, his back slides down the wall. As shown in **44j**, the relationship indication is one of a sliding touch, therefore he is not putting any weight against the wall. If he leaned against the wall, which is probable, the round relationship bows would be replaced by angular support bows.

44.5. A reverse situation occurs in **44k**, illustrated in **44l**. Lying on his back, very close to the wall, with his legs contracted, close to his chest, and soles of his feet on the wall, the performer walks his feet up the wall until his legs are stretched. His center of weight has risen to a leg-length above the floor (the point of support) and the unit of chest-to-feet is forward high. Note the indication for the path made by the feet stated at the right of the notation.

A Wall

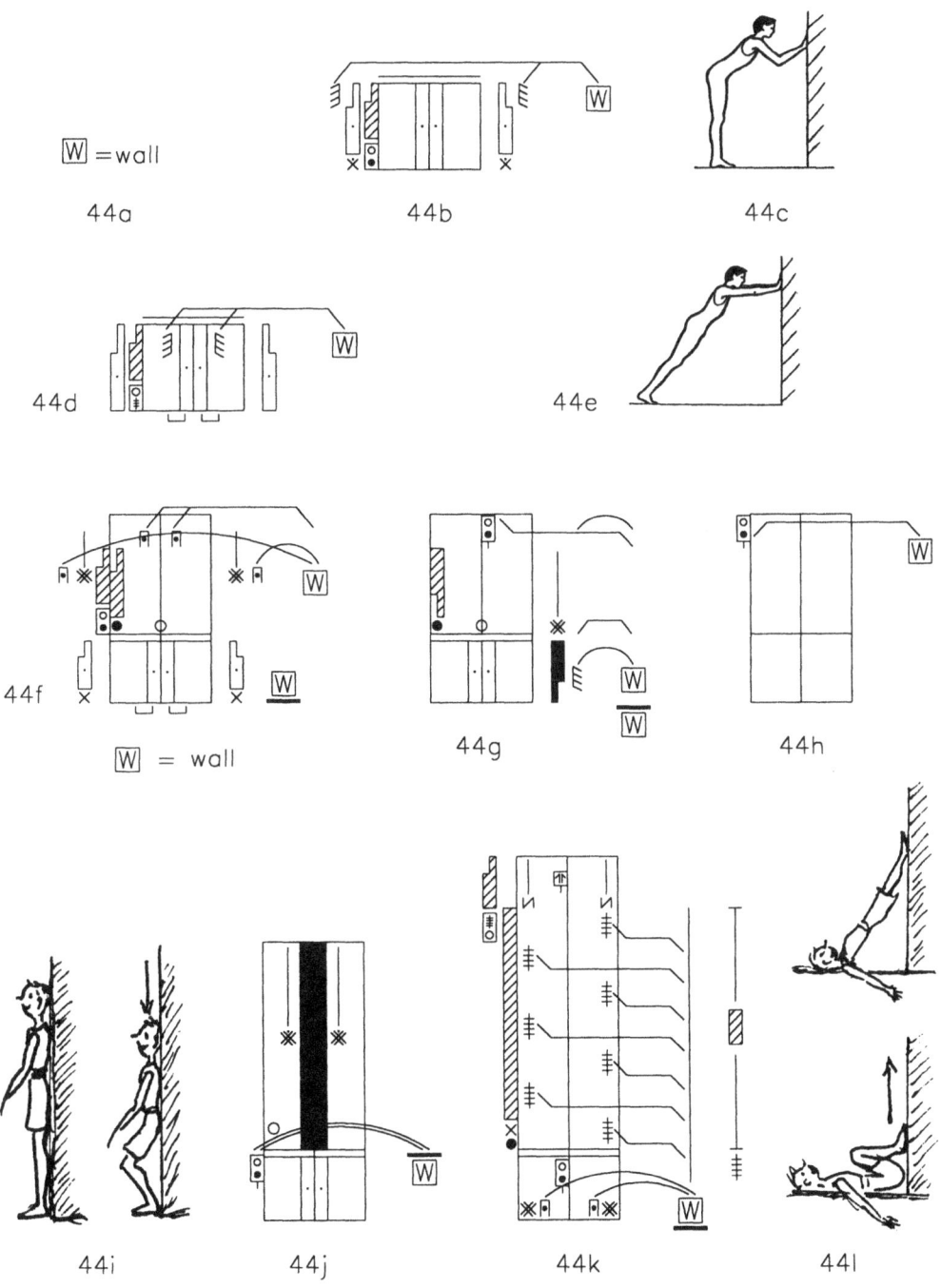

45 Stairs, a Ladder

45.1. **Moving Up or Down Stairs.** At a basic level, the instructions for walking up or down stairs can be given in words and the barest indication provided in the notation, **45a**. Here the traveling forward and upward suggest an upward slope, but no indication of stairs has been given.

45.2. Ascending or descending stairs may be a necessary part of the choreography, as it is, for example, in Nijinsky's ballet *L'Après-midi d'un Faune*. There the Faun has six steps to negotiate, descending by walking backward and later ascending with forward steps. Ex. **45b**[81] shows the start of his first descent. Here the word 'stair' is used, and a simple statement of change in level for the steps is given combined with the indication of traveling backward and downward. Each step starts taking weight in middle level, then lowers as the next step begins.

45.3. If space on the page allows, walking up stairs could be indicated as in **45c**. Here each of the stairs is shown, and, as the person is progressing forward, the alignment with the appropriate stair is possible. Of course, if the drawing is taken literally, the impression is given of very high stairs.

45.4. More practical for walking up or down is to use an indication of a stair and to give each its appropriate number, **45d**. For dances which take place on stairs, this is vital. Ex. **45d** also spells out in more detail the movement of **45b**; here each leg is shown to extend backward to reach for the next step. Similarly, in **45e** lifting the knee before each upward step is given, and **45f** indicates the more usual walking forward downstairs.

Advanced Labanotation

Moving Up or Down Stairs

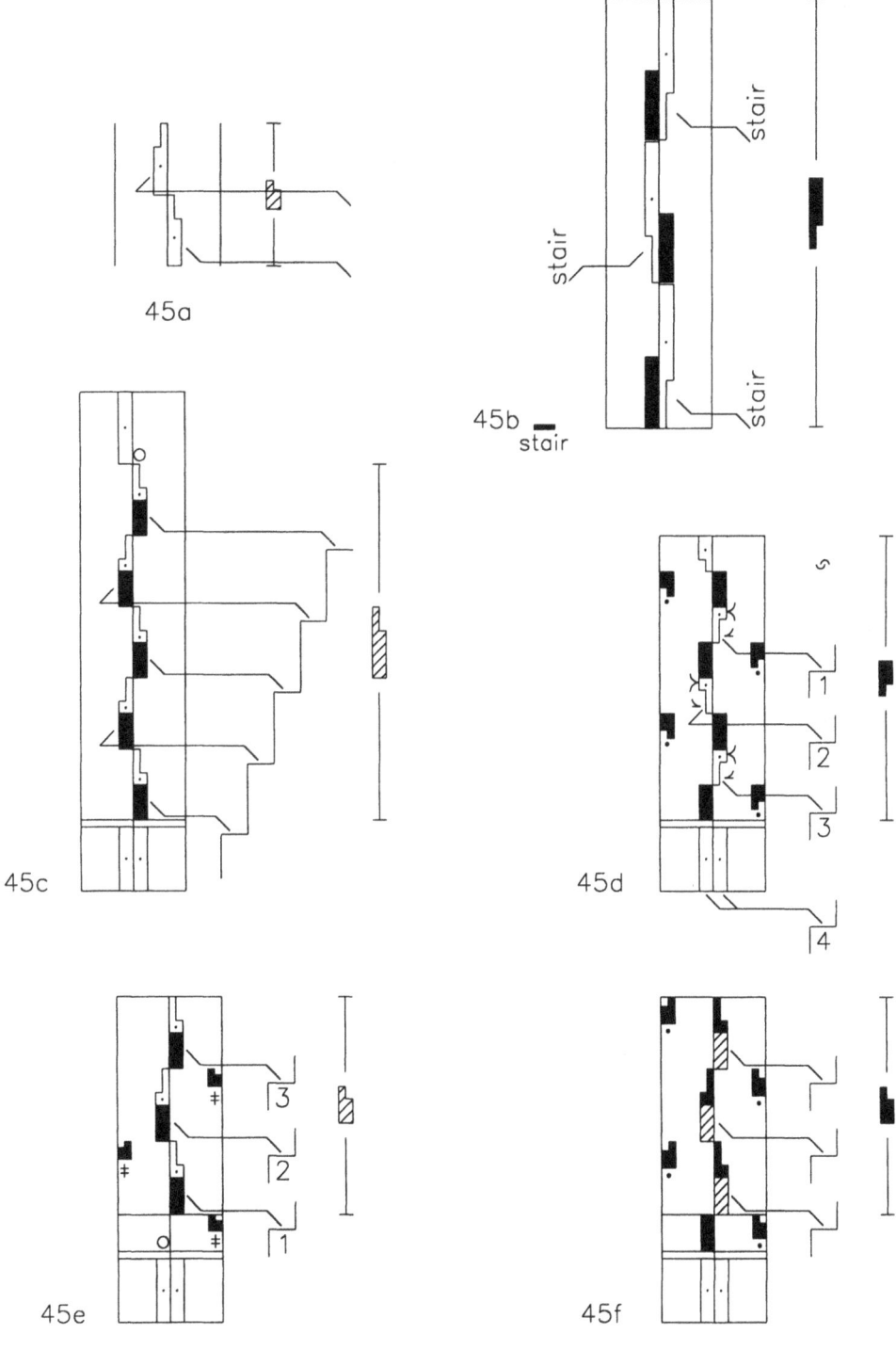

45.5. Climbing a Ladder. A general verbal statement can be given for climbing a ladder, when timing and style are not important. However, to be more specific, indication of the rungs needs to be established. This can be done as an extraction from a drawing of a ladder, **45g**, the rungs being numbered underneath or at the side. Depending on the slant of a ladder, the path when mounting will be either forward high, when the ladder is resting at an angle against a wall, as in **45h**, or straight up in the case of a vertical, built-in ladder, **45i**. In these examples no indications are given for the arms.

45.6. The action of the legs can be spelled out, as in **45j**. Here the usual backward placement of the center of weight and the slight forward tilt of the torso are shown. The activity of the hands are indicated separately to the right. Because the hands must grasp much higher than the rung on which the foot is being placed, an extra indication for the ladder is required in order to coordinate the timing. Here placement is on the right with the hand indications being placed close to it on left and right.

45.7. The disparity between where on the ladder the hands hold and the passage of time up the page, illustrated in **45k**, means that, for greater precision in depicting where the hand is grasping at a given moment, abstract indications may be needed for the rungs. In this way coordination in timing can be more easily stated. Ex. **45l** illustrates such use. This device can also be used for the feet. While pictorial representations are desirable, abstract indications can prove to be clearer and more precise.

45.8. In these examples the hands are shown as grasping the rungs. Often in climbing it is the upright struts between the rungs that are grasped. This can be shown as in **45m**.

Advanced Labanotation

Climbing a Ladder

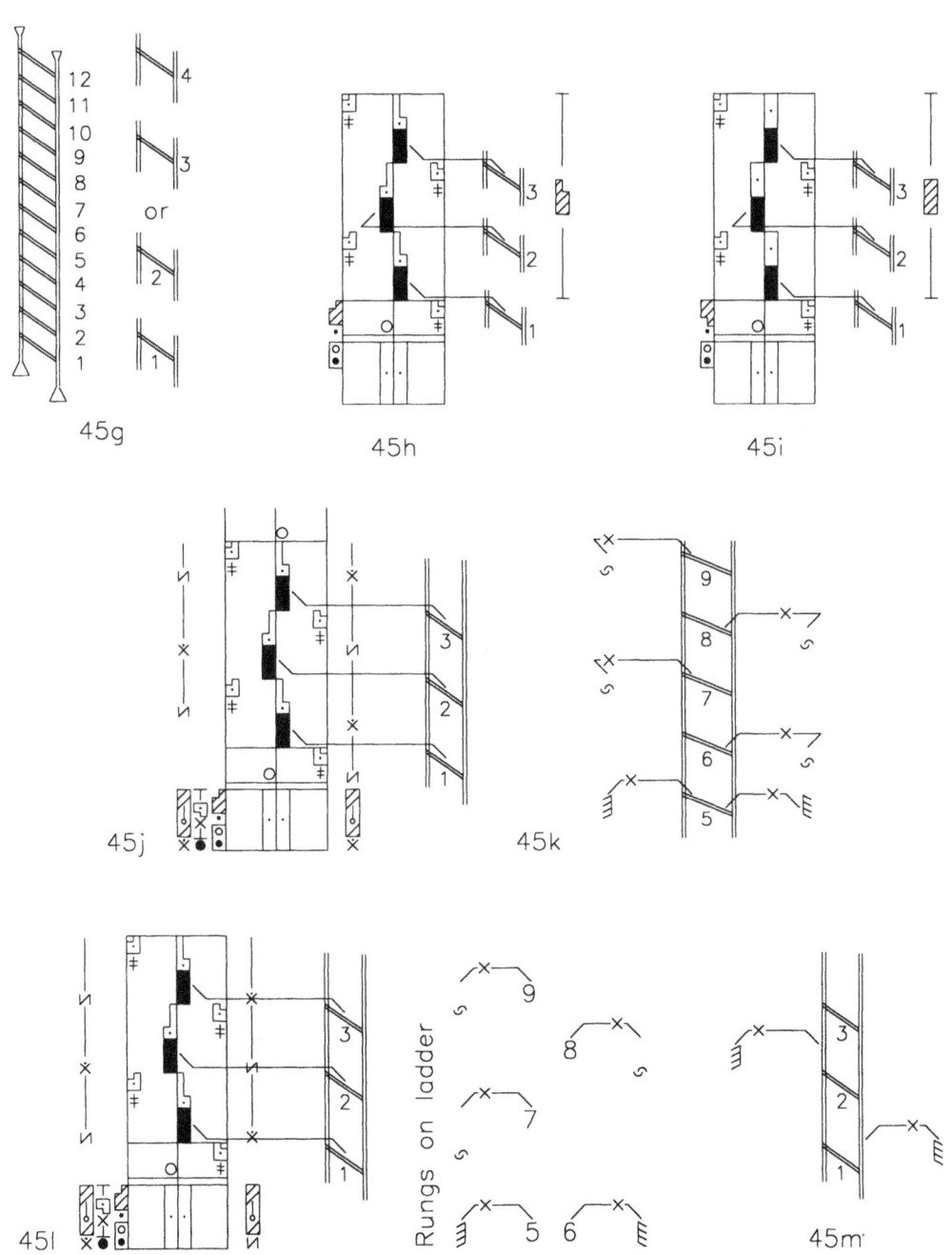

46 A Rope

46.1. When description of the technique required to climb a rope is not needed, a brief statement for climbing a rope can be given by showing grasping the rope with hands and ankles and indicating a path traveling upward. Climbing up a rope is shown in detail in **46a**. Except when the ankles and the hands are major supports and hence placed in the support column, they have been given specific placement to the right of the staff to be closer to the indication of the rope, thus facilitating placement of the contact bows. In this placement outside the staff, use has been made of the double hand sign and also the double ankle sign meaning both: both hands, both ankles respectively. The grasp for the hands is quite straightforward - they grasp from the side and in front. By using the double body part signs for hands and ankles sliding, one sliding relationship indication will take care of both.

46.2. The abbreviation used in this sequence for grasping with the ankles is explained in **46b**. The legs enclose the rope, passing between the knees and the crossed ankles; either ankle can, of course, be in front. Here the left ankle is shown to be grasping through adducting from in front and to the right; the grasp of the right ankle, both when taking weight and when sliding, is behind and to the left of the rope. These parts are shown here to be pressing the rope from opposite sides. Also pressing from either side are the knees. In the abbreviated form within the staff, the grasping is shown with the standard 'x' symbol.

46.3. The sequence of **46a** starts facing the rope. In preparation for climbing, the arms move up, the right hand higher than the left; they become principal supports. With a slight spring, the legs and arms draw up (contract), the hands now being the main support. The ankles 'embrace' the rope, taking weight. With the ankles now being the main support, the arms and legs extend, the ankles having a spot hold while the hands slide up the rope, an upward path being shown for the hands.

46.4. Both hands now become the main support and have a spot hold while the legs and arms contract and the ankles slide upward to become the next support. This sequence then repeats. The overall activity, the upward path for the body-as-a-whole, is also stated, placed between the staff and the rope indication.

Advanced Labanotation

46.5. Sliding down a rope or pole can be achieved in stages, the reverse of **46a**. A more rapid descent, given in **46c**, will result from both hands and ankles sliding at the same time. The landing is specifically shown to be on the floor, represented by the T in a box.

A Rope

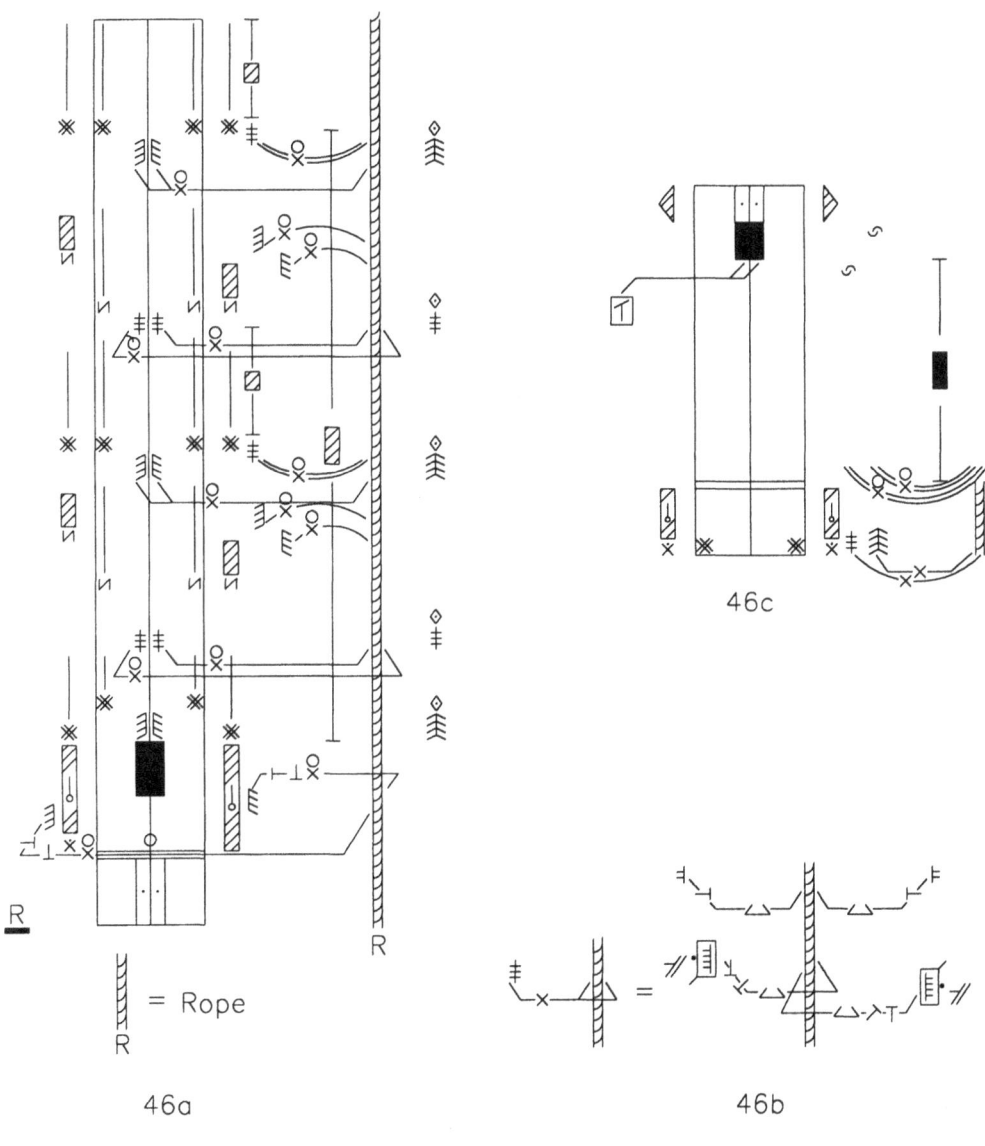

46a

46b

46c

47 A Pole

47.1. Reading Material - Bamboo Grove.[82] The following excerpts from the score of *Bamboo Grove* provide good examples of handling a pole. The glossary at the start, **47a**, indicates the lettered sections of the pole; the end section E is also marked with a thick black line. Where the pole is grasped, the movements of the pole and its relationship to the floor are indicated in three separate columns for the pole to the right of the main score. (See also endnote[83])

47.2. In the starting position of **47b** the directions for the upper and lower arms are clearly stated as well as where the pole is grasped by each hand.[84] In lowering the upper arms slightly to hit the end of the pole on the floor, and subsequently raising them, it is important that the lower arms remain spatially side horizontal. Note the horizontal line below the pole representing the floor.

47.3. Just before count 3 the right hand releases and the right arm moves down, while the left hand carries the pole upward, both arms being on the center track. The right hand now grasps the end section E before the performer makes a turning fall into a lunge to the right side with the torso tilted to the left. During this turn the pole makes a $^3/_8$ forward somersault, the left hand sliding along the pole to grasp section C. The free end of the pole (A), now pointing left side low, hits the floor.

47.4. The right foot picks up and, with a falling action, steps again on the same place; note use here of the 'same spot' caret. There follows a repeated dragging step, traveling to the right during which the end of the pole slides on the floor. As the right hand releases the pole, the left hand passively allows the weight of the pole to slip so that the left hand ends grasping section E. In this dragging step the left foot approaches the state of closing into place but does not achieve it; however, the sliding inward does take some weight. The right foot releases before the falling motion into another sideward step, which travels to the right, as does the next one. The center of weight is shown to retain the same level during this whole passage; it is canceled as the turn to the left takes place.

47.5. The phrase ends with the flexed left leg crossing to the right behind the right leg. This movement includes a rotation of the pelvis to the left. The transition into the next movement is a half turn to the left during which there is a space hold for the torso and left upper leg. For these last movements the pole is given no specific instruction but the previous sliding is canceled.

Advanced Labanotation

Reading Material - Bamboo Grove

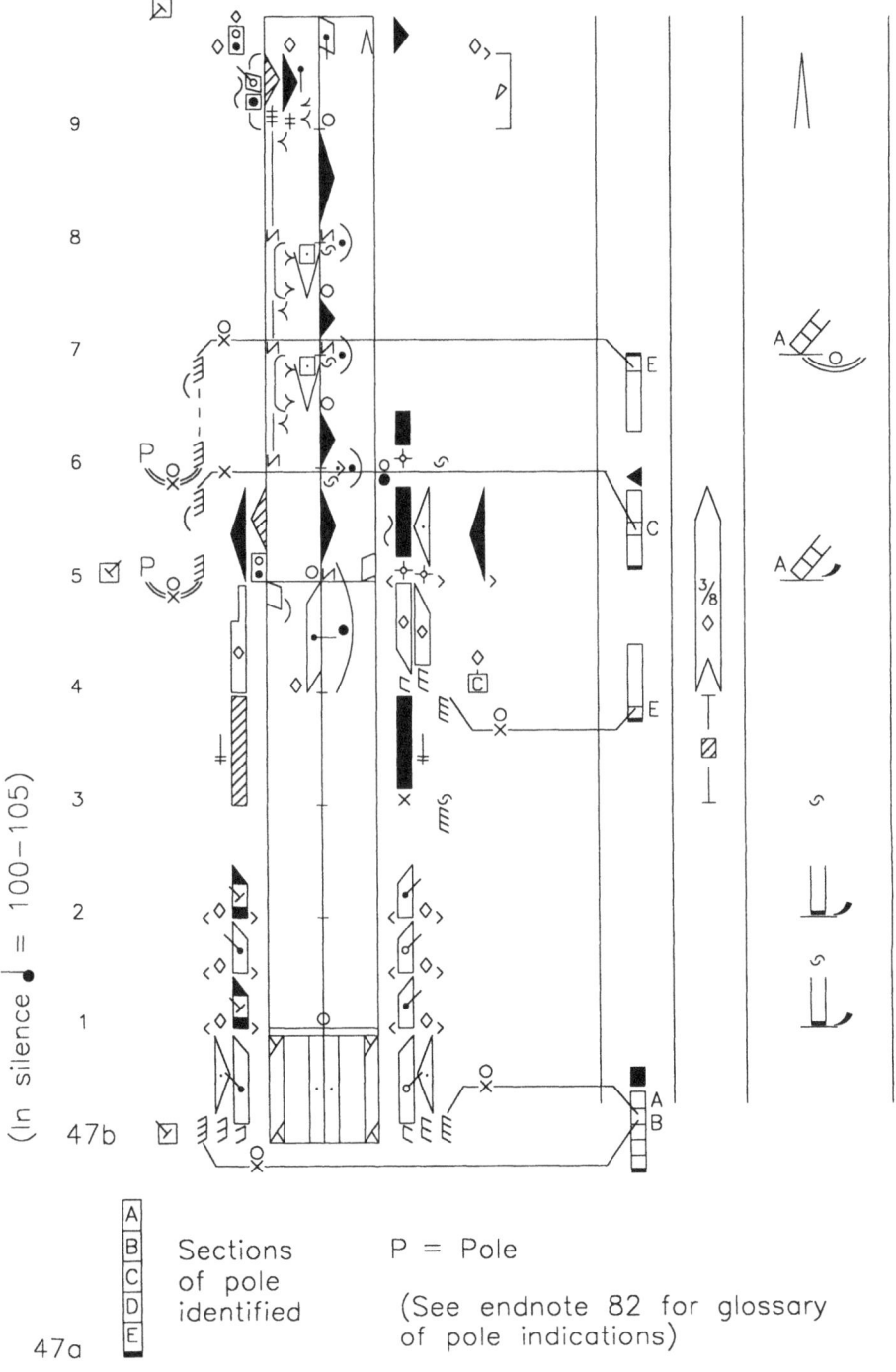

47a Sections of pole identified P = Pole

(See endnote 82 for glossary of pole indications)

47.6. The next excerpt from *Bamboo Grove*, **47c**, features the male solo in which some specific movements for the pole are given. Indications for the parts of the pole are as before. Coming from a low kneel, torso folded forward and arms sideward, rather low, the man holds the pole at sections B and D. That the pole is sideward horizontal can be deduced from this opening position; however, the direction of E is also given.

47.7. As the performer's left leg slowly gestures sideward, his right hand slides along the pole to the right, ending grasping section E. He then releases his left hand, takes his right arm across to the low left diagonal direction, bringing the A end of the pole to the floor. Putting weight onto his left foot, but remaining low, he steps into second position with his right foot, as his right arm makes a semi-circular movement causing the pole to slide along the floor in a semi-circular arc to the right. Because of the torso twist to the right, directions for the arm gesture and for the pole are both taken from the Constant Key.

47.8. Taking his left arm across to his right side, the performer's left hand grasps the pole at E, while his right hand releases. With his right hand close to the shoulder (place middle direction) he grasps the pole from the left side. The left arm rises to place high, led by the elbow, pulling the pole up as if with great effort (strength). At the same time the right hand slides down the pole ending by grasping part A. As this occurs, the torso folds to the right and the performer rises to a middle level 2nd position on the feet. The pole is now vertical and sections A, B and C are behind him (near the back of his torso).

47.9. The performer's arms now lift to a high sideward V shape causing the pole to start a half cartwheel path to the left. As this path finishes, weight is transferred to the left foot in low level while the right leg takes a position with the ankle on the left thigh. The left hand slides to grasp the center of the pole; the A end now up, the B section touches in front of the left shoulder. The lower arm moves across to the left side, behind the head; note passive elbow indication.

47.10. As he returns to the middle level 2nd position, the performer's left hand slides back toward the end, ending at section D, arms again up sideward. The pole then makes a half cartwheel path to the right, during which the right hand slides to the C section as the arm comes down to place low, bringing the A end to the floor and the E end touching in front of the right shoulder. The left elbow is passive so that the lower arm comes across to the right side behind the head. At the end of each half cartwheel path there is a pause to register the shape which has been established.

Advanced Labanotation

Reading Material - Bamboo Grove

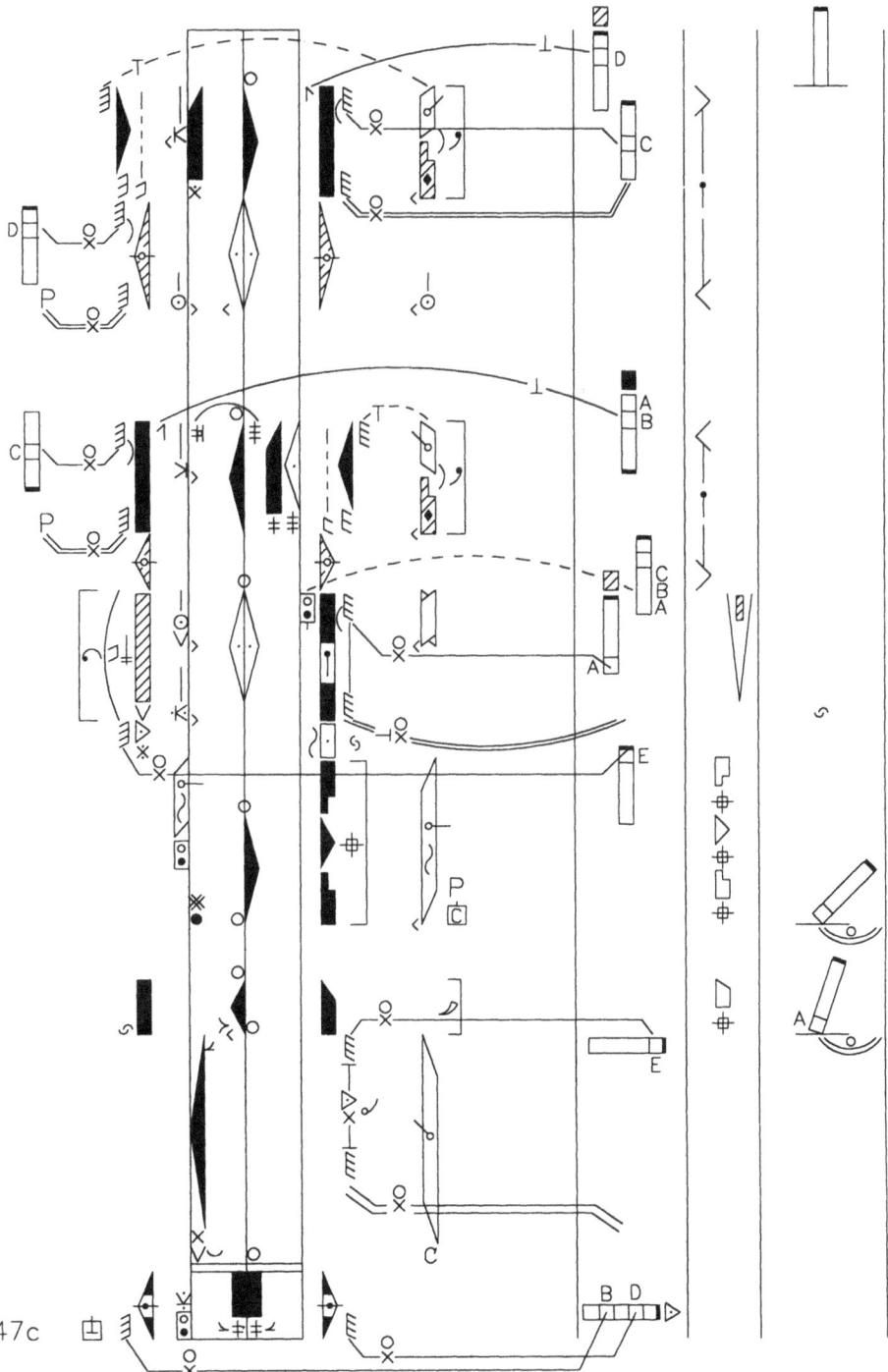

47c

47.11. The next excerpt from *Bamboo Grove*, **47d**, gives the overall sequence in which the pole is shown to fall from side to side, to be leaned on as well as standing alone for one count before someone entering quickly grasps it. This section of the dance involves additional people; only one performer has been shown here, with another performer entering at the end of this section, page 195.

47.12. The performer starts with the feet together, the pole in front of him being grasped by both hands at the B segment, arms bent in front of the body, a similar position to that in **47b**, the E end of the pole supporting on the floor. As both hands let go, the pole falls to the right and is caught in his right hand as the performer takes a falling lunge to the right and catches the top end of the pole. As he closes to his left foot in a slightly open 1st position, his arms resume their previous position and the pole is brought upright. This same pattern is then performed to the left.

47.13. With a little springing step in place, left foot to right with knees lifted, the upper arms also lift slightly bringing the pole off the ground. The pole must remain vertical. After a pause the upper arms move down slightly, causing the pole to hit the floor on count 8.

Reading Material - Bamboo Grove

47d

47.14. A half-turn spring from the left foot to the right ends in a wide lunge with the left leg backward and straight; in this lunge position the unit ankle-to-head inclines forward high in one line. During the spring the pole changes from being on the performer's left side to being again in front of him. The right foot then steps next to the left foot, shown here from Direction from Body Part (DBP), causing the weight to be taken on the pole. Observe here the center of weight indication showing that more of the performer's body weight is now supported on the pole. Note use here of the center of weight sign on the supporting bow to show that more of the performer's weight is on the pole. (See the <u>Advanced Labanotation</u> issue on center of weight.)

47.15. As the left foot steps forward with a falling action into a lunge, weight is taken off the pole, but the hands do not release, shown by the 'release weight' sign indicating that weight is released without letting go the hand grasps.

47.16. Releasing the pole from both hands, the performer turns away, swiveling on both feet before a long step forward on the right foot. At this moment, with an accent he opens his arms very wide (i.e. slightly backward) and extends and spreads his hands. During this count the pole stands unsupported. From the upstage left wing the next performer enters, turns to face downstage right and, placing himself with the pole in front of him, grasps the pole with the same arm position as the first dancer used at the start. At this moment the first performer lunges forward into a low kneel, his torso forward and rounded, his arms across his body, the right above the left.

Advanced Labanotation

Reading Material - Bamboo Grove (concluded)

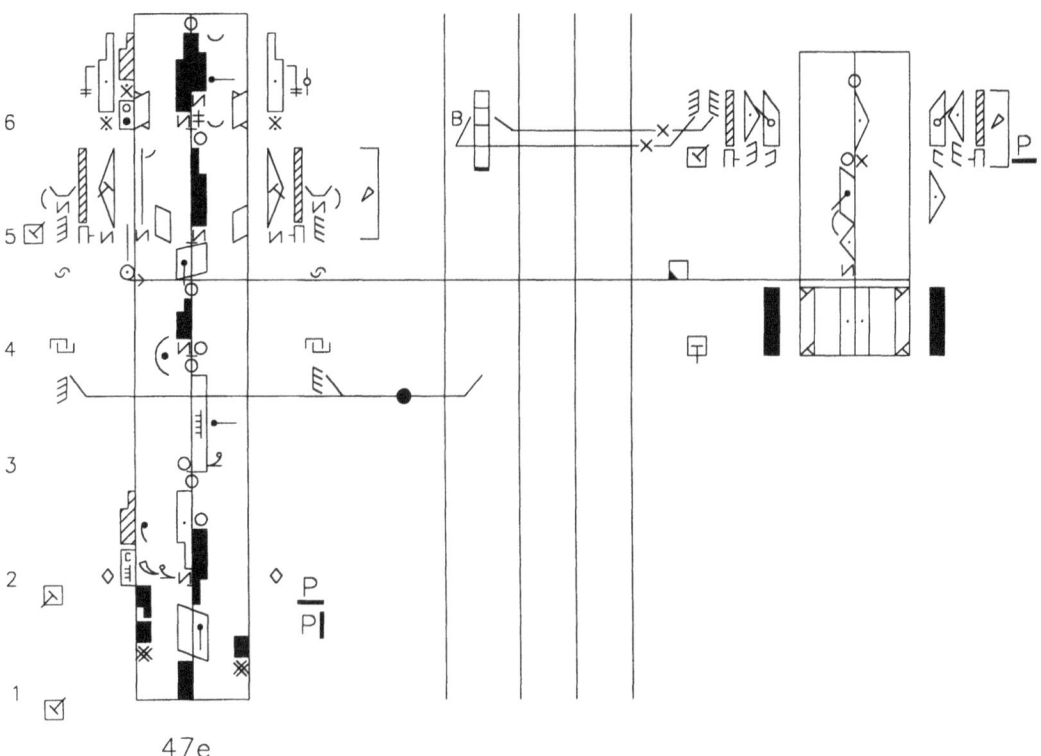

47e

48 A Box

48.1. Depending on the size, a box may be a small enough object to be handled, placed on a table, etc.; or it may be a large box into which things are placed or on which performers are supported. The following examples illustrate lying on a large box in different positions. In **48a** the person is lying on her back; the box is short enough to allow her arms and legs to hang over. In the prone position of **48b** only the arms can hang down. Lying on the right side is shown in **48c**. Each of these three examples takes direction from the Standard Cross.

48.2. In **48d** a person indicated as P is in a low box. It may be a rosin box, as in a ballet studio, in which case only the feet go inside. In **48e**, after stepping inside, the feet are shown to be making use of the rosin, the leg rotations causing the feet to slide in the rosin.

48.3. A box may be quite big, large enough for a person to step inside and entirely disappear from view, as in **48f**. Here person P steps inside a large box and then crouches down. Note the addition here of the indication of A for the audience. At the start they are seeing P; then P is not to be seen. P has actively moved away from the view (eyes) of the audience. A moment later P rises up and can be seen by the audience.

48.4. The ordinary addressing sign of **48g** can also be written as **48h**. From the toward and away signs of **48i**, the special signs of **48j** and **48k** are derived, **48j** meaning an addressing (relating) toward, while **48k** means relating away.[85] For example, in **48l** P averts his/her eyes from B. The ordinary addressing sign of **48h** does not contain the message 'away'.

A Box

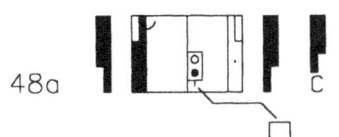 48a
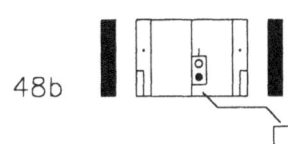 48b
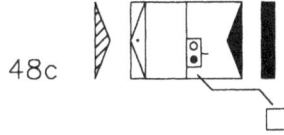 48c

48d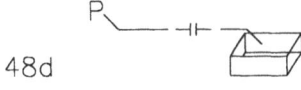

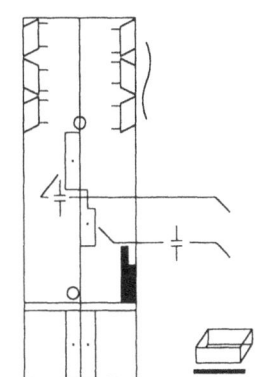 48e

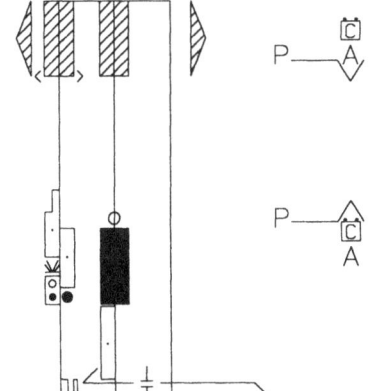

48f

B = box   A = audience

48l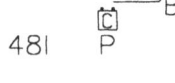
48k
48j
48i   V, Λ
48h
48g

48.5. Reading Material - New Dance.[86] It is not unusual for a stage set to include static boxes; a good example occurs in Doris Humphrey's choreography for 'Variations and Conclusion' from *New Dance*. Being an integral part of the choreography, full information concerning the sizes of the boxes is given in the score. Here the information on their location and numbering is given for the dancers. Ex. **48m** shows the view as from the audience, and **48n** gives the dancers' plan as seen from above.

48.6. Ex. **48o** shows the beginning of Variation II. Male dancer C is already standing on box 2, with his left leg on box 5. He slowly turns his torso as he follows dancer D as she makes her way toward box 1. On count 5 dancer C is now facing downstage left (note the use of the secret turn sign to show the new front chosen after the torso turn). C sits on box 5, his left lower leg tucked behind, his right palm on box 5, his right foot touching box 2.

48.7. As the group opens into two lines, sinking in a false split to the floor, dancer D makes her way through them, taking her fifth step onto box 1 and her sixth step onto box 2 where she ends, facing front.

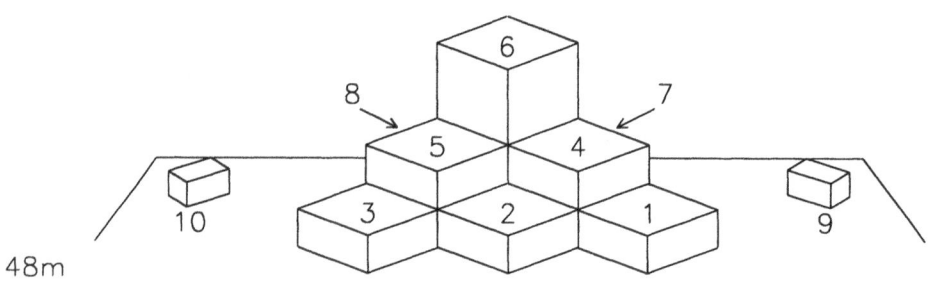

48m

FRONT VIEW AS SEEN FROM THE AUDIENCE

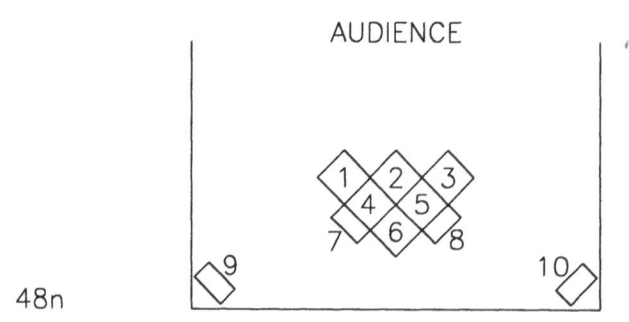

48n

AERIAL VIEW AS SEEN FROM THE STAGE

Advanced Labanotation

Reading Material - New Dance

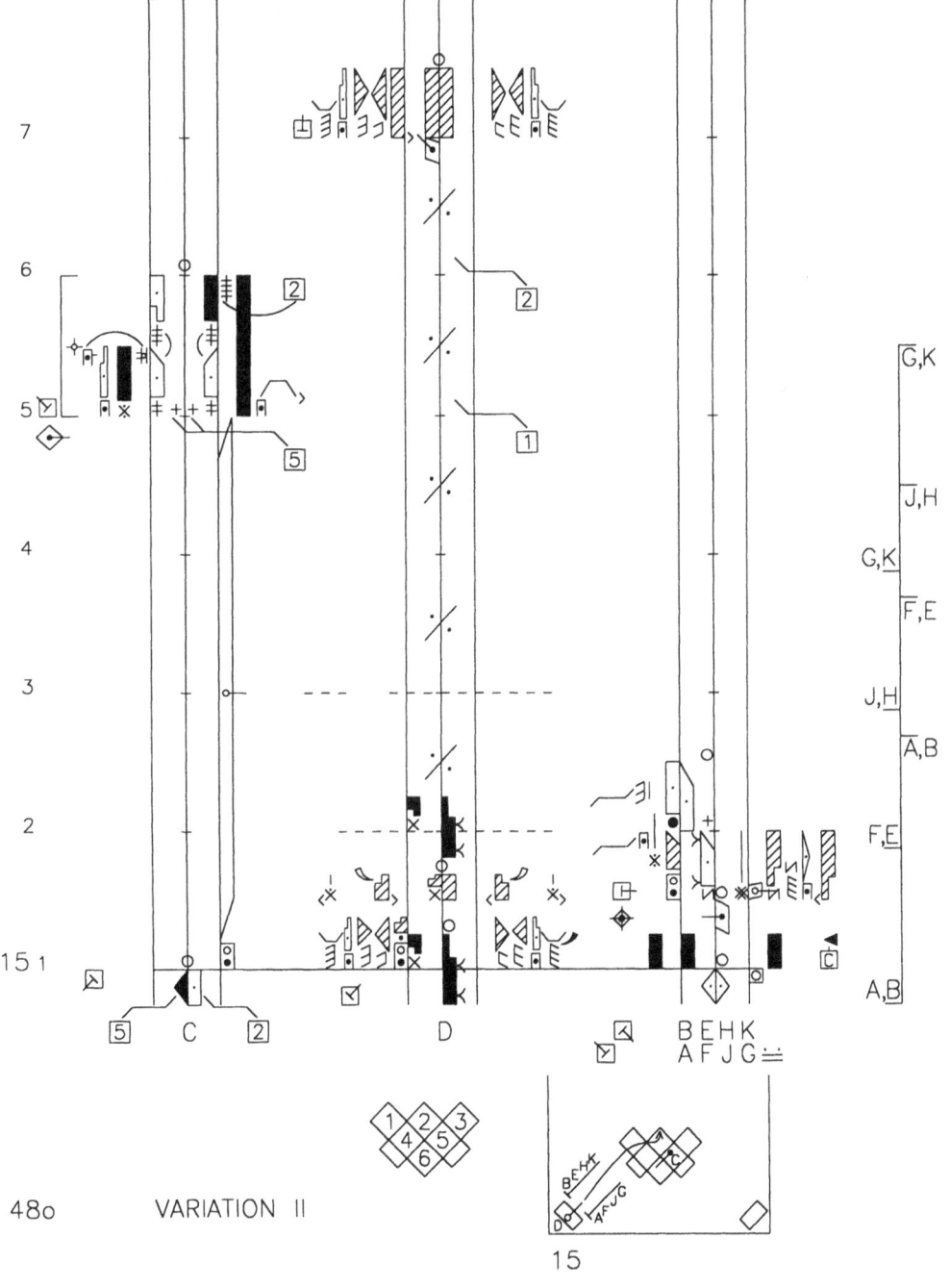

48o VARIATION II

48.8. Ex. **48p** is also an excerpt from Humphrey's 'Variations and Conclusion' from *New Dance*. This shows part of the trio with H and her two male companions, E and K. The previous soloists D and F are already seated on boxes 4 and 5, while C is now on box 6. This excerpt begins with E and K running across the front of the stage to catch up with H. Then, with K leading (note the circular path signs for E with K linked to the start to show K is the leader), they run onto the lower boxes, ending on boxes 1, 2 and 3. K ends with his right foot on box 2 and his left foot on box 1. E ends with his right foot on box 3 and his left foot on 2. H steps onto box 3 and then 2, before stepping onto the thighs of E and K who hold her waist to give her balance. Note use of the ad lib. signs for timing: the duration of those movements next to which the timing ad lib. sign is placed do not have to be exact; the important thing is to arrive at the end of the phrase.

Advanced Labanotation

Reading Material - New Dance

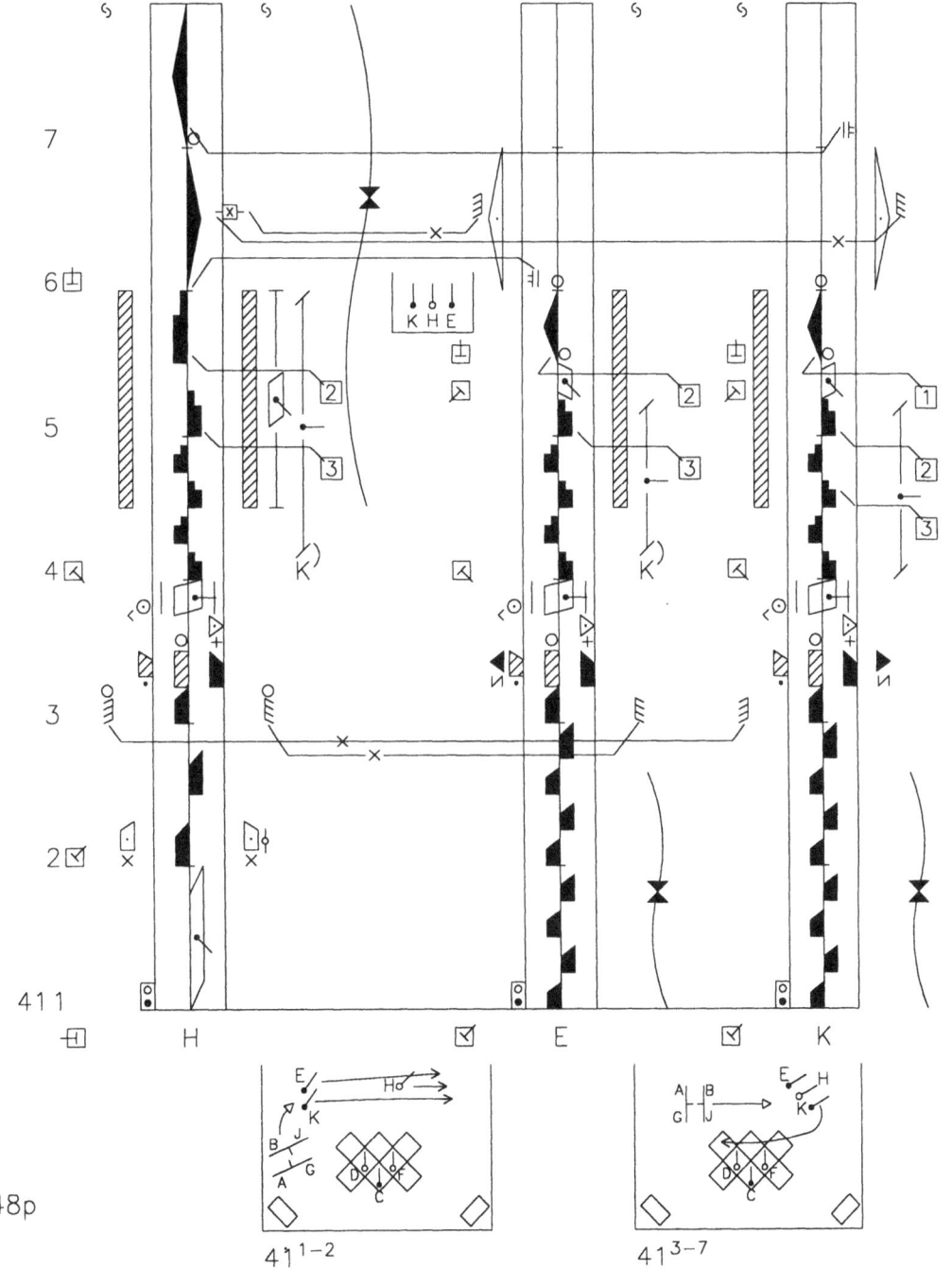

48p

49 An Imaginary Prop

49.1. Imaginary props appear in many mimed sequences, the skill of the performer making the viewers able to 'see' the absent prop. For example, the performer picks up a heavy suitcase, sits down, opens it up, discovers wads of money inside, which he gleefully throws in the air, and then scrambles around to pick it all up; or a clown may pick a flower, smell it, caress it, and then hand it to his ladylove. When sequences like these need to be performed in a particular choreographed way and possibly also to music, the need arises for some representation of the imagined object. A good device is to draw the imagined prop with dotted lines, but this may not be visually clear. This is not applied to the use of letters here to represent the prop. In the first example here the imagined object is a rose.

49.2. A note must be given at the start of the score to state that this is an imagined prop. On paper the prop may appear the same as a real object; this is important in order to indicate the parts of the object. In the case of a rose, these are the stem, the flower itself and the petals. In the key of **49a**, these parts have been given letters, such definition being needed. R stands for the rose as a whole; **a** and **b** are parts of the stem; **c** is the flower with **d** the center (top) of the flower, and **e** represents a petal. G is an imaginary girl friend. Use of this key to indicate parts of the rose facilitates direct reference to those parts which pictorial drawings do not so readily provide.

49.3. The study of **49b** follows the relationship of the clown to his imaginary rose. He walks forward, holding the rose out to the side. Bringing it in front of himself, he smells it (nose above and near the center of the rose) and then holds it away while he revels in the fragrance (head inclined, eyes looking heavenward). He then begins to change hands, grasping higher up on the stem with his left hand, but he draws it away suddenly (the thorn was sharp), and shakes his hand to get rid of the pain. He looks again at the blossom and admires it, caressing it with his left hand. Note the use here of design drawing for the circular hand movement. The palm facing and wrist flexion are shown as being resultant, since the relationship to the rose is the main activity.

An Imaginary Prop

R = imaginary rose
a,b = parts of stem
c = the flower
d = the center of the flower
e = a petal
G = imaginary girl friend

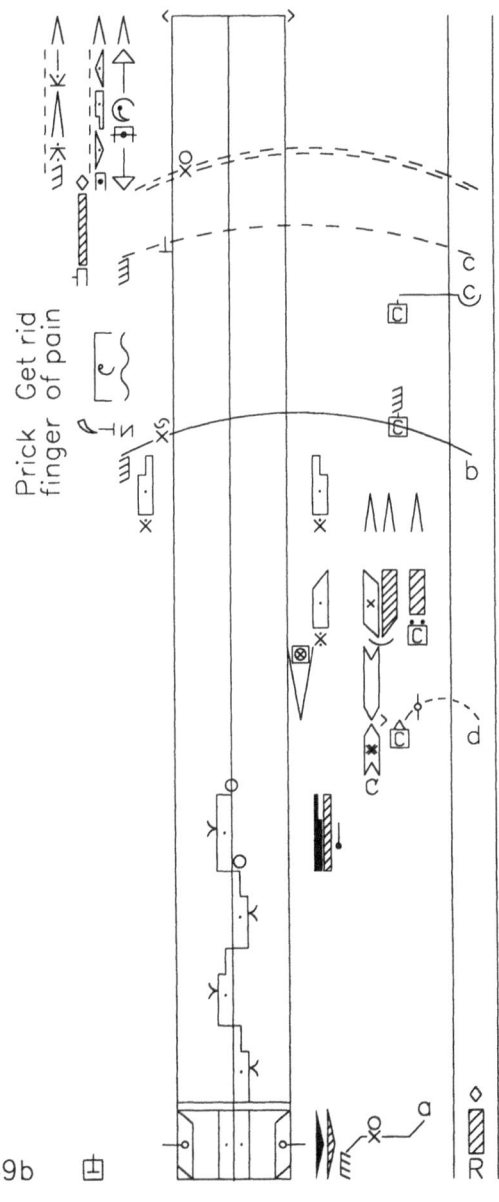

49.4. With his left hand at his heart (the left forward part of the chest) the clown holds the flower aloft in enjoyment. But a petal (e) falls to the floor. He looks at it, bends down and daintily picks it up between thumb and first finger. He holds it out to the side, still looking at it, deciding what to do.

49.5. With both arms in front the clown places the petal above the rose, and releasing it, he 'drops it in'. He touches his right shoulder and, inclining his head slightly, he looks at the petal closely. He decides this will not work (small head rotations saying "no"), turns the rose upside down (a half cartwheel to the left for the rose) and watches the petal as it drops to the floor. He then resumes his opening position. Suddenly seeing his imaginary girl, he walks over to her and, extending his arm, offers the rose to her.

Advanced Labanotation

An Imaginary Prop (concluded)

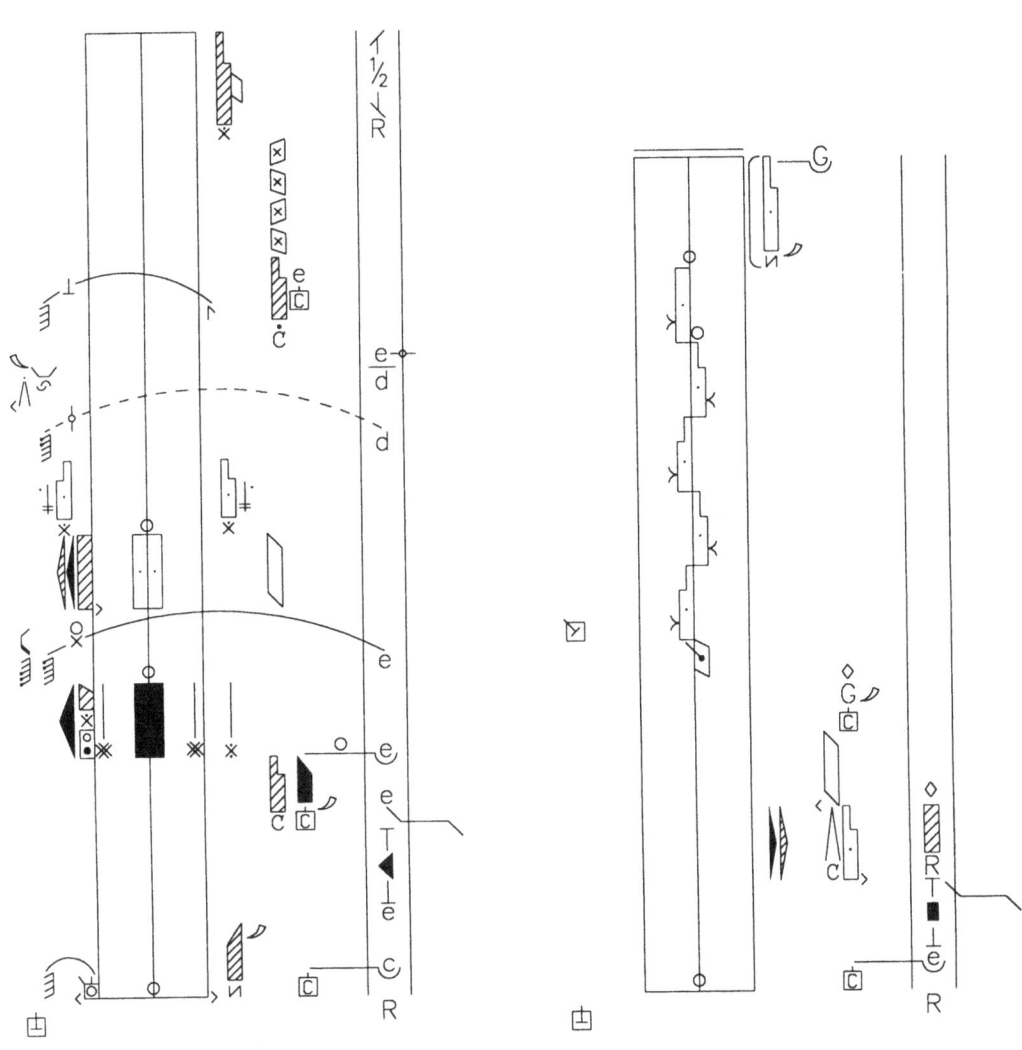

49b

Appendix: Historical Background on Labanotation Textbooks

The authoritative textbook *Labanotation - The System of Analyzing and Recording Movement*, was first published in 1954. The revised and expanded version, published in 1970 (reprinted in 1977) drew attention to a number of topics which were to be dealt with in greater detail in a subsequent publication, referred to as "Part Two". The need for such statements was high-lighted by the reaction of a group in Japan, who, when studying the 1954 Labanotation textbook, assumed that it presented the whole system. Since no handling of long sleeves was included, they decided that the system did not meet their needs. It was therefore important to make clear that much more existed. Labanotation did indeed have the capacity of meeting their needs, and in a wider context it was necessary to draw attention to the fact that the system was applicable across the whole spectrum of movement.

Detailed information on advanced Labanotation usage has not been generally available. Three volumes on advanced topics were published in 1991 and the present series continues the detailed and more advanced material along the same lines.

Labanotation and *Kinetography Laban*, *Motif Description* and *Structured Description*

The above terms may need some clarification. The specific subject of this book is *Labanotation*, the name given in the United States to the system of movement notation originated by Rudolf Laban and first published in 1928. Many European notators and dance scholars refer to the system as *Kinetography Laban*. There are some differences between Labanotation and Kinetography in notation usages, and occasionally in symbols and rules, and since 1959 the International Council of Kinetography Laban (ICKL) has provided a successful platform for discussions between practitioners on unification and further applications of the system. Differences are now small so that mutual understanding of scores is ensured. Kinetography rules and usages are catalogued in Albrecht Knust's 1979 Dictionary (see Bibliography) and in the 1999 ICKL paper given by Jacqueline Challet-Haas, published in the Proceedings of this conference.

The aim of the present series of texts is to provide a guide to the *Structured Description* of movement, the fully-fledged notation offering a determinate description of the movement progression by detailing choreographed (or otherwise set) actions. A different and complementary approach is provided by *Motif Description (Motif Writing)*, which uses symbols to represent movement ideas and concepts and to provide a general statement concerning the theme or motivation of a movement.

The term Labanotation is used in this book to refer to the notation system in general and not to mark an opposition with Kinetography or Motif Writing, except where specifically stated.

Source materials

Advanced Labanotation contains, whenever possible, systematic discussion of other usages and, where appropriate, comments on the history of symbols and rules and the reason for their inclusion in the Labanotation system. The material presented is based on all available textbooks, on earlier writings of Knust and Maria Szentpál, as well as on personal discussions and correspondence with specialists such as Sigurd Leeder, Valerie Preston-Dunlop and members of the Dance Notation Bureau in New York and the Dance Notation Bureau Extension at Ohio State University. Another major source of information are the proceedings of twenty ICKL Conferences.

Much use is made of the comprehensive theoretical account of the system by Knust, summarized in his *Dictionary of Kinetography Laban/Labanotation* (1979), and his earlier publications including his eight-volume encyclopedia of 1946-50 entitled *Handbuch der Kinetographie Laban*. The textbook *Dance Notation. Kinetography Laban* by Szentpál, published in Hungarian between 1969 and 1976 is unfortunately not readily accessible to readers outside Hungary, but Szentpál generously provided an English translation for her many colleagues.

In many cases, writing an advanced text of this kind has meant breaking new ground: the intricacies of handling a fan, manipulating stage props and identifying object parts, for instance, were not adequately covered, and some not included at all, in the 1979 Knust Dictionary. Some recent developments in the system such as 'DBP' (Direction in relation to the location of Body Part) track pins and symbols for 'design drawing' came too late to be included in Knust's 1979 Dictionary.

The Advanced Labanotation series offers the latest research on the Labanotation system and hence is completely up-to-date as of the date of publication.

Research Involved

A major concern in the research for this book has been the comparison of one rule against another to check applicability in all contexts. Often this has led to discoveries producing new arguments for or against a certain way of writing.

Labanotation is rapidly developing and is accepted as a tool in recording, research and in education. Each of these fields has specific requirements. There is a call for maximum flexibility in the notation system, so that it can provide general and simple statements for particular purposes and at the same time be very precise where such specificity is required. In dance research the need for precision has increased to the point where we are obliged to consider questions about the system that only ten years ago did not seem important, let alone when the fundamentals of the system were devised. In this new text we have tried to take these different needs into account while respecting the system as it has been handed down to us and is now used by people all over the world.

Notes

These annotations are mainly of three kinds. Firstly, they identify other major *rules and usages*. Secondly, they mark symbols and rules that have been *recently introduced* or *not described in other sources*, the origins of these being given. And finally, they give the *references of particular notation excerpts*.

On important or controversial issues, a short discussion of rationale is included. Sometimes, old ways of writing are briefly mentioned.

Research of other usages systematically involved *Táncjelírás, Laban Kinetográfia* by Szentpál and the *Dictionary of Kinetography Laban (Labanotation)* by Knust (see Bibliography). Where needed, other sources were also used.

Numbers in parentheses at the end of each note indicate where the note is in the text. The following abbreviations identify sources, for full bibliographic information see Bibliography.

References
- H83   Hutchinson 1983
- H91   Hutchinson 1991
- ICKL   International Council of Kinetography Laban
- K45-50 Knust 1945-1950
- K79   Knust 1979
- LNTR   *The Labanotator*
- S76   Szentpál 1969-76

- AHG   Ann Hutchinson Guest
- AK   Albrecht Knust
- KIN   Kinetography Laban
- LN   Labanotation

1. The need to indicate degrees of nearness has not arisen in the examples included in this book. However, the examples given below illustrate the choices available. Each is, of course, a relative statement. Ex. a) means quite near; b) states very near, almost touching. Less used are c), near, but at a slight distance, and d) the intention of nearness but still somewhat at a distance. (3.1)

2. The validity for Horizontal (Relationship) Bows, established at ICKL 1989, was based on the rule for contact bows with leg gestures. It is thus as follows:
A. When an action terminates in a relationship expressed with a horizontal bow, e.g. contact, support, nearness, the relationship remains valid for as long as the position resulting from the previous action is maintained.
B. When the relationship occurs part way through an action, the relationship is passing and occurs only at the moment where the relationship bow occurs.
C. Two relationship bows during an action indicate a passing or sliding relationship. The placement of the bows indicate the start and finish of the passing or sliding. The two bows may also be shown as a double bow at the start of the movement and a retention sign used to maintain the passing or sliding. The retention must then be specifically canceled; it will not usually be canceled by context.
D. When showing separated consecutive relationships during an action, or during a change of direction, a release sign must be used after each bow to distinguish consecutive touches from sliding. When no spatial change occurs, the release signs are not needed unless a specific rhythm is to be established. (4.2)

3. This usage was first presented in LNTR No. 31, June 1980. (5.6)

4. The question comes up as to whether carets need to be added at the end of the contact bow to make quite clear that reference is to the same prop. As a rule such reference is perfectly clear without stating "the same part" (i.e. using a caret) each time, thus keeping the score less cluttered. (6.2)

5. AK established the rule: if an object is held at one end, that end is drawn pointing towards the bottom of the page, and the free end is drawn pointing towards the top of the page, i.e. towards the direction sign written above the object's sketch. This direction sign indicates the direction of the object's free end (K79: 630). Current thinking is that application of this rule should be flexible; there is often the need to draw the object in other orientations which may be easier to read. (7.7)

6. Relationship of the hand in contacting an object was previously written as a). The relationship of the pin for above to the contact bow could be generally understood, but needed to be more precise. Placement above the hand, as in b) was also used but could now be understood to indicate a slight upward movement of the hand, not connected to the contact bow. The present appropriate placement is between the hand (or other body part) and the relationship bow, as in c). Placing the pin within the bow itself, as in d), also leaves no doubt as to what the pin refers and is therefore often the preferred usage. (8.6)

7. In the past the practise has been to draw supporting and touching bows from the object to the support column to indicate that it was supporting on or touching the floor. This is shown in **9h**. The new method of swinging the bow out beyond all columns has proved to be clearer and more practical. (9.3)

8. From S76, Part 2, Lesson XIX: 18. (9.5)

9. ibid.: 17. (9.5)

10. The sign for 'release of weight' is derived from the angular 'taking weight' bow (see the <u>Advanced Labanotation</u> issue on center of weight). (9.8)

11. Taken from S76, Part 2, Lesson XIX: 7. (9.9)

12. Paths for objects are always passive in that they are caused by an action of the perfomer or by gravity. It is logical, therefore, to write them as passive paths, i.e with dotted vertical lines. However, because objects do not initiate actions, the question of active or passive does not arise. For visual reasons a solid vertical line is used for the paths of objects in this book. (10.2)

13. The rule of an object automatically being carried along when a related body part moves does not exist in KIN. The KIN rule is that an automatic space hold is understood for a stated gestural direction; this also applies to objects. Therefore in KIN the hand will adjust so that the stick will be pointing forward all the time. (11.2)

14. From S76, Part 2, Lesson XIX: 9. (11.6)

15. If uncertain of the direction of rotation for an arm, always make note of the physical direction of the rotation and perform the same with the arm hanging down; the direction of the rotation can then be clearly seen. (12.1)

16. Because a stick has no front or back, no right or left sides, it is not possible to describe this rotation from the object's cross of directions; the movement must relate to the peformer's Standard Cross of Axes and rotational abilities. (12.2)

17. It would appear that for this somersault rotation of the stick, the movement

could better be described as a rotation around its longitudinal axis, as in **12b** or **12d**. The following experiment will reveal the problem: release the left hand, turn the stick in the direction of a) below. Grasp the stick with the left hand, turn the stick in the direction of a). Lower your left arm and turn the stick in the same physical direction and you will find that the stick is *now turning to the left*; this would require the turn sign of b). (12.2)

18. Notated in 1965 by AHG as taught by gymnast expert Philip Rolt. (13.2)

19. The path sign of a) was put forward in LNTR No. 8, 1961, the sign being based on the two diagonal points of b), with c) the other diagonal path, based on d). In actual use, preference has been for indicating the axis of the circular path or the surface on which the diagonal path lies. (13.7)

20. From S76, Part 2, Lesson XIX: 22. (13.10)

21. ibid.: 15. (13.11)

22. For Time Signs see ICKL 1991 (Technical Report I:1). (13.12)

23. Examples of baton manipulations are contributed by Billie Mahoney. (13.13)

24. For movements of a range of objects described through Design Drawing see H91. (15.1)

25. These two examples are taken from S76, Part 2, Lesson XIX: 12, 13. So-called 'lopsided' figure eight patterns are typical of Hungarian men's dances.

However, there are different 'schools' on how these should be performed; the differences lie mainly in how the hand and arm coordinate to achieve the desired result. In this book the KIN usages of Maria Szentpál have been adjusted into standard LN. (15.6)

26. From *The Green Table* by Kurt Jooss (1932), updated score notated by Gretchen Schumacker, 1980 (scene 2 'Farewells', measure 75). This example was also used in H91. See also note 62. (15.8)

27. Examples of baton manipulations are contributed by Billie Mahoney. (15.9)

28. From K79: 627. (16.1)

29. From S76, Part 2, Lesson XIX: 20. (16.3)

30. These examples are from S76, Part 2, Lesson XIX, where the author has chosen to designate the props in this manner. Other possibilities exist, i.e. to repeat the drawing of the crossed sticks without referring to them as B. (17.1)

31. From S76, Part 2, Lesson XIX: 29. (17.2)

32. ibid.: 26. (17.3)

33. Choreographed by Fergus Early, this dance was used for the Royal Academy of Dancing Grade One examinations in 1981. (18.1)

34. Collapsable umbrellas, which are more complex to handle, are not being dealt with here. However, by including contraction signs the different states can be shown. (19.3)

35. This example is based on notation by Sheila Marion, 1979, revised 1998. Courtesy of Sheila Marion. (20.6)

36. Originally, a plain wide sign within the carrying bow was used. In K79, pp. 236 and 591, the wording is: "A wide sign within the carrying sign indicates holding by means of a spreading out movement". (21.2)

37. From K79: 592c, d. (21.3)

38. These examples are based on those in S76, Part 2, Lesson XIX: 25, 28, fig. 3. The Hungarian letter representing the bottle, ü, representing the word 'üveg'

for bottle, used in the original notation has been changed to the English B. (21.4)

39. These signs are derived from K45-50, Part K, p. 1574. (22.7)

40. This meaning for the double X sign is a special usage, established by Knust, K45-50, Part J. It is also used for such gestures as running the fingers through dry ingredients in cooking. (23.1)

41. The 'within' sign means that part or all of the hand is inside the object. The penetrating sign is only used when the object is grasped between the shafts (not tips) of the fingers. If penetration is all the way to the roots of the fingers, the fingers sign is used, as opposed to the hand sign. (For grasping, see the <u>Advanced Labanotation</u> issue on hands and fingers.) (23.3)

42. From K79: 3441', m', n'. (23.5)

43. From *Le Beau Danube* by Léonide Massine (1924), notated by AHG, 1971 (Scene One 'Strollers, Children, Artists', measures 85-89). (24.2)

44. Sign devised by AHG for this need, 1999. (25.4)

45. In K79: 551 for person b, a plain horizontal line is drawn across the whole staff; in LN the end of the horizontal line is angled so that it does not look like a bar line. (25.4)

46. Using the above pin to designate the embroidered side of the pillow contrasts with the use of a black circle for the decorated side of a fan. For a fan which may involve much manipulation, the black circle relates to the palm sign which addresses the stated direction. The embroidered side of the pillow, indicated by the above pin, frequently is presented to (addresses) the audience and thus has an expressive significance. (27.3)

47. A 'grasp' is usually indicated by a) or b); these involve flexion of the hand, fingers, or arm, etc. Two body parts can 'grasp' i.e. hold an object by pressing together, no flexion occurring. In such cases the lateral adduction sign of c) or the sagittal adduction sign of d) can be used. (28.1)

48. See K79: 344a-n'. (28.5)

49. From *Coppélia*, original choreography by Arthur Saint-Léon (1870), notated by Allan Miles, 1965, revised 1970. (30.4)

50. From a girl's Jiaozhou Yangge Dance from Shandong Province, China, notated by Zhang Lingling and Tan Lianying, 1982. (30.5)

51. The Japanese do not seem to mind that it is actually the eighth and not the seventh rib counting from the other side. The term *shichi-san* was borrowed from a *Kabuki* term which refers to a point on the *Hanamichi*, the runaway that goes into the audience. Important scenes are played at the *shichi-san* point, which is, on a scale of ten, three units away from the stage and seven units from the back of the house. (30.19)

52. This is a direct departure from the standard LN rule that direction is judged from the point of grasp, the point of support. (30.25)

53. From Hanayagi, 1981. (30.33)

54. From *Ikkaku Sennin* by Zenou Komparu (1964), notated by Odette Blum and Lucy Venable, assisted by Judith Bissell and Raymond Cook, 1965, revised by Carl Wolz and Ann Hutchinson Guest, 2001. Courtesy of Odette Blum and Lucy Venable. (30.51)

55. The fan used in the Noh Theatre is different from the *sensu*, the fan used in Kabuki and Nihou Buyoh. Called *ogi*, it has fewer ribs, no pin, and a larger paper area. However, for writing and reading purposes, the method used for the *sensu* is satisfactory. Note from Carl Wolz. (30.51)

56. Feminine pronouns are used here because the role is "Lady Senda." The role is always played by a man. Women never perform in Noh; however, it may be studied by wealthy matrons or students as a hobby. Note by Carl Wolz. (30.52)

57. Exs. **31a-31f** are taken from Louise Chan Wong Shuk Chun's 1982 MA Thesis. Other ribbon examples from this thesis were used in H91. (31.2)

58. For situations of the design in space see H91: 9.7-10. (31.3)

59. The sign for body-as-a-whole, example a), was derived from the basic three-line staff which represents the body. This indication, which is needed for Motif descriptions, was considered in 2001 not to be an appropriate sign, lacking any

organic sense or body reference. Therefore, in line with symbols used by Laban Movement Analysis practitioners, based on the figure 8, b) which is an abstraction from the sign for the whole torso, c), the symbol of d) was put forward and generally approved to be the sign encompassing the body-as-a-whole. (31.6)

a) ⊔⊔ b) 8 c) ⦙ d) ⊗

60. From *Day on Earth* by Doris Humphrey (1947), notated by Muriel Topaz, 1959, revised 1978 and 1981 (Third Movement, measures 119-134). In the light of further research and experience the version given here is a modification of the original. (32.1)

61. From Garcia and Hutchinson Guest, 1991. (34.7)

62. Choreographed by Tamara Karsavina for the Royal Academy of Dancing for Grade IV, notated by AHG, limited publication, 1981. (34.10)

63. *The Green Table*, a ballet in eight scenes by Kurt Jooss (1932), originally notated by AHG, 1938 (Scene 1 'The Gentlemen in Black', measures 101-103). A more detailed, up-to-date score was recorded by Gretchen Schumacker, 1980, when it was restaged by Anna Markard for the Hartford Ballet. (34.16)

64. This example is a variation of one given in S76, Part 2, Lesson XIX: 11. (35.1)

65. Exs. **35b-35g** are from *The Green Table* (see note 63) ('The Dance of the Partisan'). (35.2)

66. Based on K79: 584a. (36.1)

67. From *L'Après-midi d'un Faune* by Vaslav Nijinsky (1912), Labanotation translation by Hutchinson Guest and Jeschke, 1991 (measures 88-89). This sequence for the fifth, leading nymph (N5) has been condensed in time. (36.2)

68. When a skirt is worn it is carried (supported) by the body, not by the grasping hand. It has been thought in the past that each such holding of part of the skirt should be written with an angular support bow. (37.3)

69. From S76, Part 2, Lesson XIX: 3. (37.4)

70. The inverted pelvis sign indicates that the direction of the movement is judged from the top of the pelvis (near the waist) instead of the usual description of direction taken from the hip joint up. (37.4)

71. From *The Three-Cornered Hat* by Léonide Massine (1919), notated by Odette Blum, 1967, completed by Jocelyne Asselbourg, 1973. Courtesy of Lorca Massine. (37.5)

72. From S76, Part 2, Lesson XIX: 23. (37.7)

73. Choreographed by Lam Ah Mui, this dance was notated by Louise Chan Wong Shuk Chun as part of her 1982 MA thesis in which much historical background and performance details are given. Excerpts **38b** (p. 308, measure 1) and **38c** (p. 309, measure 7) have been slightly modified for our purposes here. (38.2)

74. The original of this example was in a phrase of eight counts; here it is condensed to six counts to fit on the page. (38.6)

75. From *Minikin Fair* by Paul Taylor (1989), notated by Sandra Aberkalns, 1989. Courtesy of Paul Taylor. (39.1)

76. From H83, p.250. (40.3)

77. From *Continuous Project, Altered Daily* by Yvonne Rainer (1969), notated by Barbara Katz ('Chair, Pillow'). (40.4)

78. From *The Green Table* (see note 63). (41.1)

79. The original of this sequence comes from K45-50, Part K, p. 1632. Some modifications have been made for inclusion here. A small card table was used. (41.6)

80. It is common in dance circles to use the French spelling for the ballet bar. (43.1)

81. From *L'Après-midi d'un Faune* by Vaslav Nijinsky (1912), Labanotation translation by Hutchinson Guest and Jeschke, 1991 (measures 42-43, 100-101). (45.2)

82. From *Bamboo Grove* by Ming-Shen Ku (1988), modified from the notation by Mary Corey, 1989 ('Entrances' 8-9 and pp. 8-9). For the purposes of this

Advanced Labanotation textbook, these pages from the score have been reworked to reflect current usage. Teaching notes and word descriptions, which are clearly expressed in the notation, have been omitted. The score was commissioned by the Department of Theatre and Dance at the University of Hawaii at Manoa. Permission to use the score must be sought. (47.1)

83. The following are the pictorial pole indications provided by Mary Corey for this score. (47.1)

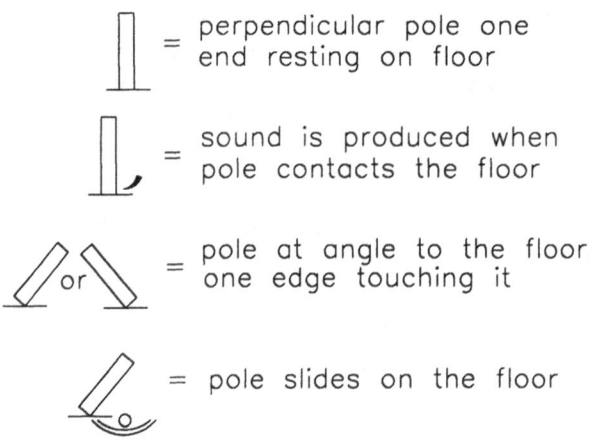

84. Length of pole: when the pole is standing, for most dancers the pole end should reach the middle of the performer's face. Exactly where each dancer grasps the pole is, in most cases, dependent on the height of the dancer. (47.2)

85. The angular address bow, in which the 'toward' and 'away' signs replace the curved bow, was originated by AHG and first presented in the Advanced Labanotation issue on hands and fingers. (48.4)

86. From *New Dance* by Doris Humphrey (1935), notated by AHG and Els Grelinger, notator trainee, 1948, with additions, clarifications and alternate versions by Lucy Venable, 1950 ('Variations and Conclusion'). (48.5)

Bibliography

Chan Wong Shuk Chun, Louise. *From the "Yue Di" Dance to the "Adventures on the Silk Road": A Perspective on the History & Forms of Chinese Dance with Recordings in Labanotation*, unpublished MA Thesis, 1982.

Garcia, Josefina and Hutchinson Guest, Ann. *Two Mexican Dances*, Cervera Press, London, 1991.

Hanayagi, Chiyo. *Nihon Buyo no Kison (Japanese Dance Basics)*, Tokyo Shoseki, Inc., Tokyo, 1981.

Hutchinson, Ann. Notebooks from Jan. 1936 - July 1938, while at the Jooss-Leeder Dance School.

Hutchinson, Ann. *Labanotation, The System of Analyzing and Recording Movement*, Theatre Arts Books, New York, 1970. (1st published 1954; revised 3rd edition published in 1977.)

Hutchinson Guest, Ann. *Children's Grade Dances in Labanotation*, Royal Academy of Dancing, London, 1981.

Hutchinson Guest, Ann. *Your Move, A New Approach to the Study of Movement and Dance*, Gordon and Breach, London, 1983. (3rd reprinting with corrections, 1995.)

Hutchinson Guest, Ann and van Haarst, Rob. <u>Advanced Labanotation</u>, *Shape, Design, Trace Patterns*, Vol. 1, Part 2, Harwood Academic Publishers, 1991.

Hutchinson Guest, Ann and Jeschke, Claudia. *Nijinsky's Faune Restored*, Gordon and Breach, London, 1991.

Hutchinson Guest, Ann. *A History of the Development of the Laban Notation System*, Cervera Press Publication, London, 1995.

Knust, Albrecht. *HandBuch der Kinetographie Laban*, unpublished manuscript (8 vol.), written mainly between 1945 and 1950.

Knust, Albrecht. *Handbook of Kinetography Laban*, translated by Valerie Preston, unpublished (1 vol.), 1951.

Knust, Albrecht. *Abriss der Kinetographie Laban* (2 vol.), Das Tanzarchiv, Hamburg, 1956.

Knust, Albrecht. *Handbook of Kinetography Laban* (1 vol.) (English edition), Das Tanzarchiv, Hamburg, 1958.

Knust, Albrecht. *A Dictionary of Kinetography Laban (Labanotation)* (2 vol.), MacDonald and Evans, 1979. (2nd edition: Institut Choreologie, Poznan, Poland, 1997.)

Laban, Rudolf. *Schrifttanz, Methodik, Orthographie, Erläuterungen*, Universal Edition, Wien, Leipzig, 1928.

The Labanotator, bulletin, London, Nos. 1-25 published 1957-65 by the Dance Notation Bureau, New York; Nos. 26-77 published 1978-1994 by the Language of Dance Centre, London.

Preston-Dunlop, Valerie. *An Introduction to Kinetography Laban*, Laban Art of Movement Guild, London, 1963.

Proceedings of the Biennial Conferences of the International Council of Kinetography Laban (ICKL), 1959-1999.

Szentpál, Maria. *Táncjelírás. Laban-kinetográfia* (Dance Notation. Kinetography Laban), Népmüvelési Propaganda Iroda, Budapest, 1969-76 (3 vol.; vol. I 2nd. ed.; 1st ed. 1964).

Index

1.3, 5.2	etc. refer to paragraph numbers
1e, 6a	etc. refer to example numbers
*S*1, *S*2	etc. refer to section numbers
*n*1, *n*2	etc. refer to end note numbers
p.1, p.2	etc. refer to page numbers

\-   replaces the entry word(s)

In the longer listings, the more relevant references are placed first, separated from the others by a semi-colon (;).

Accent, double sign, 16.3
Act of skipping with a rope, 24.1
Action stroke, 4.5
'Active' end of a stick, 15.6
Actual contact, touching, 3.1
Acurate, detailed drawing, 2.1
Additional clarity in writing change of direction for prop, 11.5
Addressing, 3.1, 20.5
- gliding, 37.7
- sign, 48.4
  - drawn across whole staff, 25.4
  - to indicate watching, 20.5
Adduction
- of fingers, 28.1
- sign, 22.5
Ad. lib
- line for finger movement, 22.13
- sign, 5.6, 15.8, 30.19
Advanced Labanotation, 8.1, 9.7, 13.9, 14.1, 26.3, 28.1, 43.4, 44.1, 47.14
Aiming position for gun, 18.2-3
Albert, 39.1
Angling sign, 43.4
Angular
- bow, 3.4, 8.10
- ,support bow, 9.2
Ankle sign, double, 46.1
'Any rib' sign, 30.19
Apple
- ,biting into an, 28.5
- ,handling an, *S*28
- ,holding an, 28.5
- ,teeth penetrating, 28.5
Appropriate action, 25.4
Arm/s
- and stick direction the same, 8.6

Arm/s (cont.)
- circles, 38.5
- ,sagittal, 38.6
- gestures
  - circular paths for, 13.1
- in opposite sleeve to keep warm, 34.15
- inside a sleeve, 23.5
- lower weight on, 41.2
- rotation of a prop, 12.1
  - when overhead, 12.1
- rotations (twist), 29.2
- slides through sleeve, 34.14
Armpit
- holding stick, 8.10
- sleeve pressing under, 38.6
- supporting stick, 8.11
Arrow to indicate from which side fan is opening, 30.30
Ashtray
- ,cigarette above, 28.3
- ,cigarette contacts, 28.4
Asian dance/s, 29.1
- ,long sleeves featured in, 38.1
- use of a fan, 30.1
Assemblé, 42.3
Assisted balance, 9.3
'Attack' with stick, 16.3
Attention-grabbing rattling sound of tambourine, 26.4
Augmented areas of a fan, 30.16
Aural interest of clashing props, 16.1
Axe, 13.10
Axis of the circle, 13.6

Backward flourish, 16.2
Balance assisted, 9.3
Balkan folk dances, 35.1

Balletic use of fan, 30.4
Ball/s, 7.1
- balancing with index finger, 7.1
- bouncing up to be caught, 20.3
- grasped from below, 20.2
- grasping with hand, 7.1
- ,handling a, S20
- hit from behind, 20.4
- in lateral plane, 20.6
- juggling, 20.6
- path in air, 20.2
  - indicated by design drawing, 20.6
- rolling
  - along the body, 20.7
  - along the floor, 20.4
  - indications, 20.4

Bamboo Grove, 47.1-16, n81
Bar, hanging over a, 43.5
Barre, S43
- ,both hands grasping the, 43.3
- center of weight placement, 43.4
- ,hand resting on, 43.1
- ,hand sliping along, 43.2
- ,placing weight on, 43.4
- stretching exercises, 43.4

Barrel of gun, 18.2, 18.6
Basket
- fingers
  - carrying with penetration, 23.1
  - penetrating the spaces, 23.1
- grasping from above, 23.1
- ,handling a, S23
- 'inside', 'in the center' sign, 23.3-5
- open wickerwork, 23.1
- penetrating, 23.1
- supporting bow, 23.1-2
- ,wastepaper, 23.1

Baton, 13.13, 15.9
- ,ball of, 15.9-10
- forward sagittal circle, 15.9
- 'tail' of, 15.10
- twirling, 13.13

Beaker, 21.1
Beating of swords, sticks, 16.1
Belt, 34.4
- grasping the waist, 34.4
- ,stuffing a scarf into a, 35.4

Biting into an apple, 28.5
Blanket
- completely covering person, 33.3
- gathered across body, 33.2
- ,handling a, S33
- sign for
  - a shape, 33.1
  - folding and lateral closing, 33.1
- wrapped around body, 33.3

Blessing, use of *sensu*, 30.48
Body-as-a-whole, 17.2, 25.4
- movement, 40.3
- sign, 31.6

Body Cross analysis for fan, 30.11
- path for, 46.4

Body Key used for prop, 12.4, 22.15

Body unit, ankles to chest, 44.1
Book
- balancing on head, 22.1
- Body Cross of Axes, 22.12
- Body Key, 22.15
- bottom edge, 22.7
- carried on palm, 22.2
- cartwheel, 22.14
- center fold, 22.2
- closed, 22.1
- ,column for, 22.5
- Constant Key, 22.16
- Cross of Axes, 22.12, 22.15
- 'face down', 22.8
- folded
  - backwards, 22.5, 22.8
  - inside out, 22.8
- general orientation, 22.6
- grasped from behind, 22.4
- gutter, 22.7
- ,half-opened, 22.2, 22.4
- ,handling a, S22
- ,hands grasping lower edge of, 22.3
- hanging down, 22.4
- ,holding on both palms, 22.3
- ,identification
  - of a, 22.2
  - of edges, 22.2, 22.6-7
  - of parts of a, 22.6-8
  - of surfaces, 22.6
- indication of orientation combined with degrees of contracting, 22.11
- inner center, 22.7
- inner spine opening laterally, 22.9
- longitudinal axes, 22.15
- lying on a table, 22.1
- ,moving for the, 22.13
- natural closing, 22.8
- one side closes, 22.5
- open, 22.1
- ,orientation of, 22.2-3, 22.10-11
- outside cover, 22.7
- paperback, 22.8
- performer's Standard Key, 22.15-16
- recto page, 22.7
- resting on elbow, 22.2
- revolving counterclockwise, 22.13
- ,rotating a, 22.12-16
- rotation
  - judged around - axis, 22.15
  - two forms at one time, 22.16
- somersault, 22.14-15
- spine, 22.6-7
- staff for, 22.8
- Standard Key, 22.16
- surfaces, 22.6
- verso page, 22.7
- ,vertical, 22.4
- 'wing', 22.7-8

Bottle
- as focal point, 21.4
- identification of areas on either side, 21.5

Bottle (cont.)
- ,leg above, 21.5
- ,relating to a, S21
- ,traveling around a, 21.4

Bouncing (ball), 20.3
Bouquet of flowers, 23.4
Bow
- ,official, 34.15
- with handkerchief, 34.13

Bow, 3.3
- active part thickened, 3.5
- angular, 3.4
- avoid crossing staff, 6.1
- contact, 9.5
- ,dotted nearness, 13.10
- double, 9.6
  - supporting, 10.1
- drawn to appropriate part, 21.1
- linked to landing step, 21.5
- ,relationship, 4.1
- swung to indicate part of prop contacted, 5.7

Bowl, 23.4
Box, S48
- ,crouching inside, 48.3
- foot touching, 48.6
- ,palm on, 48.6
- ,performers supported on, 48.1
- Reading Example, 48.5-8
- ,run onto, 48.8
- ,sitting on, 48.6, 48.8
- ,size of, 48.1, 48.3
- ,standing on, 48.6
- ,rosin, 48.2

Breathing, 28.2-3
Brief passing relationship, 4.4
Broom
- handle, 9.9
- head, 9.9

Brushing the floor with a stick, 9.6
Bugaku, 30.8
'Bunched finger' position of hand, 8.7
Butt of gun, 18.2-3
- supported at front of right shoulder, 18.3

Cabriole, 39.9
Cancellation
- automatic, 16.3
- of hold sign, 4.5, 8.12
- of retained relationship, 4.6
- rule, 8.12

Cancelling supporting on object, 42.1
Candles
- ,circling lighted, S29
- resting on palm, 29.2
- reverse circling, 29.3

Cane, 13.13
Caressing rose, 49.3
Carrying
- a book without grasping, 22.2
- a vase with two handles, 21.3

Carrying (cont.)
- an object on a fan, 30.15-16
- object along, 11.2-4, 19.7

Cartwheel
- axes, 13.7
- for book, 22.14
- for pillow, 27.5
- pattern for twirling a stick, 13.11-12
- rotataions of a cane, 13.13

Catching a ball, 20.1, 20.5
Center, in the, 23.3
Center of gravity in a *sensu*, 30.18
Center of weight
- backward placement, 45.6
- sign on supporting bow, 47.14

Chair
- as focal point for orientation, 40.4
- facing, 40.6-7
- falling backwards to floor, 40.2
- foot placed on seat, 40.2
- gestures toward, away, 40.3
- ,grasps the front edge of, 40.7
- ,hand touches back of, 40.2
- ,Reading Study Using a, 40.3
- Pillow, 40.4-7
- ,relationship to, 40.3
- ,sitting on, 40.5
- ,stepping on, 40.5
- tilt, 40.2
- ,using a, S40
- visual representation, 40.2

Changes of orientation, 7.8
Chest, passive reaction, 29.2
Chi, 30.12, 30.14
Chichibone, 30.19, 30.22
China bowls, 23.3
Chinese dance, 30.5-6, 31.1
- *Long Sleeve Dance*, 38.2-36

Choice of description for writing movement of objects, 11.1
Cigarette
- above ashtray, 28.3
- base end, 28.1
- changes in finger hold, 28.1
- contacts ashtray, 28.4
- finger taps off ashes, 28.3
- grasping with two fingers, 28.1
- ,handling a, S28
- identification of parts, 28.1
- ,letting go of, 28.4
- lit end, 28.1
- manner of holding, 28.3
- middle, 28.1
- ,mouth 'grasping', 28.2
- stubbed out, 28.4

Circled 'below' pin, 27.3
Circles focal point, 17.1
Circling
- amount indicated with fraction, 17.2
- leg above bottle, 21.5
- lighted candles, S29
  - body participation, 29.3

Circling (cont.)
- saucers of water, 29.1-3
- sign
  - ,object placed in, 21.4
- without turning, 17.2

Circular
- path
  - for arm gestures, 13.1
  - for a stick, S13
- props, 25.1
- tray, 25.1

Clashing of sticks or swords, 16.1

Climbing
- a ladder, 45.5-8
- a rope, 46.1-5
- up stairs, 45.1-4

'Closed' arm circles, 13.4
Closing one side of a book, 22.5

Cloth
- dotted line to indicate a fold, 32.1, 32.5
- finger edges sliding across, 32.6
- flicked, 32.7
- ,folding a large, S32
- forward somersault path, 32.6
- grasping
  - the center of the edge, 32.4
  - two corners, 32.4
- illustration of prop, 32.2
- indication of parts, 32.1
- lateral closing, 32.3
- resting on front of torso, 32.5
- resultant upward path, 32.2
- turning, 32.4, 32.7

Clothing, Part III
Column, 6.2
- for book, 22.5
- on prop staff, 19.7

Commonly used objects, 2.2

Constant
- Cross of Axes, 15.8, 24.3, 38.5
  - for directions, 7.4
- Key, 9.1, 22.16, 25.6

Contact
- ,actual, 3.1
- bow, 9.5
- ,freedom of, 5.6
- object and part of torso, 8.9
- ,specific statements of, 5.6
- with enclosing, grasping, 3.1
- with penetrating, interlacing, 3.1
- with the floor using a stick, S9

Continuous
- contact, 4.5
  - of ball with body, 20.7
- moving
  - a stick, 13.12
  - relationship, 4.5

Continuous Project, Altered Daily, n76
Coppélia, 30.4
Counterclockwise revolution of book, 22.13
Cover of umbrella, 19.5

Cover of umbrella (cont.)
- ,edge of, 19.5-6

Cross of Axes for a book, 22.12
Crossed sticks on the floor, 17.1-2

Crutch
- additional support columns, 39.14
- column outside staff, 39.12
- ,'step' on, 39.13
- ,support column for, 39.13
- taking weight, 39.12
- two crutches, 39.14
- ,using a, 39.12-13

Cup, 2.1
Cushion, 27.1

Dance with a fan and handkerchief, 30.5-6
Day on Earth, 32.1
Defensive position, 16.3
Definition of prop, S1
Degree of opening for an umbrella, 19.4
Describing the desired change for an object, 11.1
Design drawing, 13.9, 15.5, 20.6
- description of reverse circle, 15.7
- figure eight patterns, 15.1
- for a false leg, 39.8
- for a hat, 34.3
- for a ribbon, 31.3
- for a skirt, 37.5
- in the air, 14.1
- loop-like, 14.2
- modification of size, 31.4
- on the floor, 14.2
- ,path of ball through the air, 20.6

Deviate diagonally from sagittal line, 15.6

Diagonal
- circles, 13.7
- deviation from sagittal line, 15.6

Direction
- from body part (DBP), 47.14
- from which a grasp takes place, 8.4
- of grasp, 8.4, 8.6
- of object when thrown, 10.4
- of rotation of prop, 12.1
- of the *sensu*, 30.25
- orientation of object, S7
- relating to free end, 7.7
- symbols
  - for circular paths, 13.1-4
  - small, 37.2
  - to identify orientation, 7.2

Distance
- inside an object, 23.3
- of travel, 20.4

Dotted line to represent a fold, 32.1, 32.5

Double
- accent sign, 16.3
- ankle sign, 46.1
- bow, 9.6
- closing symbol, 30.29

Double (cont.)
- hand sign, 46.1
- pin for 'within', 23.5
- relationship sign, 4.4
- spreading symbol, 30.29
- supporting bow, 10.1
- swing of skipping rope, 24.1

Downward path
- for bouquet of flowers, 23.4
- for stick, 10.3

Drawing
- accurate, detailed, 2.1
- of an umbrella, 19.1
  - to convey closed or open state, 19.1
- ,three-dimensional, 5.3

Dropping a stick, 10.3
- path of stick affected by arm movements, 10.3

Duration of relationship, S4
- brief passing, moving, 4.4
- cancellation, 4.6
- continuous moving, 4.5
- momentary, 4.2
- retained, 4.3
- timing, 4.1

Early, Fergus, n33
Edges of a book, 22.2
Effort
- sign for dabbing, 34.5
- ,use of, 47.8

Elbow, placing weight on, 41.2
Eliptical track for juggling balls, 20.6
Embroidered pillow or cushion, 27.1
Established terminology, 3.1-2
European dances, 26.1
Eyes looking, 18.3
Extension, three-dimensional, 21.2

Facing of the *sensu*, 30.26-28
Fairy's wand, 11.6
Falling against wall, 44.3
- forward, 44.2

False leg, 39.1-11
- arm used to manipulate leg, 39.3
- design drawing, 39.8
- enlarged staff, 39.2
- lateral circular arc with, 39.11
- leg passing above false leg, 39.8
- meeting line for relationship with feet, 39.5
- relationship with two feet, 39.7
- springing, 39.5
- swinging, 39.8
- torso inclines as result of leg movement, 39.4
- ,weight maintained on, 39.11

Fan
- ,augmented areas of, 30.16
- ,balletic use of, 30.4
- basic hold, 30.38
- ,Body Cross analysis for, 30.11

Fan (cont.)
- ,carrying objects on, 30.15-16
- ,cartwheel revolution, 30.47
- closed state, 30.3, 30.29-30
- closing, 30.53
- column indication, 30.27
- dance with - and handkerchief, 30.5-6
- direction column, 30.30
- edges, 30.27
- facing direction and movements, 30.31
- facing indication, 30.28
- Japanese
  - dance, 30.7
  - fan, 30.8-56
- ,handling a, S30
- 'Hawk's Beak' grasp, 30.6, 30.51, 30.53-54
- identification of parts, 30.1
- in Asian dance, 30.1
- open state, 30.3
- orientation, 30.3
- pointing with a, 30.44
- presigns for direction indications, 30.28
  - cancellation, 30.28
- reading example, 30.4
- ,representation of a, 30.2-4
- ,revolutions of a, 30.45-47
- rotation, Standard System reference, 30.3
- somersault, 30.46
- spreading and closing signs, 30.3, 30.30
- ,staff for, 30.31-32
- symbolic representation, 30.3
- system of reference, 30.3
- touching frequently, 30.32
- visual representation, 30.2

Far inside an object, 23.3
Feet walking up wall, 44.5
Fencing, 16.2
Figure eight patterns with a stick, S15
- 'dead point' in circle, 15.6
- direct way of writing, 15.1
- design drawing description, 15.7
- ,flat, 15.9
- ,'lopsided', 15.6
- reverse circle, 15.7
- sagittal, 15.9
  - design, 15.2, 15.4
- slant, 15.3

Finger/s
- carrying a basket with penetration, 23.1
- edges sliding across cloth, 32.6
- grasping a cigarette, 28.1
- manipulation of a stick, 12.5
- mid-finger segments, 26.3
- penetrating
  - the hair at the temple, 23.5
  - the spaces of a basket, 23.1
- rotated outwards, 8.6

Finger/s (cont.)
- tapping off cigarette ashes, 28.4
- tips, led by, 29.2
- twirl, 13.13

Flag, 15.8
Flat 'figure eight', 15.9
Flexibility of arm, 29.1
Flexions of the wrist in rotating a stick, 12.2
Flicking skirt in circular manner, 37.5
Floor
- brushed with a stick, 9.6
- ,contact of stick with, S9
- hitting with a stick, 9.5
- ,line below pole representing, 47.2
- ,understood supporting on, 42.1
- sign for, 6.3, 9.1, 20.3

Floor plan
- ,location of object on, 7.4
- ,small, 21.5

Fluent continuity shown by notation, 13.1
Focal point
- ,bottle as, 21.4
- of circle, 17.1

Focus on prop important, 12.1
Fold indicated by dotted line, 32.1, 32.5
Folding
- a book backwards, 22.8
- a large cloth, S32
- and lateral closing sign, 33.1
- one sided, 22.5

Folk dances, 26.1
Forms of relating to a prop, S3
Four-legged performer, 39.1-2
Free end
- ,directions relating to, 7.7
- of stick, 9.5, 11.5, 15.1

Freedom in place of contact, 5.6
Functioning
- edge or surface, 7.11
- end, 7.11

Gallant gesture with a hat, 34.3
Gate, hanging over a, 43.5
Gathering a cloth across body, 33.2
Gentlemen in Black scene, 34.17, 41.1, n62
Girl's Russian Dance, 34.10
Gliding addressing, 37.7
Glossary, 2.1, 19.6
- indication of a gun, 18.1

Glossarizing unfamiliar signs, 16.3
Grasp/ing
- a chair, 40.7
- a cloth, 32.2
  - at the center of the edge, 32.4
  - at two corners, 32.4
- a fan, 30.6, 30.34-36
  - areas fequently used, 30.14-15
  - basic hold, 30.38
  - flat hold, 30.41
  - flat lifted hold, 30.48

Grasp/ing (cont.)
- a fan (cont.)
  - Grasping Hold, 30.37
  - 'Hawk's Beak', 30.6, 30.34, 30.51, 30.53
  - Holding the End, 30.36
  - Middle Hold, 30.35
  - Middle Rib Hold, 30.39
  - Naka-mochi, 30.35
  - Nakabone-mochi, 30.39
  - Nigiri-mochi, 30.37
  - Oyabone-mochi, 30.38
  - paper end of the closed fan, 30.36
  - Parent Rib Hold, 30.38
  - Pinching Hold, 30.40
  - ribs, 30.21
  - Saki-mochi, 30.36
  - Taira-mochi, 30.41, 30.48
  - Taira-kazashi-mocchi, 30.48
  - Tsumami-mochi, 30.40
- a rose, 49.3
- action of the palms, 21.3
- any part, 37.2
- ball from below, 20.2
- basket from above, 23.1
- beaker, 21.1
- book at top and bottom ends, 22.15
- ,brief, 4.2
- by the barrel, 18.6
- center fold of half-opened book, 22.2
- cigarette
  - with mouth, 28.2
  - with two fingers, 28.1
- ,comfortable, 8.3
- ,direction of, 8.4, 8.6
- edge of umbrella cover, 19.5
- from above, 8.4, 22.4
- from behind, 22.4
- from the left, 21.1
- general statement, 8.4
- handle of cup or mug, 21.1
- hoop, 25.2
- lattice gate, 23.2
- lower edge of a book, 22.3
- pocket edge, 34.16-17
- ,quick alternation of, 6.1
- shown pictorially for a skirt, 37.2
- ,sliding, 10.2
- ,supporting, 4.5
- tambourine from above, 26.2
- waist grasped by belt, 34.4
- with index and middle finger, 37.3
- with stretched fingers, 36.3
- with thumb and index finger, 37.3

Gravity, 10.5
Greater specificity for part of prop, 5.3
Green Table, The, 15.8, 34.16, 41.1, n26, n62, n64
Gun
- aiming position, 18.2
- barrel, 18.2
  - ,hand sliding along, 18.3
- ,butt of the, 18.2

Gun (cont.)
- ,butt of the, (cont.)
  - supported, 18.3
- drawing, 18.1
- ,handling a prop, S18
- 'shouldered', 18.2, 18.6
- trigger, 18.3
Gymnastics, 31.1

Hahabone, 30.19, 30.22
Hair
- ,fingers penetrating, 23.5
- sign for, 23.5
Half-opened book, 22.2, 22.4
Hanayagi Chiyo, 30.33
Hand/s
- adjustments when holding a stick, 8.3
- as major support, 44.1
- 'bunched finger' position, 8.7
- 'creep' along scarf, 35.3
- direction approaching object, 8.4
- double - sign, 46.1
- grasping
  - book, 22.3-4
  - hoop, 25.2
  - trigger of gun, 18.3, 18.5
- grip, 11.1
- inserted into lower sleeve, 34.15
- inside a pocket, 23.5
- movements and positions, 8.1
  - during skipping with a rope, 24.1
- ,palm of, 13.13
- prop, Part II; 1.1-2
- rotating, 21.1
- sign in support column, 9.7
- slides along barrel of a gun, 18.3
- sliding along fold in veil, 36.4
- sliding down rope, 46.5
- sliding on a stick, 10.1-2
- ,stick slipping within, 10.2
- touching edge of book, 22.4
- use when holding a stick, 8.3
- ,valley of, 15.9
- ,vertical displacement of, 29.2
Handkerchief, 34.5-6
- ,Dance with Fan and, 30.5-6
- flicks, 34.13
  - across right instep, 34.11
- placed in pocket, 34.6
- Reading Examples, 34.10-13
- used to blot the brow, 34.5
- waved, 34.13
  - for ornamental purposes, 34.5
Handle
- of umbrella, 19.2
- of parasol, 19.6
Handling
- apple, S28
- ball, S20
- basket, S23
  - with fingers penetrating the spaces, 23.1

Handling (cont.)
- blanket, S33
- book, S22
- cigarette, S28
- fan, S30
- hoop, S25
- long ribbon, S31
- long sleeves, S38
- pillow, S27
- prop gun, S18
- scarf, S35
- skirt, S37
- tambourine, S26
- umbrella, S19
- veil, S36
Hanging over a bar, 43.5
Hat, 34.1-3
- brim, indication of, 34.7
- ,circling around, 34.7
- ,gallant gesture with, 34.3
- *Mexican Hat Dance*, 34.7
- path indicated through design drawing, 34.3
- picked up by brim, 34.2
- Reading Example, 34.7-9
- resting on a table, 34.2
- supported on head, 34.1
- tapped
  - on brim with toe, 34.8
  - on crown, 34.2
- ,wearing a, 34.1
'Hawk's Beak' grasp, 30.6, 30.34, 30.51
Head, part of, 23.5
Heaven (*ten*), 30.12
Hips supported on parallel bar, 43.6
Hitting
- swords, sticks, S16
  - with a partner, 16.2-3
- tambourine, 26.3
- the floor, 9.5
Holding, see grasping
- apple, 28.5
- book
  - by the lateral edges, 'wings', 22.8
  - on both palms, 22.3
  - ,simple manner of, 22.8
- fan, areas used in, 30.14
- hoop, 25.6
- object in the middle, 7.10
- ,releasing a, 8.12
- right angle relationship, 8.5
- scarf, 35.1-2
- stick
  - horizontally, 8.8
  - with armpit, 8.10
  - with the fingers, 12.4
- support, 3.1, 3.5
- through body parts coming together, 3.1
- through extending, 3.1
- ,use of hand in, 8.3, 8.6-7
Hold sign, 9.5, 16.3

Hold sign (cont.)
- cancellation, 4.6, 8.12, 16.3
- ,placement of, 4.3

Hone, 30.10

Hoop
- duck through - to other side, 25.5
- ,handling a, S25
- held upright in sagittal plane, 25.3
- hit by a stick, 25.5
- ,holding a, 25.6
- in sagittal plane, 25.3
- ,large, 25.4
- ,limb passing through a, 25.4
- loss of momentum, 25.6
- movements
  - judged from performer's System of Reference, 25.2
  - described in terms of Constant Key, 25.6
- orientation, 25.2
- rolling along the ground, 25.5
- rotary movement, 25.6
- sign for 'through', 25.4
- somersault rotation, 25.2-3
- ,spot holds for hands, 25.4
- throwing and catching, 25.3
- turn around vertical axis, 25.2
- ,whole body passing through a, 25.4

Horizontal
- circle, 13.6
  - under the legs, 13.10
- pinwheel, 15.10

Humphrey, Doris, 32.1, 48.5, 48.8, *n*59, *n*85

Hungarian dances
- male dances, 15.6
- relating to a bottle, 21.4
- use of pillow or cushion, 27.1
- use of sticks·in, 17.3

Identifying
  - the ribs on the *sensu*, 30.19
  - the sides of the *sensu*, 30.26

Ikkaku Sennin, 30.51

Imaginary prop, S49
- design drawing, 49.3
- drawn with dotted lines, 49.1
- in mimed sequences, 49.1
- letter representation, 49.1
- Reading Example, 49.2-5
- rose, 49.1-3

Inbuilt top and bottom of object, 7.5

Inclusion
- passive, 13.1
- shoulder, hip, 16.3

Independant circles for a stick, 13.5-9

Indian clubs
- 'at the ready', 13.4
- 'closed' circles, 13.4
- open lateral circles, 13.4
- reverse circle, 13.3
- small circles, 13.2

Indication of prop, S2; 2.1
- letters, 5.1
- numbers, 5.1
- particular features, 7.1
- special signs, 5.1

'Inside', 'in the center' sign, 21.2, 23.3
Inner subsidery column, 44.1
Intermediate areas on the *sensu*, 30.15
Intermediate points on the *sensu*, 30.13
Inward arm rotation, 12.1

Japanese
- dance, 30.7
  - *Kabuki*, 30.9, 30.33
  - *Kagura*, 30.9
  - *Nichibu*, 30.9
  - *Nihon Buyo*, 30.9, 30.33
- fan, 30.8-56
- theater
  - *Bugaku*, 30.8
  - *Noh*, 30.8
  - *Takarazuka*, 30.26

Jarabe Tapatio, 34.7
Jiaozhou Yangge Dance, *n*50
Jigami, 30.10
Jooss, Kurt, *n*26, *n*62
Juggling with two balls, 20.6

Kabuki, 30.9
Kagura, 30.9
Kaname, 30.10, 30.21
Ken, 30.23
Kerchief, 35.1
Key for rotation of fan, 30.3
Knust, Albrecht, 28.5
Kobone, 30.11
Komparu, Zenou, *n*54

Labelling stick, 11.5
Ladder, S45
- abstract indications for rungs, 45.7
- ,climbing a, 45.5-8
- general verbal statement, 45.5
- hands grasping rungs, 45.8
- indication of rungs, 45.5
- pictorial representations, 45.7

La Jolie Fille de Gand, 39.1
Lady Senda's Dance, 30.51-56
L'Après-midi d'un Faune, 36.2, 45.2, *n*66, *n*80

Lateral
- axes for a somersault, 13.6
- circle of skipping rope, 24.1
- circular path for a stick, 13.5
- closing for a cloth, 32.3
- closing and folding sign combined, 33.1
- plane for ball in the air, 20.6
- spreading of fan, 30.3

Lattice gate
- grasped, 23.2
- lifted, 23.2

Leaning
- degree of, 44.1
- on a stick, 9.7

Le Beau Danube, 24.2, n43

Leg/s
- above the bottle, 21.5
- enclosing rope, 46.2
- rope passing under, 24.1

Letter used to indicate prop, 2.1, 5.1, 19.4, 19.6

Lifting
- a lattice gate, 23.2
- an object, 21.2

Limb sign used for fan ribs, 30.19
Location of object on floor plan, 7.4
Loop-like design, 14.2
'Lopsided' figure eight patterns, 15.6
Loss of momentum of a hoop, 25.6
Loud, very, 16.3

Lower arm
- circle, 13.4
- rotates, 12.1
- signs, 13.4

Mahoney, Billie, n23, n27
Male Hungarian dances, 15.6

Manipulations
- of hoop, 25.4
- of a stick, 7.5

Manner of grasping, holding stick, S8
'Marching' position for gun, 18.2, 18.4
Massine, Léonide, n43, n70
Meeting line, 9.4, 25.5
Mexican Hat Dance, 34.7
Middle, in the, 21.1, 23.3
Mimed sequence, 49.1
Minikin Fair, 39.1, n74

Momentary
- relationship, 4.2
- touch, 4.2

Momentum, loss of, 25.6
'More or less' sign, 15.8
Motif Description for study using a chair, 40.3
Moto, 30.21

Mouth
- 'grasping' a cigarette, 28.2
- ,sign for, 28.5

Movements of the *sensu*, 30.24
Mug, 21.1

Naka, 30.12
Nakabone, 30.19

Nearness
- and enclosing, 3.1
- proximity, 3.1

Neck
- scarf grasping, 35.5
- scarf wound around, 35.6

New Dance, 48.5, 48.8, n85
Nichibu, 30.9
Nijinsky, Vaslav, 36.2-4, 45.2, n66, n80

Nihon Buyo, 30.9
Noh, 30.8
Number identification, 5.1, 19.6

Object
- appropriate part, 21.1
- carried along, 11.2-4
- contacting part of torso, 8.9
- direction when thrown, 10.4
- drawn as though transparent, 23.3
- functioning edge, end or surface, 7.11
- holding in the middle, 7.10
- identifyable parts, 19.6-7
- inbuilt front and back, 7.6
- inbuilt top and bottom, 7.6
- 'inside' the, 23.5
- major support, 9.7
- orientation, S7
- partially supporting person, 9.7
- partly rigid and moveable, 22.6
- ,perspective drawing of, 27.2
- placed in circling sign, 21.4
- placement on stage, 7.4
- point of attachment, 7.7
- relating to
  - the body, 24.1
  - mouth, 28.1
- repeated redrawing, 2.1
- rigid, 7.2
- spatial retention for, 9.10
- ,spot hold for, 9.8-9
- totally supporting person, 9.7

Omote, 30.10, 30.17, 30.26-28
Open wickerwork basket, 23.1
Opening, degrees of, 19.3
Orientation of object, S7
- book, 22.2-4, 22.6, 22.10
- ,changes in, 7.8
- hoop, 25.2
- tambourine, 26.1
- use of direction symbols, 7.2
- with no defined end or surface, 7.2

Ornamental movement, 29.1
Ornamentation of rope when skipping, 24.1
Orthography, 2.1, 3.3-5
- quick alternation of grasp, 6.1

Outward arm rotation, 12.1
Oyabone, 30.10, 30.12, 30.19, 30.26-27
Overcurve for juggling balls, 20.6
Overlapping sequential movements, 38.4

Palm/s
- carrying a book, 22.2-3
- carrying a saucer, 29.2
- grasping, 21.3
- hitting a tambourine, 26.3

Paperback book, 22.8

Parallel bars
- ,sitting, hips supporting on, 43.6

Parasol, 19.1, 19.6-7
- 'batted' back by hand, 19.7
- space hold for vertical direction, 19.7

Parasol (cont.)
- traveling, 19.7

Part/s
- of prop touched, grasped, carried, S5
- within the mouth, 28.5

Participation of body when circling candles, 29.3

Partner with swords, sticks, 16.2-3

Passive inclusion of lower arm, 13.1

Path
- ,backward, sagittal, 13.6
- for body-as-a-whole, 46.4
- forward somersault for rope, 24.3
- lies at a three-dimensional slant, 13.8
- of object, 20.2
  - affected by arm movements, 10.3
  - in air, 20.2
  - passing under or over a limb, 13.10
  - when thrown, 10.4
- sign for sticks, 13.1

Pattern, wave-like, 14.2

Penetrating, 23.1
- nearness, 3.1

Performer's (person's)
- point of view, 20.4
- Standard Cross of Axes, 7.2, 12.2
- Standard Key, 22.15-16
- Standard System of Reference, 12.4, 22.12, 22.15, 25.2

Personal prop, 1.1, 1.3

Perspective drawing of object, 27.2

Pictogram of an umbrella, 19.3

Pillow
- cartwheel, 27.4
- ,drawing of a, 27.2
- dropping, 40.6
- ,handling a, S27
- held vertically by opposite corners, 27.5
- hugged with both arms, 27.5
- on lap, 40.5
- orientation, 27.1
- ,parts of a, 27.3
- picked up by corner, 40.6
- placed on the chair, 40.6
- placed on the floor, 40.5
- ,Reading Example with Chair and, 40.4-7
- ,sitting on, 40.6

Pin/s
- and contact/supporting bow, 21.1
- for parts of *sensu*, 30.11
- metal, *kaname*, 30.10
- to specify direction of relationship, 8.1

Pinwheel pattern, 15.9-10

Pistol,
- in pocket jacket, 34.16-17
- grasped, 34.16

Placement
- of hold sign, 4.3
- of object on stage, 7.4

Placement (cont.)
- of pin when grasping, 8.3
- of prop on the staff, S6

Pocket, 34.16-17
- ,inside a, 23.5
- ,grasping the edge of, 34.16-17
- ,pistol in jacket, 34.16
- ,placing a handkerchief in, 34.6
- ,placing pistol inside, 34.17

'Point of attachment', 7.7

Pole, S47
- cartwheel, 47.9-10
- catching top end of pole, 47.12
- ,columns for, 47.1
- end supporting on the floor, 47.12
- falling from side to side, 47.11
- ,grasping the, 47.8-9
- ,hand sliding along, 47.3, 47.7-8, 47.10
- ,handing a, 47.1
- hit end of - on floor, 47.2, 47.13
- ,performer's pulling the, 47.8
- Reading Material, 47.1-16
- releasing both hands, 47.16
- sliding down, 46.5
- slides to the floor, 47.4
- somersault, 47.3
- stands unsupported, 47.16
- ,weight
  - supported on, 47.14
  - taken off, 47.15

Pre-staff
- diagram, 17.1, 17.3
- indication, 2.1, 20.2

Pressing rope, 46.2

Prop
- column, 6.2
- definition, 1.1-4
- designating specific parts through numbers or letters, 19.5
- determine orientation, 7.1
- horizontal placement, 19.2
- identification of features, 7.1
- ,indication of, 2.1
- no longer supporting on, 42.1
- part touched, S5
- pictorial drawing, 2.1
  - examples, 2.2
  - part of - contacted, 5.7
- placement on staff, S6
- redrawing, 6.5
- ,relating to, 3.1
- ,rotation of, 12.1
- spatial relationship to performer, 12.2
- ,specific column for parts of, 19.6
- ,static, 6.4, Part IV
- ,use of static, 6.4
- vertical placement, 19.2
- with insufficient identifying features, 22.12
- written below staff, 6.1

Rainer, Yvonne, *n*76

Reading Examples
- box, 48.5-8
- fan, 30.4
- handkerchief, 34.10-13
- hat, 34.7-9
- imaginary prop, 49.2-5
- pole, 47.1-16
- table, 41.6-10

Reading Study, Chair, 40.3
Recto page, 22.7
Red Ribbon Dance, 31.2-6
Redrawing of object, 2.1, 6.5
Relating
- to a bottle, 21.4
- to a cup, jar or bottle, S21
- to a prop, S3
- to sticks on the floor, S17

Relationship
- active part, 3.5
- bow, 4.1
  - double, 4.4
  - placement of pin, 8.3
- duration, 4.1-6
- of prop to performer, 12.2
- of stick on floor to performer, 9.4
- pin in bow, 3.3
- to a hoop, 25.5
- signs, 3.1
  - ,modifications to, 3.3

'Release weight' sign, 47.14
Releasing a hold, 8.12, 10.3
Resultant upward path for a cloth, 32.2
Retained relationship, 4.3
Revolution of fan,
- around vertical axis, 30.55
- Basic Turning of the Pin, 30.49
- cartwheel on lateral axis, 30.45, 30.47, 30.49
- horizontal circle, 30.56
- *kaname-gaeshi no kihon*, 30.49
- *mae-tonbo*, 30.46
- placement of sign in fan direction column, 30.45
- somersault on sagittal axis, 30.45-46, 30.54, 30.56
- *yoko-tombo*, 30.47

Rhythmic gymnastics, 31.1
Rhythmically beat swords, 16.1
Rib/s
- edges, 30.20
- on *sensu*, 30.19
- points, 30.21
- ,spaces between, 30.23

Ribbon,
- arc overhead, 31.6
- fluttering up and down quickly, 31.5
- handling a, S31
- inward spiralling shape, 31.6
- ,leg 'piercing' circle made by, 31.4
- Red Ribbon Dance, 31.2-6
- somersault paths, 31.3
- three-dimensional figure eight patterns, 31.3

Riffle (toy), 18.1
Right angle relationship, 8.5
Rigid object, 7.2, 7.6
- spatial orientation, 8.8

Ring, 25.1
Rolling
- a ball, 20.1
- along the body, 20.7
- a hoop along the ground, 25.5
- into palm of hand, 13.13

Rope, S46
- arms in climbing, 46.3
- ankle
  - grasp taking weight, 46.3
  - grasp through adducting, 46.2
  - sliding down, 46.5
- ,climbing a, 46.1
- grasping with hands and ankles, 46.1-2
- legs enclose the rope, 46.2
- pressing with knees, 46.2
- ,skipping, S24
- ,staff for the, 24.3
- sliding down, 46.5

Rotary movement of a hoop dies out, 25.6
Rotating
- a book, 22.12-16
- turning a stick, S12

Rotation
- for a fan, 30.3
- of arm, 12.1, 12.3
- of book, 22.12-16
  - two forms at one time, 22.16
- of direction of prop, 12.1

Rotational state, 11.1
Rug, S42
- no longer a supporting surface, 42.1
- ,stepping from - on to floor, 42.1
- ,stepping on to a, 42.1
- still a supporting surface, 42.3

Sagittal
- axes for a cartwheel, 13.6
- circling of skipping rope, 24.1
  - passing under legs, 24.1
- design, 15.2
- figure eight, 15.4, 15.9
- path, 13.6
- pinwheel pattern, 15.9
- plane, hoop held in, 25.3

Saint-Léon, Arthur, n49
Saki, 30.12, 30.28
'Same spot' caret, 47.4
Saucer
- of water, 29.1
- resting on palm, 29.2

Scarf
- circles clockwise in the air, 35.1
- dropped, caught at elbows, 35.7
- encircling throat, 35.5
- grasping neck, 35.5
- handling a, S35

Scarf (cont.)
- held in the fingers, 35.1
- indication for where - is held, 35.2
- resting on shoulders, 35.7
- stuffing a - into a belt, 35.4
- wind around neck, 35.6

Schematic drawing, pictogram, 2.1, 19.5
Scottish dance, use of swords in, 17.3
Sensu, 30.9-56
- ,addressing with the, 30.44
- area below pin, 30.12
- ,areas of the, 30.14
  - used in grasping, 30.14-15
- ,area surfaces of the, 30.17
- arrow indicating side from which to open, 30.30
- back of fan, 30.10, 30.17
- bamboo ribs, 30.10
- bottom center of paper, 30.12
- ,carrying objects on, 30.15-16
- *chi* (earth), 30.12
- *chichibone* (Father Rib), 30.19, 30.22
- ,closed, 30.9, 30.28
  - ,grasping the, 30.34-36
- ,closing the, 30.43
  - *tojiru*, closing the, 30.43
- ,direction of the, 30.25
  - analysed from Standard Cross Axes, 30.25
  - analysed from Constant Cross of Axes, 30.25
- edges, 30.27
- ,facing of the, 30.26-28
  ,column for, 30.27
- front of fan, 30.10, 30.17, 30.26
- fully closed, 30.29
- fully open, 30.29
- ,grasping the - ways of, 30.33
- *hahabone* (Mother Rib), 30.19, 30.22
- heaven (*ten*, part of), 30.12
- *hone* (ribs), 30.10
- identifying the ribs, 30.19
- intermediate areas, 30.15
- intermediate points, 30.13
- *jigami* (paper), 30.10
- *kaname* (Metal Pin), 30.10, 30.18
  - weight, 30.18
- *ken* (space between ribs), 30.23
- *kobone* (thinner ribs), 30.10
- ,manipulation of open, 30.48-50
- metal pin, 30.10, 30.18
- *moto* (base), 30.21
- ,movements of the, 30.24
  - preferred method of writing, 30.27
- *naka* (bottom edge of paper), 30.12
- *nakabone* (middle ribs), 30.19
- negative space between ribs, 30.23
- *omote* (the front side), 30.10, 30.17, 30.26
- ,open, 30.9
- ,open or closed state of the, 30.29-30

Sensu (cont.)
- ,opening the,
  - *akeru* (way of opening), 30.42
  - *ikken-ake* (opening one space), 30.42
  - smoothly, 30.42
- *oyabone* (parent rib), 30.10, 30.12, 30.19
- paper, 30.10
- ,parts of the, 30.10
- ,points of the, 30.11-13
- ,revolutions of the, 30.45-47, 30.49
- rib/s, 30.19
  - 'any rib' sign for, 30.19
  - edges, 30.20
  - how many to open or close, 30.29
  - points, 30.20
  - ,spaces between, 30.23
  - surfaces, 30.22
- *saki* (side corner), 30.12, 30.28
- seven-three rib, 30.19
- *shichi-san-bone*, 30.19
- side corner, 30.12
- side middle, 30.12
- staff for *sensu*, 30.31-32
- *ten* (top center), 30.12, 30.28
  - used for pointing, 30.44
- top center, 30.12
- ,throwing the, 30.45
- *ura* (back), 30.10, 30.17
- weighted part, 30.18

Sequential movements, overlapping, 38.4
Shaking a tambourine, 26.4
Shape, sign for, 33.1
Shepherd's crook, 9.10, 11.6
Shichi-san-bone (third rib), 30.19
Shoulder/s
- and hip inclusion, 16.3
- scarf resting on, 35.7
- section arched touching stick, 8.9
- sleeve resting on, 38.3
'Shouldering' the gun, 18.2, 18.6
Sitting on a parallel bar, 43.6
Size
- modification of, 31.4
- of design, 15.1
Sketch drawn prop, 2.1
Skipping
- hand movements, 24.1
- higher jump, 24.1
- lateral circle, 24.1
- double swing, 24.1
- ,forward somersault paths for, 24.3
- long, 24.3
- passing under legs, 24.1
- Reading Example, 24.2
- staff, 24.3
- sagittal circles, 24.1
- ,turning of the - rope, 24.3
- with three people, 24.3
Skirt
- any part grasped, 37.2
- being grasped, 37.2

Skirt (cont.)
- column, 37.1
- ,drawing representing, 37.1
- flicking in a circular manner, 37.5
- fold in front, open out, 37.4
- ,grasping
  - part shown pictorially, 37.2
  - with fingers, 37.3
- handling a, S37
- ,not actually touching, 37.7
Slant/ing, 8.6
- , of figure of eight, 15.3
Sleeve, 34.14
- arm inside, 23.5
- ,arm sliding through, 34.14
- Chinese *Long - Dance*, 38.2-6
- flicking action, 38.1, 38.6
- flipped by wrist action, 38.3-4
- ,hand inserted into lower part of sleeve, 34.14
- motion of, 38.1
- passes under arm pit, 38.6
- resting on shoulder, 38.3
- slide across shoulder, 38.3
- stick held within, 38.1
- twist of the hand, 38.3
Sliding
- down a rope or pole, 46.5
- hands - on a stick, 10.1-2
- support, 4.5
Smelling a rose, 49.3
Smoothing, 4.5
Sombrero, 34.7
Somersault
- for book, 22.14-15
- for hoop, 25.2-3
- path, 13.7, 15.4
  - ,standard axes for, 13.7
- rotations for stick, 12.2-3
Space hold sign, 9.10, 11.4
- combined with equal sign 13.4
- for vertical direction of parasol, 19.7
- in path sign, 17.2
Space measurement signs, distance inside an object, 23.3
Spatial
- orientation of rigid prop, 8.8
- retention for object, 9.10
Speed, time sign for, 13.12
Spot hold
- for manipulating hoop, 25.4
- for object, 9.8-9
- over carrying grasp, 13.2
- used for hands, 43.3
Spreading hand inside a vase, 21.2
Springing onto hat brim, 34.8
Staff
- enlarged for false leg, 39.2
- for book, 22.8
- for the fan, 30.31-32
  - placement of symbols on, 30.31
  - second staff for two *sensu*, 30.32
- for the prop, 19.7

Staff (cont.)
- for skipping rope, 24.3
- for umbrella, 19.4
- placement of prop indications, S6
- ,prop written below, 6.1
Stage
- ,placement of object on, 7.4
- props, Part IV; 1.1, 1.4
Stairs, S45
- ascending, 45.1
- descending
  - by walking backwards, 45.2
  - by walking forwards, 45.4
- ,drawing of, 45.3
- ,indication of, 45.4
- ,moving up and down, 45.1-4
- ,numbering, 45.4
- ,walking up, 45.3
Stance Key, 27.5, 38.6
Standard Cross, System of Reference, 30.3 48.1
- Key, 21.1
Stick/s, 13.13, 15.9
- 'active' end, 15.6
- ,armpit holding, 8.10
- ,armpit supporting, 8.11
- ,brushing the floor with a, 9.6
- ,circular paths for a, S13
- contact with the floor, S9
- ,continuously moving a, 13.12
- crossed on the floor, 17.1-3
- ,dancer circling, 17.2
- direction same as arm, 8.6
- direction when thrown, 10.4
- ,downward path for, 10.3
- ,dropping a, 10.3
- figure eight patterns, S15
- ,finger manipulation of a, 12.4
- 'free end', 9.5, 15.1
- ,gravity affecting aim of, 10.5
- ,hand use when holding a, 8.3
- ,hands sliding on a, 10.1-2
- held by fingers, 12.5
- held within long sleeves, 38.1
- ,hitting, S16
  - a hoop, 25.5
  - the floor, 9.5
- identification of ends being held, 7.5
- ,independent circles for a, 13.5-9
- labelled, 11.5
- ,lateral circular path for, 13.5
- ,leaning on a, 9.7
- manner of grasping, holding, S8
- on floor
  - crossed, 17.1-3
  - relating to, S17; 9.4
  - spaces between, 17.3
- orientation of, 7.2-3
- ,partner dances with, 16.3
- rotating, turning a, S12
- slanting, 8.6
- slip within hand, 10.2
- ,somersault rotations for, 12.2

Stick/s (cont.)
- tapping end of gesturing foot, 9.5
- touching back of shoulder section, 8.9
- ,throwing a, 10.4
- ,turning direction of a, 12.4
- ,twirling a, 13.11-13
  - cartwheel pattern, 13.11-12
Stoking, 4.5
Stubbing out a cigarette, 28.4
Support/ing
- a stick
  - on the floor, S9
  - with the armpit, 8.11
- bow, 9.2, 17.3, 20.7, 21.1-2
  - ,double, 10.1
  - linked to landing place, 21.5
  - to indicate penetration, 23.1
- carrying, 3.1, 3.5
- grasp, 4.5
- partial, 9.7
  - on wall, 44.2
- prop cancelled, 42.1
- ,sliding, 4.5
- through extending, 3.1
- total, 9.7
Surface for ball to roll over, 20.7
Swaying step, 37.4
Swinging Indian clubs, 13.2-4
Sword, 14.1
- backward flourish, 16.2
- clashing or beating, 16.1
- ,hitting, S16
  - with a partner, 16.2-3
- rhythmical beats, 16.1
System of Reference
- for fan, 30.3
- performer's Standard, 12.4
Symbolic representation of a fan, 30.3
Symbolise a blessing, 30.48

Table, S41
- book lying on, 22.1
- brushing leg along top, 41.5
- cartwheel, 41.8
- ,contacting, resting on, 41.1-3
- grasping
  - nearest corners, 41.7
  - nearest legs, 41.7
- landing on, 41.4
- ,leap onto, 41.5
- lifts - up, 41.9
- ,manipulating a, 41.6-10
- parts identified, 41.6
- upright position, 41.8
- Reading Example, 41.6-10
- somersault, 41.7
- ,springing off a, 41.4-5
- tilting away, 41.7
- top surface on floor, 41.7
Takarazuka, 30.26
Tambourine, S26

Tambourine (cont.)
- drum
  - identification, 26.1
  - side, 26.1
- familiar grasp, 26.2
- ,handling a, S26
- ,hitting a, 26.3
  - with mid finger segments, 26.3
  - with palms, 26.3
- orientation of, 26.1
- rattling sound, 26.4
- ,shaking a, 26.4
Tapping stick on gesturing foot, 9.5
Taylor, Paul, 39.1, n74
Teeth penetrating apple, 28.5
Ten, 30.12, 30.14, 30.17, 30.28
Terminology, established, 3.1-2
Terra, 6.3, 9.1, 20.3, 42.1
Third leg, 38.1
Three-cornered Hat, The, n70
Three-dimensional
- drawing, 5.3
- extension, 21.2
  - of umbrella, 19.3
- figure eight pattern, 31.3
- slant, 13.8
Throat, scarf encircling, 35.5
'Through' pin, 25.4-5
Throwing
- a ball, 20.1
- a hoop, 25.3
- a stick, 10.4
Ticks to indicate corners of prop, 27.3
Time signs for much speed, 13.12
Timing
- coordination for prop, 45.7
- of relationship, 4.1
Tip of umbrella, 19.2, 19.6
Torso
- contacting object, 8.9
- forward tilt, 45.6
Tossing a ball, 20.1
Touching
- a fan frequently, 30.32
- a hot stove, 4.2
- momentary, 4.2
Toy riffle, 18.1
Tracing a design, S14
- in the air, 14.1
- on the floor, 14.2
Traveling
- around a bottle, 21.4
- for the parasol, 19.7
Trigger, hand grasps at, 18.3
Turning
- a stick, S12
- direction of a stick, 12.4
- hoop around vertical axis, 25.2
- of a skipping rope, 24.3
Twirling
- a baton, 13.13
- a stick, 13.11-12

Umbrella
- closed state, 19.3
- cover, 19.5
- degrees of opening, 19.3-4
- ,drawing on an, 19.1
- edge of cover grasped, 19.5
- ,handling an, S19
- ,holding an, 19.2
- identifying parts, 19.5-6
- ,letter abreviation for an, 19.4-6
- opening, 19.3
- staff for, 19.4, 19.6
- tip, 19.2
- 'working' end, 19.1
Undercurve for juggling balls, 20.6
Upper
- body inclusion, 29.2-3
- spine, 20.7
Ura, 30.10, 30.17
Using
- a Chair, S40
- a Crutch, S39
- a False Leg, S39

Validity
- duration of relationship, S4; 4.6
'Valley' (base of thumb/index finger), 15.9
Variations and Conclusion, 48.5, 48.8
Vase
- lifting hand inside, 21.2
- with two handles, 21.3
Veil
- drops, 36.4
- ,grasping top of, 36.3
- ,hand sliding along, 36.4
- ,handling a, S36
- ,parts of, 36.3
- pick up - at top edge, 36.2
- slips
  - down, 36.4
  - onto elbows, 36.2
Verso page, 22.7
Vertical
- axes
  - for horizontal path, 13.6
  - of hoop, 25.2
- book, 22.4
- displacement of hand, 29.3
- line for an appropriate action, 25.4
Visual
- pattern ribbon makes, 31.1
- representation
  - of a fan, 30.2
  - of a prop, 18.1

Walking
- backwards down stairs, 45.2
- feet up a wall, 44.5
Wastepaper basket, 23.1
Watching, 20.5
Wave-like pattern, 14.2
Waving a handkerchief, 34.5

Wall, S44
- ,back touching, 44.4
- ,degree of leaning on, 44.1
- ,falling against a, 44.2
- ,sliding down a, 44.4
- ,walking feet up a, 44.5
Waving a handkerchief, 34.5
Wearing a hat, 34.1
Weight
- on back of torso, 44.3
- on elbow, lower arm, 41.2
- ,partial - on hands, 44.1
- remaining on false leg, 39.11
Whole body through hoop, 25.4
Wickerwork basket, 23.1
'Within' sign, 23.3, 23.5
Wolz, Carl, 30.7
Word abbreviation for prop, 2.1
Wrapping a cloth around body, 33.3
Wrist
- action flipping sleeve, 38.3-4
- circles, 13.3
- flexion
  - for rotating a stick, 12.2
  - when holding, 8.6
- manipulation of Indian clubs, 13.2
- propels, guides direction of baton, 15.10

Useful Contact Information

Language of Dance Centre
17 Holland Park
London W11 3TD
United Kingdom
Tel: +44 (0) 20 7229 3780
Fax: +44 (0) 20 7792 1794
email: info@lodc.org
www.lodc.org

Language of Dance Center
1972 Swan Pointe Drive
Traverse City
MI 49686
USA
Tel: +1 231 995 0998
Fax: +1 231 995 0998
email: Tinalodc@aol.com

Dance Notation Bureau
151 West 30th Street, Suite 202
New York NY 10001
USA
Tel: +1 212 564 0985
Fax: +1 212 904 1426
web: http://www.dancenotation.org/
e-mail: notation@mindspring.com

Dance Notation Bureau Extension
The Ohio State University
Department of Dance
1813 N. High Street
Columbus OH 43210-1307
USA
Tel: +1 614 292 7977
Fax: +1 614 292 0939
web: http://www.dance.ohio-state.edu
e-mail: marion.8@osu.edu

The Labanotation Institute
The University of Surrey
Guildford
Surrey GU2 5XH
United Kingdom
Tel: +44 (0)1483 259 351
Fax: +44 (0)1483 300 803
e-mail: J.Johnson-Jones@Surrey.ac.uk

Andy Adamson
Department of Drama and Theatre Arts
University of Birmingham
P.O. Box 363
Birmingham B15 2TT
United Kingdom
e-mail: a.j.adamson@bham.ac.uk

www.ingramcontent.com/pod-product-compliance
Lightning Source LLC
Chambersburg PA
CBHW081106080526
44587CB00021B/3470